INDIA 2039

 SAGE www.sagepublications.com

Los Angeles • London • New Delhi • Singapore • Washington DC

INDIA 2039

An affluent society in one generation

Editors:

Harinder S. Kohli

and Anil Sood

Figures, tables, and boxes

Tables

Boxes

Foreword

India is currently the second most populous country and the eleventh largest economy in the world. For the past two decades, it has enjoyed the second highest growth rate—after China—amongst the large economies. And, as happened in China, India's growth rate has continued to accelerate. As a result, India is already a dramatically different country compared to what it was just a generation ago in terms of its per capita income, the self-confidence and ambitions of its people as well as India's position in the global community of nations. In recognition of these achievements and its rising global footprint, India is now an important participant in global forums such as the G-20 Summits. The question is what would India look like one generation from now.

Many observers have declared that the 21st century will be Asia's century, partly based on their belief that India and China will sustain their recent high economic growth over the longer term. While there is a plethora of such statements as well as of studies of the Indian economy, until now there has not been any analytically rigorous, dispassionate and interdisciplinary study of India's long term social and economic future, and an analysis of what it will take India to replicate the past successes—during our own lifetimes—of countries such as Japan, Spain, Singapore, Ireland, Korea and, most recently, China. To fill this gap and building on ADB's own positive experience with the development of a vision of Asia in 2020, we commissioned the Centennial Group to prepare a long term vision of the Indian economy. That study forms the basis of this book. By sponsoring this analytic work, our objective is to provide a hopefully useful input to the country's deliberations of preparing its long term development strategy and a framework for supportive policy and institutional reforms.

The book paints a bold and inspiring scenario of India becoming an affluent society by 2039, that is, within a generation from now. It makes a persuasive case as to why such a scenario could be plausible. Even more importantly, the book very appropriately and frankly assesses the many hurdles—political, social, policy and institutional—that the country must overcome to realize this vision and lift millions of Indians from relative poverty today to enjoy the fruits of a modern and inclusive affluent society within 30 years or so. Its agenda of inter-generational issues is central to India avoiding the middle income trap that so many other countries have fallen into. However, India can successfully tackle this trap only by addressing, and addressing urgently and head on, the various facets of governance highlighted in the book.

India's future success is not only critical to more than one billion Indians but also to peoples elsewhere. Through its success, India would become a beacon of hope throughout the developing world, and greatly help achieve our dream of a world without poverty.

I congratulate the authors for an excellent job.

Haruhiko Kuroda
President
Asian Development Bank

Preface

Do we need yet another study on India? A valid question, given that there is no dearth of studies on India. Indeed, with the reports regularly produced by the plethora of committees and blue ribbon panels, multinational institutions, private financial institutions and think tanks, there is no shortage of analysis or recommendations.

So, what makes this book different? First, while any number of reports on major issues bear on the future prospects of Indian society and economy, they are mostly vertical. They treat a topic in depth but on its own, with limited or no attempt to relate it to other equally important—and perhaps even more fundamental—related topics that have a bearing on possible solutions. This book tries to connect the dots between the key issues that in our view could decide the future of Indian society. Second, multigenerational issues have received rather short shrift in other studies and in the policy debate. This study takes a much longer 30-year perspective, with a corresponding emphasis on challenges that require long gestation to address. Third, the study offers a projection not of what will be but of what India's potential is.

The point of departure is a perspective on where India could be in 30 years and the "promise" that holds for its people. If India maintains anything close to recent economic growth rates—which Japan, South Korea and now China have done in their long growth spurts—it could be one of the top three global economic powers. More important, its people could achieve the living standards of an affluent society.

This is not a preordained state of affairs. But it can happen, and that "can happen" comes with a long list of imperatives. The study also presents the alternative scenario of an India caught in the "middle income trap" if these imperatives are not fulfilled.

The study's other distinguishing features are:

- It is put together by a highly experienced international team that has no institutional or policy agenda—private, multinational or civil.
- During its preparation, the authors consulted widely with policymakers, private sector executives and political leaders at the center and in key states.
- It combines path-breaking analytical work on the lessons from other middle income countries —such as Argentina, Brazil, China, Japan, South Korea, Mexico and the Philippines—with the best work that already exists on India on many topics.
- It puts forth a framework that transcends the traditional ideological debates and gives equal priority to three overarching prerequisites for realizing the promise: maintaining social cohesion; continuously enhancing economic competitiveness; and achieving greater influence and shouldering more responsibility in global fora.
- The study focuses on issues that require long lead times and conveys that success in addressing them will critically determine whether India can deliver on its promise.

A final word on the recommendations and the tone of this study: In our recommendations we draw heavily on the experience of other countries. In doing so we are not oblivious to the fact that India's size, diversity, political system, culture and history make it different. Each country has its own claim to uniqueness. Uniqueness, however, is not a justification for inertia. So each country, while learning from the successes and failures of others, has to devise solutions and take actions that fit its particular circumstances.

The tone of our study is candid and forthright. At the risk of giving unintended offense we deliberately want to provoke discussion and hopefully concordance among the major stakeholders on the complex set of multigenerational issues. This is particularly timely and urgent given the verdict of the electorate in the recent elections. A historic opportunity for bold and far sighted action could be easily frittered away if the momentum is not seized. If the study serves to engage civil society, the press and the private sector in a vigorous ongoing debate with the government—center, state and local—on the need to act decisively on significant multigenerational issues, it will have served its purpose.

Gautam S. Kaji
Chairman, Centennial Group
Chairman, Advisory Board,
Emerging Markets Forum

Acknowledgements

This book is the result of a project of the Centennial Group, coordinated and managed by Harinder S. Kohli, under the overall guidance of Gautam Kaji.

Harinder Kohli is also a co-editor of the book, together wth Anil Sood. Other members of the core team, in alphabetical order are: Richard Ackermann (water); Vinod K. Goel and R. A. Mashelkar (tertiary education, technology development and innovation); Bimal Jalan (role of the state and governance); Homi Kharas (evolution of global economy and India through 2039—the promise); Hossein Razavi (energy revolution); Inder Sud (livable cities and governance); C. M. Vasudev, Hariharan Ramachandran, and Vivek K. Agnihotri (civil service reform); and Michael Walton (tackling inequities and creating contestable markets). Harpaul Alberto Kohli provided data analysis and support. Yanbei Yao oversaw the logistics support.

The book gained greatly from advice and counsel from members of the Advisory Group: Kemal Dervis, Bill Emmott, Rajat Gupta, Bimal Jalan, Caio Koch-Weser, Rajiv Lall, Johannes Linn, Bindu Lohani, Rajat Nag, Prabhakar Narvekar, Deepak Parekh, Andrew Sheng, Arun Shourie, and Vinod Thomas.

The final product reflects valuable comments and critique offered by a large number of people within and outside India. For practical reasons, we can name only a few: Shankar Acharya, Surjit Bhalla, Manu Bhaskaran, Jack Boorman, Prem Garg, Ishrat Husain, Claudio Loser, Srinivasa Madhur, Keshub Mahindra, Jayant Menon, Nitin Paranjpe, Bruce Ross-Larson, V. Sundararajan, and Arvind Virmani.

This book is based on a nine-volume study released at the Emerging Markets Forum meetings held in Mumbai and Delhi from June 23–26, 2009. The study was funded by a grant from the Asian Development Bank.

The book itself is the result of a collaborative and joint effort of Harinder Kohli and Anil Sood with invaluable support from Aaron Szyf. They and other authors are obligated to Sunanda Ghosh, Rekha Natarajan, Sugata Ghosh and their collegues at Sage Publications for their support and encouragement and for publishing the book under a very tight time schedule.

Finally, the authors are grateful for the inspiration and encouragement provided—and the insistence on intellectual rigor demanded—by Mr. Montek Singh Ahluwalia, Deputy Chairman, Planning Commission of India, and Mr. Haruhiko Kuroda, President of the Asian Development Bank.

Introduction:
Determined marathoner or sporadic sprinter?

Harinder S. Kohli

India now has the second fastest growing large economy in the world, surpassed only by China. Its per capita income approached $1,000 in 2007, when the economy exceeded $1 trillion for the first time. While still home to the largest number of absolute poor and with average per capita income only a ninth of the global average, India has just been classified as a lower middle-income country, a far cry from the 1970s, when it was still one of the world's poorest countries.

When measured in purchasing power terms—the measure used by many economists to do cross country comparisons—India is already the fourth largest economy in the world behind only US, China and Japan, and ahead of Germany, UK and France. India today is a global leader in information technology industry. It is also home to many world-class corporations that enjoy global brand recognition and are expanding overseas to join the club of top global companies.

India's recent economic successes are due primarily to its dynamic and competitive private sector and to the can-do spirit of the younger generation and of the newly confident middle class—despite massive failures of government on most fronts.

As an Op-Ed article in the January 2, 2009, New York Times put it, "Both the Chinese and the Indians are convinced that their prosperity will only increase in the 21st century. In China it will be induced by the state; in India's case, it may well happen despite the state."

Fundamentals driving India's growth —and hurdles

India enjoys strong fundamentals, the basic ingredients for driving economic growth over a long period, making India potentially an affluent society within a generation—fulfilling Nehru's dream of "India's tryst with destiny."

The fundamentals:

- In the next 30 years, growth in Asia will likely dominate the world economy, and the Asian economies, including India, can benefit from neighborhood effects—the fastest growing markets in the world (in East Asia) will be closer to home.
- India's domestic savings and investment rates have reached East Asian levels that, along with prudent macroeconomic policies, would drive productivity improvements and fuel rapid economic growth.
- The growth of manufacturing has finally started to pick up, broadening growth beyond its vaunted information technology sector.
- India's forthcoming "demographic dividend" and urbanization should fuel further growth.
- The rapid increase in the size of India's emerging middle class would promote entrepreneurship and fuel consumption.
- The shift in values to those typical of the middle class in higher income countries that generally underpin the political economy of reform— independent thinking, self-reliance, hard work, entrepreneurial spirit—appears to be now well underway in India.

But these strong fundamentals are hampered by some major handicaps—including infrastructure bottlenecks, poor educational and healthcare systems and, above all, massive government failures, outdated bureaucracy and poor governance.

The big unknown about future performance is whether India can address these handicaps fast enough to allow the strong fundamentals to drive economic and social progress over the longer term—or whether these handicaps will overwhelm the fundamentals and ultimately drive down the growth rates closer to the "Hindu rate of growth" seen until the 1970s.

The lessons of experience from other middle-income countries—such as Argentina, Brazil, Mexico and the Philippines—are sobering. They became mired in low or even negligible growth rates for extended periods after enjoying a spurt of high growth that enabled them to reach middle-income status. In this book, we call this phenomenon the "middle income trap."

In addition to addressing its own unique internal constraints, both real and perceived, India would need to avoid this middle income trap—successfully avoided by many countries in East Asia and a handful of countries in Europe (Japan, Hong Kong, Korea, Singapore, Taiwan, Ireland and Spain)—for it to enjoy sustained economic success that otherwise appears within its grasp.

Indeed, there is a greater than even chance that India may get mired into the middle income trap unless there is a fundamental change in the mindset, unless governance is improved dramatically, and unless concrete actions, as opposed to innocuous pronouncements, are taken soon on the issues highlighted in the book.

Need for a longer-term vision, and change in mindset

Despite India's recent success, the political and economic debate still appears hostage to the issues that the country struggled with in an environment of low growth and mass poverty. Propelled by the first generation of macroeconomic reforms launched around 1990, which plucked the low hanging fruit, India has been able to jumpstart growth. But it is still reliant on the basic institutional structures, practices and mindsets inherited from the British Raj. Major policy and institutional reforms seemingly are taken on only in times of crisis and under duress, not as part of a long-term strategy that anticipates and promotes change.

These structures and mindsets—basically intact under successive governments comprising political parties of all economic and social philosophies—need to change rapidly for the economy to maintain high growth and to mature. Indeed, a paradigm shift is long overdue.

The time has come to ground the policy debate in a longer term vision of where the country could be one generation from today and to consider how to start transforming the country's institutional, administrative and governance systems at all levels to meet the needs of a vast, dynamic, rapidly growing and young society that must wrestle with being rich and poor at the same time, being sophisticated and yet backward, and becoming a prospective global economic heavyweight but without equivalent political and military muscle.

To stimulate such debate, this book presents a longer-term vision of India's economy.

A determined marathoner or a sporadic sprinter?

The starting point of the book is the presentation of a vision of India's promise as a "determined marathoner" that overcomes the challenges and sustains recent growth rates. The alternative scenario is that of a "sporadic sprinter" that periodically puts out a burst of reforming zeal when prodded by crisis.

The payoff to the marathoner is huge: India could have the second largest economy in the world (larger than the US) of $36 trillion, and a per capita income of about $22,000 by 2039, four times what the sporadic sprinter can expect to achieve.

But, the cost of getting bogged down and becoming exhausted like a sprinter are equally huge: a per capita income of only $5,500 or less (the level reached by Brazil as far back as 1978), and an economy one fourth the size anticipated under the first scenario; only $8 trillion and thus yet another medium sized economy in the global community of nations.

In human terms, the stakes for the next generation(s) of Indians are truly staggering. Under the first scenario, the billion and half Indians living in the late 2030s will enjoy the fruits of an affluent society while under the second scenario they will have average incomes no better than South Africa of today. Put another way, if India can develop along the affluent scenario indicated here, it can eliminate poverty within 15 years, under the World Bank $1 a day poverty figure of 456 million poor in 2005 or the Indian government figure of 310 million.

Responsibility of India's current leadership

The burden of determining as to what kind of life our future generations will inherit thus falls on India's leaders of today. The critical question then is: Are they ready

to live up to their obligations by meeting the challenges before them and seizing with both hands a unique window of opportunity presented to them by the electorate in the May 2009 elections so unexpectedly? Or, would they squander the opportunity because of complacency arising from satisfaction with short-term success combined with reluctance (or inability) to challenge the status quo?

The recent work of the Commission on Growth and Development, chaired by Nobel Laureate Michael Spence, suggests that the main distinction between marathoners and sprinters is the single-minded pursuit of their economic and social objectives spanning the terms of several governments.

The marathoners did this by creating the institutional capabilities to develop and periodically re-evaluate long-term strategies, set targets, monitor achievements and adjust policies and implementation as necessary. They never lost sight of what they wished to ultimately achieve by improving their governance and building their implementation capabilities to execute their strategies. And they remained ruthlessly focused on results, outcomes and implementation effectiveness. That in turn meant that the approach had to be pragmatic rather than doctrinaire. These ingredients were present in each of the East Asian countries that successfully avoided the middle income trap.

The marathoner economies reap the rewards because they consistently and steadily pursue their objective over the long haul; the sporadic sprinter economies on the other hand are less dependable as they react to external stimuli rather than internal drive. But once growth slows, it becomes hard to revive. Marathoners, by contrast, build the momentum to grow through the middle income trap.

This has a fundamental implication for India and the Indian leadership today. India cannot wait until it has fallen into the middle income trap to initiate remedial measures to escape. Instead, it must take anticipatory measures in advance to avoid getting mired in it to begin with. Hence, the time to start worrying about the middle income trap is now.

Objective and approach of the book

This book is meant to present to India's leadership of today, in government, business, and civic society as well as the intellectuals at large, the major issues, challenges, and choices that, in our opinion, they need to confront, starting now, so as to maximize the prospects of our upcoming generations enjoying the fruits of an affluent society.

The basic premise of this book is that India can indeed be a growth marathoner, but it must understand the world it is and will be operating in and the changing shape of its economic footprint. It must start to put in place the institutions and policy frameworks consistent with a move from poverty to affluence in one generation. Few countries have achieved this, so the challenge is enormous. But no country has achieved it without serious deliberations over the ingredients for sustained growth.

Rather than getting bogged down in a spurious debate over the feasibility of either scenario or any specific numbers therein, we hope the readers will focus on what bold and ambitious strategy and actions are required to achieve an outcome proximate to the book's vision of an affluent India in one generation.

This mindset will in turn allow the readers to feel more free to ask tough what-if questions, and bring into greater relief the major structural changes that the society and economy must undergo to sustain the past decade's growth over the next three decades.

The book has five basic building blocks. The first is a model comprising some 150 countries that develops possible contours of the global economy between 2007 and 2039. The evolution of the Indian economy under two different scenarios—of the marathoner and of the sprinter—is developed through this model to help address what-if questions.

The second building block is a comparison of successful East Asian economies (that have sidestepped the middle income trap as they grew rapidly from the low to middle income status to high income status in our own lifetimes) with a number of Latin American and Middle Eastern economies that fell into the middle income trap. From this comparison, we have identified the key characteristics that seem to account for the differences.

The third building block is a review of the special characteristics of India—the world's second most populous country; a large, continental-sized economy; a diverse, multi-lingual, multi-caste and multi-religious nation; a relatively poor society; a noisy and vibrant democracy; and a free press and active civic society— that pose special challenges.

These first three building blocks in turn allow us to develop the fourth building block: the framework for our analysis that is informed both by the global experience of marathoners and sprinters as well as the challenges unique to India.

This framework emphasizes the critical importance of successfully navigating simultaneous transformations in three areas: moving from a poor society to a cohesive, affluent society; moving from a domestically oriented to a globally competitive economy and moving from a small player in global affairs to a responsible global citizen as India's global economic footprint jumps by a factor of nine in a span of 30 years.

The fifth and final building block is the identification of a number of critical multi-generational issues on which early actions are absolutely essential for India to successfully navigate these transformations. The list of such issues explored by us is by no means exhaustive. Instead, it includes issues that in our view are not yet receiving adequate attention in the policy debate in the country but the resolution of which is a necessary (though not sufficient) condition for India's future success. Solutions to all these issues have long gestation periods, and therefore work on them must be started immediately.

This book is divided into four parts, with a total of 13 chapters.

Part I provides the overall framework for the book, and offers our view of how India can avoid falling into the middle income trap. It comprises four separate chapters (chapters 1 to 4). Based on the model of the global economy mentioned earlier, chapter 1 visualizes India's promise as a marathoner. It is followed by a discussion (chapter 2) of the phenomenon of the middle income trap, and the costs to India of getting mired in it. We then identify in chapter 3 the key prerequisites for staying on the marathoner route, and discuss the three simultaneous transformations India must navigate successfully. This discussion also allows us to identify a number of key intergenerational issues that India must tackle urgently under each of these transformations. It also points out new challenges that will arise from success. The remaining parts of this book deal with those challenges:

- Much higher expectations of the public as citizens of a rich and democratic country.
- Massive appetite for natural resources (including energy).
- Huge disparities of incomes and living standards with its immediate neighbors (potentially making it a magnet for immigration for hundreds of millions).
- Much greater scrutiny from the international community as India's global footprint expands.

Part I concludes with a detailed discussion of seven facets of governance (chapter 4) that our work suggests are fundamental to satisfactory resolution of all intergenerational issues identified in our book.

Part II focuses on the challenges associated with creating a cohesive society in India. It includes three chapters that discuss at length the three most important intergenerational issues in this respect. Chapter 5 discusses issues related to the structural inequities and the dire implications of not tackling them. It concludes by suggesting key remedial measures. Chapter 6 follows with a discussion of the need to fundamentally improve the access and quality of all public services to the entire Indian nation. As a concrete test of the government's resolve and ability to do so, it suggests an initial focus on the creation of functioning cities, perhaps starting with the 100 largest metropolitan areas. Specific measures are proposed. Finally, chapter 7 discusses the environment. It proposes that the basic objective, focus and mindset of the government in its environmental policy and actions should be first and foremost to improve the quality of life under which the citizens live. The highest priority should be given to providing clean water, sewerage and sanitary conditions to everyone, and dramatically improving air quality in the major cities. It also discusses the serious problems related to water resources management and issues related to India's stance in the ongoing global negotiations on climate change.

Part III focuses on the challenges associated with creating a more globally competitive economy—not only the one-time immediate challenge but also how India may continuously climb up the global technological ladder as countries such as Japan and Korea have done in the past and China is doing now. It includes separate chapters on three key related intergenerational issues: infrastructure (chapter 8); energy (chapter 9) and tertiary education, technological development and innovation (chapter 10).

Finally, Part IV focuses on the overarching issue of governance, which in our view is the biggest hurdle to India sustaining a high growth rate over the next thirty years and becoming an affluent society. It emphasize the need for a fundamental change in the basic mindset—to an unyielding fixation on implementation, results, and accountability—which can only come about by transforming governance in three crucial and related areas: role of the state (chapter 11); decentralization or devolution of authority and accountability to the state and local (municipal and panchayat) levels as anticipated in the Indian constitution (chapter 12) and reforming the public administration and the civil service (chapter 13).

INDIA
2039

Part
I

India's
promise, and
imperatives
to achieving it

INDIA
2039

Part I

Chapter 1

India's promise

India's promise: An affluent society in one generation

Homi Kharas

Economic history in the making

In 2007, India's per capita GDP was $940 (at market exchange rates). Based on this performance, the World Bank reclassified it from a low income country to a lower middle income country in 2008. In 2007, the least affluent "advanced economy" on the International Monetary Fund's (IMF) list was Taiwan, with a GDP per capita of $16,768. Although the IMF uses other criteria as well as income to determine when an economy should be classified as "advanced," income is a good proxy.[1] On this basis India could become an advanced economy by 2035. In other words, India has the potential to go from a poor, developing country to an advanced economy within 30 years or less—a single generation.

The Indian economy passed another milestone in 2007—$1 trillion in gross output. That made India the world's 12th largest economy. In 2008, India's economy rose to $1.2 trillion. In purchasing price parity (PPP) terms, in 2008, India had the world's fourth largest economy ($3.5 trillion). By the time it becomes advanced, it might be the second largest economy (at market exchange rates). Second only to China, it could surpass the United States by 2039. In other words, India has the potential to overtake the United States within a generation, even though it is only one-seventh its size today.

Both statements are conditional, for this is what India could do, not what it will do, or even what is likely. The transformations required are formidable and unprecedented (chapter 3). But they are not beyond imagination. If India can replicate the experiences of China, Japan and South Korea, the changes are possible. But if it follows in the footsteps of middle income Brazil or Mexico, it could become stuck, with its growth slowing considerably.

The difference between India's performing up to its potential and muddling through is profound, both for India and the world. There is so much at stake that it behooves policymakers to think through very seriously what may be necessary to ensure that India sustains and accelerates its growth to its full potential.

The central questions here are: If India could fulfil its potential, what would such a trajectory look like? What would be the shape of a world with a dynamic India in its midst? Should policymakers take such a scenario seriously and do what it takes to push India along such a path?

To answer these questions, we use a global model that provides a sense of the economic trajectory of different country groups. Countries are categorized in four ways, so the model is called the four-speed world. Like all long-run models, the purpose is illustrative, to foster debate rather than predict the future. Within broad analytical categories that might shape country economic performance, there will inevitably be large variations between countries, which are left unexplained, and equally large variations for any given country over time. The purpose is not to develop forecasts or projections for any country or any time period, but to indicate the contours of the global economy over the next three decades.

Three assumptions

Three assumptions are the foundation for this analysis. First, the world is indeed in the midst of a historic but peaceful restructuring—with the relative economic weight of developing countries in general, and Asia in particular, set to become much larger. Second, the current financial turmoil, painful as it is, will be managed and global growth will resume by the end of 2009 or early 2010. Third, the difficulties that many middle income economies have had in growing rapidly to become advanced are due to deficiencies in their policies and strategies and are not structural. That is, the economic destiny of countries like India lies largely in their own hands.

Peaceful and orderly restructuring of the global economy

Most of us have lived through a period with extraordinary stability in global output. Once the post–World War II world settled down and the reconstruction of war-shattered economies was largely complete, the global economy was dominated by seven advanced countries. In 1975, following the first oil price shock and an ensuing global recession, six major industrial economies agreed to an annual meeting of senior finance officials to discuss global economic issues.[2] The following year, Canada was invited to join the group, and the G-7 came into being.

The significance of the G-7 was that the officials who gathered at the meetings represented the major economies. Their aggregate output was roughly two-thirds of global output. Whether by design or accident, these same seven countries dominated the world economy for a considerable period. In the 40 years between 1965 and 2004, their share of the global economy averaged 65 percent. There were some fluctuations, but in no year did the share move outside a narrow band of ± 3 percentage points from this average. Despite the Vietnam War, two oil shocks, the collapse of the Bretton Woods fixed exchange rate regime, 1970s stagflation, debt crises, the fall of the Soviet Union, the Plaza Accord, the emergence of the Euro zone and the dot-com crash, the

same seven countries accounted for two-thirds of global output year after year.

That extraordinary period of stability appears to have come to an end (figure 1). The IMF estimate of the G-7 global output share for 2008 is 52.7 percent, a drop of 10 percentage points in the four years since 2004. The share of developing countries rose from 22 percent to 31 percent in this same time frame. A major structural shift in the world economy seems under way. Such shifts are rare, but not without precedent. The economic historian Angus Maddison has constructed a long time series of global output[3] showing that significant shifts in the world economy have indeed taken place before (figure 2).

Before 1700, just over half the world's output was in East Asia and India (in purchasing power parity prices). India alone had a share of almost one quarter. But after the death of Emperor Aurangzeb and the decline of the Mughal empire, India's relative economic fortunes started to decline. India's nadir came in 1992, when gross Indian output accounted for only 1.01 percent of global output (in current prices). During the early Industrial Revolution, Western Europe gained more than

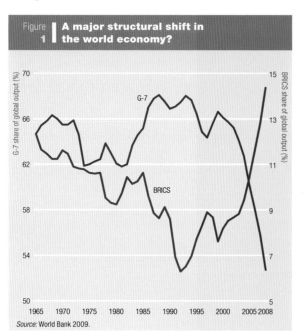

Figure 1 | A major structural shift in the world economy?

Source: World Bank 2009.

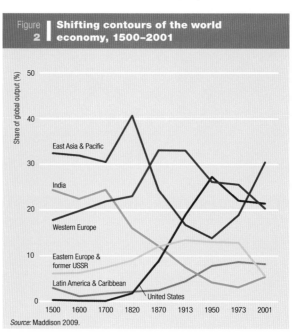

Figure 2 | Shifting contours of the world economy, 1500–2001

Source: Maddison 2009.

❝❝ Major global economic changes have occurred, but global stability has also persisted for long periods

10 percentage points of world output. The rise of the United States was even more dramatic. In the century between 1850 and 1950, it went from 5 percent of the world's economy to one-quarter—a 20-percentage point rise. More recently, East Asia has expanded, led first by Japan and then by China. East Asia's share has expanded by 15 percentage points already, with more to come.

This brief historical detour illustrates a simple point: major global economic changes have occurred, but global stability has also persisted for long periods. Some analysts have suggested that major transitions of economic power are associated with wars (witness the decline of Europe during 1913–50, when that continent suffered two world wars), while other experiences suggest that change can be peaceful (the postwar rise of East Asia).[4] Here it is simply assumed that the world economic transformation will continue to be peaceful and that India can be a part of this transformation. India has a long way to go before it regains its historical share of world output, and it should be possible for the world to accommodate rapid growth from a country with a small base. But resistance to a restructuring of major economic and political power depends in part on how many other emerging economies also grow fast. It is assumed, based on recent economic performance, that some large countries, such as Brazil and Mexico, may not.

Early and smooth end to the financial crisis
It may strike some as strange to advance scenarios of rapid, indeed accelerating, economic growth when the world economy is in the throes of its worst crisis in decades, possibly since the Great Depression. According to the IMF, advanced economies will probably see negative growth in 2009. The effects are already evident in the slower growth of developing economies. A "decoupling" of developing and advanced economies does not seem to be supported from an empirical point of view.

Why then at this time should India still consider rapid history-making growth? The answer lies largely with

today's financial crisis and the transmission mechanism from advanced to developing countries.

The financial crisis has had major effects on bank balance sheets and the willingness to supply credit throughout the economy. But with measures in place to alleviate the worst of the credit crunch, the impact on the real economy seems to be channelled through changes in demand. Aggregate demand in the United States collapsed until mid-2009 as consumers retrenched. Investment fell first as housing starts and broader construction slowed. Net exports were one bright spot in the third quarter of 2008, but that too seemed set to fade as a source of growth as the crisis spreads to other countries and affected growth in major U.S. markets. The point is that this is a problem of inadequate demand, a problem that has well tried solutions now being applied across the world—a major loosening of monetary policy and a huge fiscal stimulus to boost aggregate demand. As the book went to press, there were signs that this mega recession may finally be coming to an end thanks to these extraordinary and globally coordinated efforts.

What could be the impact of the crisis on U.S. income in, say, 30 years? The United States has faced other demand shocks, including the Great Depression. What do those experiences suggest for long-run effects of the crisis? That the long-term effects could appear mild a decade from now. Most depressions are offset by above-average growth during the recovery phase. In the United States, incomes actually overshot their long-term trend, before settling back to the pre-crisis trend line (figure 3). The permanent effect of the Great Depression on U.S. income seems to have been small. As the Council of Economic Advisers noted in its 2009 report, "Historically the strength of a recovery appears to be loosely correlated with the depth of the preceding recession. Moreover ... to the extent that a recession is deeper than the average ... most of the excess depth is offset within the first four quarters of the recovery."[5]

In other words, the effects of a crisis disappear over the long term, and long-run income reverts to the

Aggregate-demand-induced recessions tend to dissipate over time and have lower long-term effects on income than aggregate supply shocks

trend in the underlying determinants of the supply of goods—labor, capital and technical progress.

A similar pattern is found in developing countries. East Asia had been growing steadily for more than 30 years when it was hit by a crisis in several major economies—Indonesia, Malaysia, South Korea and Thailand—in 1997/98 (figure 4). Income levels in the region temporarily declined, but four years later returned to the long-run trend. Of course, performance differed across countries, but taken as a whole the crisis did not derail East Asia's impressive performance.

Analytical work confirms this visual evidence. The long-term growth trend in the United States has shown remarkable steadiness, decade after decade, averaging 1.8 percent a year with minimal variation.[6] There has been short-term variability along with the business cycle and some medium-term variability that may indicate that economic policy and technological factors can also affect growth.

The most pronounced medium-term deviation from the long-term trend in the United States was 1973 to 1995, when per capita GDP growth slowed to 0.6

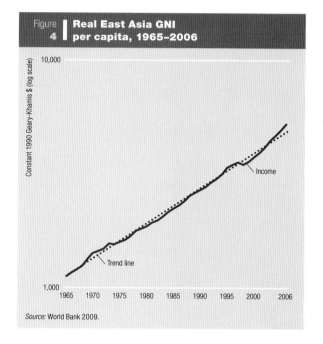

Figure 4 | Real East Asia GNI per capita, 1965–2006

Source: World Bank 2009.

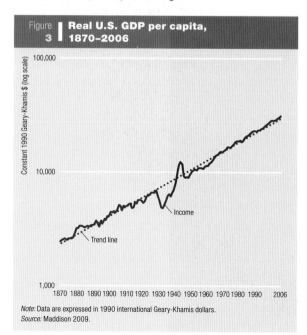

Figure 3 | Real U.S. GDP per capita, 1870–2006

Note: Data are expressed in 1990 international Geary-Khamis dollars.
Source: Maddison 2009.

percent. Unlike short-term business cycles, the economy during this phase remained close to its potential output. The slowdown was not a matter of deficient aggregate demand but of supply expanding much slower. The explanation for this slowdown (and the subsequent acceleration) remains a puzzle. But the point is that aggregate-demand-induced recessions tend to dissipate over time and have lower long-term effects on income than aggregate supply shocks. To the extent that the current financial crisis is transmitted largely through demand channels, the long-term effects should be small.

For the most part, the transmission of the crisis to developing countries is through demand. Most developing countries have chosen a cautious approach towards capital account liberalization. Their banks are less exposed to "toxic assets". As a result, the principal concern is with a slowdown in export markets. But with healthy foreign exchange reserves and modest current account deficits (surpluses in some cases), there is ample scope in many large emerging economies for a fiscal and monetary stimulus to avoid the worst effects of lower global demand growth.

> **Few countries sustain high growth for more than a generation, and even fewer continue their high growth rates once they reach middle income status**

Such a stimulus can also offset an emerging secondary channel for the crisis to spread to developing countries—through consumer and investor confidence. Lower confidence has dampened credit markets even in developing countries where bank assets had not been impaired. The lack of "animal spirits" is another classic Keynesian symptom that can be addressed through aggressive aggregate demand management and monetary and credit easing.

So, a key assumption for this analysis is that the current global recession reflects a fall in aggregate demand and not a secular stagnation or a fault in the capitalist system. If this is indeed the case, the short-term effects can be mitigated through standard policy responses, which are already being implemented in many countries. And the longer term impact on global incomes and growth should be small.

Adroit avoidance of the middle income trap
Few countries sustain high growth for more than a generation, and even fewer continue their high growth

rates once they reach middle income status. Reaching incomes associated with the advanced countries is uncommon: only six of the high-growth countries did so. More common is for growth to slow down markedly on reaching middle income. Many Latin American and Middle Eastern countries suffered this middle income country trap.

Our third assumption is that the middle income trap is a matter of country policy, not a structural phenomenon. That is, all countries are capable of emulating the high-income East Asian economies and can grow rapidly from middle income to advanced economies if they develop and implement the right strategies and policies That is, the economic destiny of countries like India lies largely in their own hands. (A more in-depth discussion of this phenomenon follows in chapter 2.)

A scenario of global growth, 2007–39: A four-speed world

A stylized view of the world classifies 145 countries into one of four categories, each with different growth

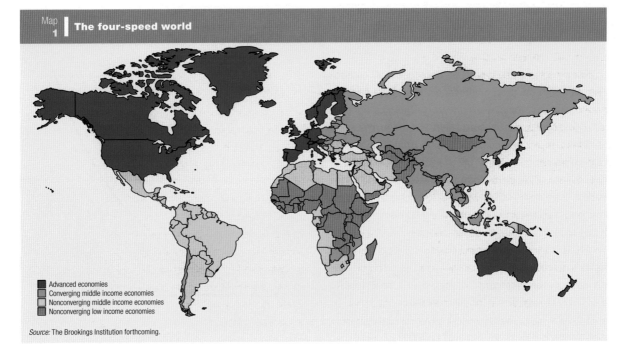

Map 1 | The four-speed world

■ Advanced economies
■ Converging middle income economies
□ Nonconverging middle income economies
■ Nonconverging low income economies

Source: The Brookings Institution forthcoming.

> **By 2039, the world would be very different from today's…. The economic center of gravity would shift to Asia**

drivers, that can be aggregated to generate a scenario of global growth (map 1; annex 1):

- Affluent countries (blue) have steadily pushed out frontier technology at 1.3 percent a year. For the United States this technical growth, coupled with more capital, has allowed labour productivity to advance at a steady 1.8 percent a year for 125 years. Other affluent countries are following suit.

- A second group of poor and middle income countries ("convergers", green) have converged with affluent countries over an extended period, demonstrating a capacity for rapid "catch-up" technology growth along with heavy investment in physical and human capital.

- Middle income countries that have had sporadic periods of growth offset by spells of slower growth—those caught in the middle income trap—are a third category (yellow). Many of these countries have significant natural resources and grow when commodity prices rise, but stall when prices fall.

- The fourth category (orange) is poor countries that for a variety of reasons associated with landlockedness, poor governance and conflict find growth elusive.

Each region in the world has countries in all categories, although the distribution varies. Most East Asian economies, and India, are in the convergers category.

The global economy surpassed $62 trillion, measured at market exchange rates, in 2008, dominated by the United States, with a $14.3 trillion economy, just under one-quarter of the global total. India was the world's 11th largest economy in 2008, with a GDP exceeding $1.2 trillion, or 2 percent of global output, just surpassing South Korea (which has only 49 million people).

By 2039, the world would be very different from today's. It would be significantly wealthier, with per capita incomes averaging $23,400, nearly three times the $8,500 today. The economic center of gravity would shift to Asia, which today accounts for 22 percent of global activity, but by 2039 could account for more than

half. Three giant economies, China, India and Japan, would lead Asia's resurgence. But other large countries like Indonesia and Vietnam would also have significant economic mass. Even Malaysia and Thailand could have economies larger than what Spain has today.

The rise of Asia would not be unprecedented. Indeed, it would bring Asia's economic share into line with its population share and restore the balance of global economic activity to that in the 18th and early 19th centuries, before the Industrial Revolution led to the great divergence of incomes across countries.

The converse of Asia's rise would be a fall in the share of the G-7 economies. Their global income share has fallen to new post–World War II lows, and by 2039 it could be just over 30 percent.

To appreciate the likelihood of this enormous change, consider the following facts. Taking out the effect of general inflation, the global economy reached $20 trillion (in 2007 dollars) in 1973, after the first oil price shock (figure 5). It took 22 years to double to $40 trillion by 1995—with 3.2 percent annual growth. Over the last

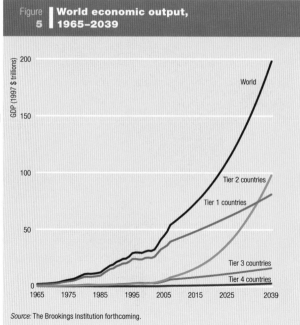

Figure 5 | World economic output, 1965–2039

Source: The Brookings Institution forthcoming.

> **Overall global growth will accelerate simply because of the larger share in global output from fast growing countries**

12 years, from 1995 to 2007, annual growth has been 3.5 percent. Over the last 5 years, global growth has been 7.5 percent, thanks to a major run-up in commodity prices, strong growth in developing countries and significant currency appreciation against the U.S. dollar in many parts of the world. To get to $200 trillion by 2039, global growth from 2008 would need to be 3.9 percent.

The reason for expecting an acceleration of global growth is that the share of rapidly growing economies has now risen to almost half of total output, while the share of slow growing countries has fallen. The model used here assumes that affluent country growth will slow in the next 30 years to 2.3 percent, from 2.5 percent over the last 10 years. Meanwhile the "convergers" could grow at 8.2 percent, close to the 8.4 percent over the last 10 years.

In other words, although growth is slowing in individual country groups, overall global growth will accelerate simply because of the larger share in global output from fast growing countries.

Not all recent growth is attributed to "convergers". High oil and commodity prices have also driven nominal global GDP higher and boosted many emerging economies. Some of the fastest increases in GDP have come in economies like Brazil. In 2007, Brazilian GDP was $1.3 trillion, twice the size of its 2004 economy. This expansion was due to the rise in prices for Brazil's commodity exports, coupled with a sharp appreciation in Brazilian exchange rates. Such growth is clearly cyclical, not structural. Commodity price levels may continue at 2007 levels (abstracting from the sharp boom and bust cycle of 2008), but the rate of change of commodity prices will not be higher than general inflation. That is why Brazil and other resource intensive countries remain classified in the middle income trap, despite strong recent growth.

One reason developing countries are growing faster than developed countries is that they are younger— still at an early phase in their demographic transition. Global demographic shifts are inexorably changing the distribution of global economic activity. Today's affluent countries accounted for 22 percent of the world's people in 1965, but only account for 15 percent today, and their share is forecast to shrink to one-eighth of the world total by 2039. Overall, the world will add 2 billion people by 2039. But the population in today's affluent countries will grow by only an estimated 100 million. Ninety-five percent of the population increase (excluding migration) will be in developing countries.

India's promise

India had consistent annual growth of 3.5 percent during 1950–79, the "Hindu" rate of growth. In the ensuing two decades, growth increased to 5.5 percent. There is still considerable controversy about the role of economic reforms in this acceleration. Some argue that growth preceded reforms.[7] Others point to much higher growth rates in 1994–97, coinciding with the major post-reform period.[8] Regardless, it took most observers by surprise when India accelerated sharply to 8.5 percent a year between 2003 and 2007.

The episodes of "structural" changes in India's growth suggest that the past is not prologue. Any estimation of growth potential based on historical growth rates would have missed two turning points in Indian growth performance: in the early 1980s and in 2003.

The model here suggests that India could accelerate its potential growth even further to 8.5 percent per capita for the next 30 years. With population growing at about 1 percent, this implies a real GDP growth of around 9.5 percent. At these growth rates, the Indian economy would increase by a factor of 19. In real terms it would reach $20 trillion, one and a half times as big as the U.S. economy today.

Even that underestimates India's potential global footprint. Because of real exchange rate appreciation, India's actual economic size by 2039 could be more than $36 trillion in 2007 dollars—or more than half of today's global output. At that level, India would be generating one-sixth of 2039 global output, about the same proportion as its population. In other words, India would no longer be a poor country with a minor global economic footprint—it would be an average income economy, with a large global footprint. And with the

> **India's per capita income in 2039 could be more than $22,000.... India could go from poverty to affluence in one generation**

Table 1 | From poverty to affluence in one generation

	2007	2039
Global output	$62 trillion	$200 trillion
Asia's share	20% or more	50% or more
Average income		
Global	$8,500	$23,400
India	$940	$22,000
India's rank	12th largest economy	2nd largest economy
India's footprint in global economy	<2%	>17%

Source: Authors' calculations.

world affluent on average by 2039, India too would be affluent (table 1). India's per capita income in 2039 could be more than $22,000, adjusted for inflation and real exchange rate movements. In other words, India could go from poverty to affluence in one generation.

The long-term growth scenario here is consistent with India's medium-term growth forecasts. The 11th Five-Year Plan, developed by the Planning Commission in November 2007 to provide a macroeconomic scenario for 2008–12, envisages growth of 9 percent. But the Prime Minister has pushed for 10 percent growth to accelerate the reduction in Indian poverty. India's former Chief Economic Adviser in the Ministry of Finance, Dr. Arvind Virmani, proposes 9 percent as the sustainable trend level for the next five years, but notes that the trend level for growth has been rising.[9] As early as 2001, a McKinsey report on India indicated that a 10 percent growth rate was achievable, driven by productivity improvements stemming largely from removing distortions in land and product markets.[10] The IMF, in a recent review of Indian growth potential, shows that scholars have systematically been raising their estimates of India's long-run prospects: Rodrik and Subramanian (2004) to 7.3–7.6 percent; Bosworth and Collins (2006) to 8–8.4 percent; International Monetary Fund (2006) to 8.7–9 percent; and Poddar and Yi (2007) to 9.5–9.8 percent.[11]

Comparisons with other middle income economies

To give some sense of whether these growth rates are achievable, it helps to compare India's projected performance with its past. Over 2003–07, the Indian economy grew from $680 billion to $1.1 trillion (adjusted for inflation)—or 12.8 percent in real dollars. This is higher than the 8.5 percent real growth rate officially registered by India because of the appreciation of the Indian rupee. Under the model scenario, India would need to grow at 11.5 percent in dollar terms—that is, slower than over those four years.

It also helps to compare India's projected growth with growth spurts in China, Japan, South Korea and Taiwan (figure 6).

- Taiwan had a per capita GDP of $1,442 in 1965 (the earliest point in our data sample). Thirty years later, in 1995, its GDP per capita was $17,500. The average annual growth rate over this 30 years was 8.7 percent.

- China's decision to open its economy and accelerate reforms can be dated to 1993, the year after Deng Xiaopeng's "Tour through the South". This is also the year when most prices were liberalized and the third plenum of the 14th Party Congress officially committed to move towards a "socialist market economy". In 1993, China's income per capita was $531. Fifteen

> **India has been following in China's footsteps, with a lag of a decade**

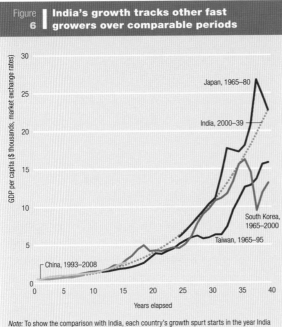

Figure 6 | India's growth tracks other fast growers over comparable periods

Note: To show the comparison with India, each country's growth spurt starts in the year India would have the same starting income.
Source: World Bank 2009.

Under the model scenario, India continues to match for the next 15 years what China, and earlier South Korea, have already done. The scenario for India is almost identical to the 30-year actual performance for South Korea, until the 1997 crisis knocked it from its long-run trajectory. And the projected scenario for India from 2024 onward matches (or slightly underperforms) Japan's growth surge from 1965 to 1980. The main conclusion is that India's recent experience and the other fast growing economies suggest that this scenario is feasible.

Reasons for optimism

There are many reasons to be optimistic about Indian growth:

- The global economy could be set for faster long-term growth, thanks to the structural change towards developing countries; growth in Asia will dominate, with India benefiting from neighbourhood effects—the fastest growing markets in the world will be closer to home.
- Indian investment levels and manufacturing growth have started to pick up.

years later, China is expected to reach $2,720, with average annual growth at 11.5 percent.

- South Korea began its reforms in the early 1960s. In 1965 its income was around $700. By 1996, just before the Asian crisis, its income had risen to $16,230, with average annual growth of 10.7 percent over 31 years.
- Japan was a much more advanced economy than India in 1965. It already had a per capita income of $6,050, a level that the model does not expect India to reach until 2024. For the next 15 years, 1965–80, Japan's income grew at 9.2 percent and in 1980 it reached $22,700, almost exactly the same as the income India could reach in 2039.

For almost 20 years India has been following in China's footsteps, with a lag of a decade. In 1991 India's per capita income was almost exactly the same as China's was in 1981. In 2008 India's income may reach $1,060, mirroring China's in 1998 (figure 7).

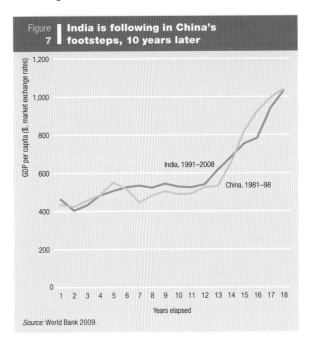

Figure 7 | India is following in China's footsteps, 10 years later

Source: World Bank 2009.

> **Indian fixed investment has sharply increased in the past few years, steadily rising from 22 percent of GDP in the 1980s to 25 percent in the 1990s to more than 35 percent in recent years**

- India has turned the corner on public sector debt—the share of interest in GDP that must be financed from budget resources has fallen since 2002, leaving more fiscal space for infrastructure spending (although the stimulus package cut into that space).
- Indian demographics and urbanization are favourable.
- India's emerging middle class can drive growth in the same way as in other countries.
- The shift in values that underpins the political economy of reform appears to be well in hand in India.

A shift toward Asia

To understand the effect of the shift of global economic mass towards Asia, look at India-China trade,[12] which has been growing at more than 50 percent a year since 2002, to reach about $37 billion in 2007. While overall trade was growing rapidly in both countries, the growth rate of bilateral India–China trade was twice the average growth in total exports from either country. China is already India's top trading partner. After adjusting for partner GDP, the propensity to trade between China and India is also higher than for any other major trading partner. Already, there are significant acquisitions by Indian companies in China and vice-versa. As these business ties deepen, the underpinnings of future trade growth will become stronger.

In other words, India's proximity to China, and by extension to the whole of East Asia, will be a factor in its projected growth acceleration.

Rising manufacturing growth and investment rates

One factor that has traditionally held back aggregate growth in India has been the mediocre performance of its manufacturing and the relatively low level of investment and gross capital formation. From 1960 to 2005 Indian manufacturing never saw 10 consecutive years averaging more than 7 percent growth. Many other countries—including such underperformers as Brazil,

Côte d'Ivoire, Ethiopia, Kenya, Mexico, Pakistan, the Philippines and Tanzania—had peak decadal manufacturing growth that exceeded India. As a result, Indian manufacturing's share of GDP in 2006 was just 26 percent (compared with 48 percent in China). That may have changed. Indian manufacturing growth in 2007 reached 12.5 percent. And subsectors dependent on engineering and information technology show considerable strength—auto parts, machinery, chemicals and other areas where supply chains with international firms are important.

Many reasons have been given for India's faster manufacturing growth. Some emphasize reforms and an outward orientation. Others point to macroeconomic factors such as low inflation, a depreciated rupee and low real interest rates. Still others point to the resolution of infrastructure bottlenecks. Doubtless all have played a role. It is no longer necessary to question whether India can be unique in achieving rapid growth without strong manufacturing growth. The Indian model of service-led growth is giving way to a more traditional development model where both industry and services drive growth and job creation.

Reflecting this movement, Indian fixed investment has sharply increased in the past few years, steadily rising from 22 percent of GDP in the 1980s to 25 percent in the 1990s to more than 35 percent in recent years. While still short of the levels attained in China and Vietnam, the acceleration of capital formation in India should position it well for future growth.

A leading Indian economic commentator Surjit Bhalla has argued persuasively that investment in India has responded to a more depreciated real exchange rate (increasing the rate of return on tradables like manufacturing) and to lower real interest rates (reducing the cost of capital).[13] Such analysis underpins the notion that proper policies are required to sustain Indian growth at the levels outlined here. Growth will not happen automatically.

> **India is set to reap a demographic dividend. Its labour force should grow by more than 1.7 percent a year over the next 30 years**

Fiscal space to build Infrastructure

Investment has risen largely because of private sector response. But the public sector has also played a role. Public deficits have come down from around 6 percent of GDP in the 1980s and 1990s to less than 4 percent in the last four years through 2007. With the government investing only about 5 percent of GDP each year in infrastructure, the bottlenecks have risen to significant proportions. But India may now be creating the fiscal space to expand infrastructure spending as well as the ability to develop new partnerships with the private sector to provide funding and expertise. Public-private partnerships have been a model for rapid infrastructure expansion throughout the successful East Asian development experiences.

A demographic dividend

India is set to reap a demographic dividend. Its labour force should grow by more than 1.7 percent a year over the next 30 years, while population growth is just over 1.2 percent. So, the ratio of working-age population to total population is on the upswing. In addition, India still has a relatively low labour force participation rate of 61 percent. As the population becomes more urban, affluent and educated, participation rates are likely to rise. Goldman Sachs forecasts that 500 million people will be added to India's cities by 2039. It notes that 10 of the world's fastest growing 30 urban areas are in India. To see the impact of demographics and urbanization on labour force participation, look at China, which has a labour force participation rate of 82 percent and a labour force of more than 800 million, compared with India's 516 million. Higher labour force participation could add another full percentage point to India's labour force growth over the next 20 years, bringing it up to 2.7 percent.

The demographic dividend takes many forms. It provides for a rapid reduction in poverty as the dependency ratio shrinks. It gives families the means to save, accumulate and invest in their own well-being. Perhaps most important, it permits greater investment in children

and human capital—the foundation for Indian growth for the next generation.

An emerging middle class

It is typical in development that the demographic dividend coincides with the emergence of a middle class. Much has been written about the boost to growth from a large middle class. There are political economy arguments suggesting that a middle class base raises the importance of economic growth in policymaking ("it's the economy, stupid"). Others emphasize the economic aspects of the middle class, providing the source of domestic demand, especially for consumer durables—cars, motorcycles, televisions, air conditioners, mobile phones and refrigerators—that in turn boost manufacturing. The middle class also demands housing, shopping malls and other infrastructure, and can afford to take an annual vacation, boosting services. They save for their own retirement, for housing and for their children's education, providing the resources for fixed capital formation, especially when there are two-income families. In short, most examples of rapid sustained economic growth coincide with the development and expansion of the middle class.

India could witness a dramatic expansion of its middle class, from 5–10 percent of its population today to 90 percent in 30 years. With a population of 1.6 billion forecast for 2039, India could add well over 1 billion people to its middle class ranks by 2039 (figure 8). The figure shows that today very few Indian households would have incomes exceeding $5 a day. But between 2015 and 2025, more than half of all Indian families would pass this threshold, swelling the ranks of the middle class substantially.

While there are several definitions of middle class, including sociological ones, it is convenient to use a single income metric to measure the size. The analysis here uses a measure that spans those living in households with incomes more than $10 a day per capita and less than $100 a day, in purchasing power. This definition,

| Figure 8 | India's middle class could expand by well over one billion by 2039 |

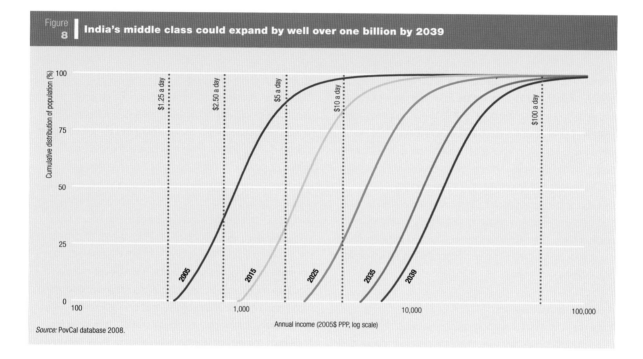

Source: PovCal database 2008.

by construction somewhat arbitrary, has several useful features.

It mirrors the common use of $1 a day to define an international poverty line, originally constructed by taking an average of national poverty lines for the 10 poorest countries. In similar fashion, the $10 lower threshold for the middle class is set at the average poverty line for the most affluent countries in the world. The argument is that all those considered poor should be excluded from the middle class. But those above the $10 threshold are likely to be able to spend on discretionary items like consumer durables.

By using purchasing power parities, the measure of the middle class is held constant across countries, useful for comparing the size of the middle class in one country with that in another.

At the other end of the scale, the middle class cut-off would represent an income of $146,000 for a family of four. It seems reasonable to argue that those above this level are affluent.

Based on this definition, India is on the verge of becoming a middle class nation. Given the high threshold for entry into the middle class, only a small proportion of the population, perhaps the top 10 percent, can be called middle class by international standards. Of course, for India, with its huge population, that means a large absolute number of people. But over the following decades, the share of the middle class rises rapidly until almost the whole country is in this category by the end of our scenario.

Very broadly, it seems that India is just at the cusp of the explosion of the middle class, a strong force for sustained growth.

Others have also highlighted India's burgeoning middle class. The McKinsey Global Institute, in a 2007 report, suggested that India's middle class would rise from 50 million to 583 million by 2025.[14] According to McKinsey, this middle class comprises government officials, college graduates, affluent farmers, traders, business people and professionals. These groups choose what they will consume, and are not driven by the necessities of life. Such

❝❝ **Despite the strong fundamentals and reasons for optimism, the high growth rates that underpin India's promise are by no means pre-ordained**

Table 2	India's changing values			
Values		1990	1995	2001
Is democracy good for the economy? (% no)			60	40
Is it important that your job be interesting (% yes)			47	74
Is it important to be allowed initiative in your job? (% yes)			46	64
What is most important for your child to get ahead?				
Independence (% yes)		30		56
Hard work (% yes)		67		85
Thrift and saving (% yes)		24		62
Determination and perseverance (% yes)		28		46

Source: World Values Survey, various years.

discretionary choices, reflecting the tastes of the new Indian middle class, will dominate consumption patterns.

Changing values

Most analysts think about the middle class in terms of values as well as incomes. The World Values Survey provides some information on how Indian society is changing. In 1995, 60 percent of the Indian sample of 1,275 respondents believed that in a democracy (such as India's) the economic system was doomed to run badly. A mere six years later, in 2001, this pattern was reversed: 60 percent of respondents disagreed with the statement (table 2).

In 1995, only 47 percent of respondents felt it important that their job be interesting. They valued pay and security as the only important elements of jobs. By 2001, while pay and security remained important, 74 percent called job interest important. The proportion of respondents who felt that the opportunity to use initiative in a job was important rose from 46 percent to 64 percent between 1995 and 2001. These data suggest a changing work ethic. Where interest and initiative are important, it is likely that labour productivity and job satisfaction will also be high.

Parents also feel that the qualities their children will need to get ahead have changed. From 1990 to 2001,

there has been a striking increase in those answering that the following quality was important for their children: independence (30 percent to 56 percent), hard work (67 percent to 85 percent), thrift and saving (24 percent to 62 percent) and determination and perseverance (28 percent to 46 percent). In other words, the changing values associated with middle income families are already visible in India, and these changing values are conducive to economic development.

A determined marathoner not a sporadic sprinter

Despite the strong fundamentals and reasons for optimism, the high growth rates that underpin India's promise are by no means pre-ordained. As an illustration of the distance to be travelled for India to meet its promise for 2039, consider that it will need to achieve social indicators and measures of economic competitiveness similar to those of South Korea today (table 3).

India would have to follow the path of a "determined marathoner" rather than that of a "sporadic sprinter." Marathoners build the momentum to grow through traps and challenges that lie in their way. They then reap the rewards. Sprinters become exhausted and pause to catch their breath. Once their growth is slowed, it becomes hard to revive. The main distinction between

> **India will need to overcome numerous challenges in order to persistently follow the path of the marathoner and realize its promise**

Table 3 | Achieving South Korea's social and economic indicators

Indicator	India today	Korea today
School enrolment, tertiary (% of relevant age group)	11.8	91
Literacy rate, adult total (% of people ages 15 and older)	61	na
Hospital beds (per 1,000 people)	0.9	7.1
Physicians (per 1,000 people)	0.6	1.6
Urban population (% of total population)	29	81
Population in urban agglomerations > 1 million (% of total population)	12	51
Improved sanitation facilities (% of population with access)	33	na
Electrical outages (days)	67.00	0.04
Electric power transmission and distribution losses (% of output)	25.0	3.5
Mobile phone subscribers (per 100 people)	15	83
Broadband subscribers (per 100 people)	0.2	29.0
Clean energy consumption (% of total)	2.4	18.0
Carbon dioxide emissions (kilogrammes per 2005 PPP $ of GDP)	0.60	0.47
PM10, country level (air pollution: particulate matter, micrograms per cubic metre)	68	37
Water productivity (2000 $ GDP per cubic metre of total freshwater withdrawal)	1	31
Research and development expenditure (% of GDP)	0.9	3.2
Scientific and technical journal articles (per million people)	13	341
Researchers in research and development (per million people)	119	3,723

Note: na is not available.
Source: Centennial Group, 2009.

marathoners and sprinters is in the institutional capabilities to develop long-term strategies and the implementation capabilities to execute these strategies.

India will need to overcome numerous challenges in order to persistently follow the path of the marathoner and realize its promise. These challenges can be broadly described under two, admittedly, overlapping headings:

- Avoiding the middle income trap
- Managing multiple transformations simultaneously

The next two chapters will focus on these challenges.

At the core of these challenges, lies the overarching imperative of improving governance. This will be discussed in chapter 4.

Annex 1
Model for global growth

The model presented here for global growth consists of separate projections for 145 different countries. The projection methodology assumes a constant-returns-to-scale Cobb-Douglas production function with growth dependent on capital investment, labour force growth, and technological improvements.[15] These three factors are commonly used for growth models. Goldman Sachs' 2003 study "Dreaming with BRICs: The Path to 2050" and PriceWaterhouseCoopers' 2008 report "The World in 2050: Beyond the BRICs" use similar methodologies.[16] The basic approach is simple. Most countries have data on investment rates from which it is easy to project the speed with which their capital stock is growing. The United Nations has detailed population projection figures for all countries from which key demographic statistics and labour force growth can be gleaned. What remains is the estimation of technological improvements.

Following Goldman Sachs and others, we assume that the rate of technological improvement in each country has two components. First, the global technology frontier is shifting out with new advances in science, new products and new processes. Second, most countries are operating within this global frontier and can catch-up rapidly. Like others, the rate at which catch-up occurs is taken to be inversely proportional to the gap between the per capita income level of the country and that of the United States, represented as the global leader in technology. That is, countries with very low income levels can catch up fast, while countries closer to the United States will see their technological improvement slow.

The rate at which the global technology frontier moves out is taken as 1.3 percent a year. Given the historical rate of capital deepening in the United States, this parameter yields an estimate for U.S. labour productivity growth of 1.8 percent, the average long-run, stable rate observed for the past 125 years. In this sense, the model does not rely on any "new economy, information technology" assumptions and is calibrated to replicate the long-run history of global growth.

By assigning rapid technological progress to all countries with income levels below that of the United States, the model would tend to produce rapid rates of convergence in income levels across the world. As a matter of practice, this has not occurred. Convergence has been limited to a subset of countries. Some countries have shifted resources into high productivity activities demanded by the world. In this way, their productivity growth has been driven by domestic structural changes that have leveraged the global economy to produce rapid technical change. It is useful to call this group of countries "convergers" because the strategies they have adopted, including an outward orientation, appear to have resulted in income convergence with advanced countries.[17]

As argued earlier, there is also a group of middle income countries that appear to have become trapped and are either not converging with the affluent countries or are converging very slowly. Last, there are a number of poor countries which, for reasons of conflict, poor governance or adverse geography have stagnated in poverty.

This gives a typology of four groups of countries:
- Advanced economies, with low rates of technological progress.
- Converging developing economies closing the income gap with the United States.
- Middle income developing economies with no convergence trends.
- Low income developing economies with no convergence trends.

The classification of countries into these categories depends on their income in 2005 (the model's base year), and their demonstrated tendency towards convergence.

Countries that have had sustained growth of more than 3.5 percent per capita over 25 years are included in the convergence group.[18] Map 1 shows how each country is classified into four-speed world categories. Each colour represents one of the four country groupings.

To build global output, individual country output must be aggregated using some exchange rate. Because data will be presented at market exchange rates (which are actually observed), rather than in PPP terms (which can be highly sensitive to measurement error in the cross-country comparison of prices), the dollar value of output is adjusted to reflect trends in real exchange rates.

It is common to assume that real exchange rates will appreciate in countries where productivity growth is faster than in the United States. There is, however, a major debate among economists as to the speed at which real exchange rates will move. The most recent work (which also appears to have the best historical track record) fits a nonlinear relationship between the real exchange rate and per capita income growth differentials. The parameters from that estimation are used to project the real exchange rate forward over time and to calculate the dollar value of output for each country at market exchange rates. This formulation assumes that the real exchange rate was in some equilibrium initially. The base is the three-year average of 2004–07, but this period contains significant current account deficits in the United States. The United States may require a more depreciated currency than in the model scenarios. If so, the model will overestimate the time needed for India to overtake the U.S. and become the world's second largest economy in current dollars.

To summarize, the model identifies five drivers of global economic growth:

- Technological advance in affluent countries at the rate of 1.3 percent a year.[19]
- Catch-up technology in a group of fast growing globalizers who are in the midst of shifting resources from low to higher productivity activities; the speed of catch-up depends on each country's income relative to the United States.

- Capital accumulation, derived by assuming each country maintains its investment rate at its historical average.
- Country-specific demographic changes of the 15–64 age group, assuming constant labour force participation rates in each country.
- Real exchange rate changes as economies grow and domestic prices rise.

What are the main differences between this four-speed world and other global models?

- The sample includes 145 countries.[20] Many countries have a small GDP but large populations, and the larger sample allows a better understanding of the interaction between demographic trends and economic trends. It also means that trends can be computed for geographic regions and local neighbourhoods, like South Asia.
- It is not assumed that all countries converge with the United States. Importantly, Brazil and Mexico are classified for now as being caught in the middle income trap rather than as being part of the group of converging globalizers.
- Parameters for capital accumulation, real exchange rate appreciation and total factor productivity growth are based on actual data and estimations, rather than on ad hoc assumptions. For example, in its 2003 study Goldman Sachs assumed an investment rate for India of 22 percent of GDP and a growth rate of 6 percent. In actuality, India's investment rate today has risen to 36.7 percent, and even in the face of the current crisis, 6 percent growth seems low.[21]

The modelling framework may appear overly deterministic and devoid of policy content, but several of the variables reflect policy choices. For example, some analysts emphasize the role of undervalued exchange rates in promoting rapid growth over long periods.[22] In this model, undervalued exchange rates lower a country's income relative to the United States and induce more rapid technological growth. As another example, openness and other reform measures will show up in higher investment rates as businesses enter new sectors. Implementation effectiveness, governance and institutional development are captured by giving higher rates of technical progress to countries with demonstrated high levels of growth which are indicative of their institutional depth. So, deep policymaking structures are captured in the model through higher rates of technological change and investment, even though actual policies themselves are not specified.

INDIA 2039

Part I

Chapter 2

Realizing the potential: Avoiding the middle income trap

Realizing the potential: Avoiding the middle income trap

Homi Kharas

Few countries sustain high growth for more than a generation, and even fewer continue their high growth rates once they reach middle income status. The Commission on Growth and Development's recent review of growth in developing countries identified just 13 countries that sustained growth of more than 7 percent for at least 25 years in the postwar period.[1] They have five common characteristics: openness to the global economy in knowledge and trade; macroeconomic stability; a "future orientation", exemplified by high rates of saving and investment; a reliance on markets and market-based prices to allocate resources; and leadership committed to growth and inclusion with a reasonable capacity for administration. These success factors, deep-rooted in local institutions, are necessary, but not sufficient, for continued growth. Some countries with these characteristics grew fast, but could not sustain that growth. Some East Asian middle income countries suffered severe setbacks in 1997/98, and Brazil has yet to regain sustained rapid growth after its disastrous hyperinflationary episodes of the 1980s.

Reaching incomes associated with the advanced countries is uncommon: only six of the high-growth countries did so. More common is for growth to slow down markedly on reaching middle income level. Many Latin American and Middle Eastern countries suffered the fate of falling into a slow-growth, middle income country trap (figure 1). Why this is so common is, however, less understood.

High growth East Asian countries vs Latin American countries in middle income trap

Figure 1 plots the per capita income levels of three groups of countries between 1900 and 2000: the eight largest Latin American countries that have reached middle income status (Argentina, Brazil, Chile, Colombia, Mexico, Peru, Uruguay and Venezuela), five East Asian economies that have reached high income status after growing rapidly through the middle income stage (Hong Kong, Japan, Singapore, South Korea and Taiwan) and the five current middle income countries in East Asia (China, Indonesia, Malaysia, the Philippines and Thailand).

In the early 1970s the average per capita income of the five high income East Asian economies and the eight Latin American countries was roughly the same: about $5,000 in PPP terms, though the East Asian countries had a larger dispersion (see figure 1). Over the next three decades the East Asian economies went on to become affluent while the Latin American economies stagnated.

By the early 2000s the other five fast growing middle income East Asian countries had caught up with the Latin American countries, and coincidentally the range of incomes of countries in the two regions was almost identical. This makes it logical to ask what the five high income East Asian countries did to transit through the middle income stages of development, what the Latin American countries did wrong and what today's middle income East Asian countries might learn from those experiences.

Some features differentiating middle income from low income growth are clear. Growth tends to become more capital intensive and skill intensive. The domestic market expands and becomes a more important engine, especially for service growth. Wages start to rise, most rapidly

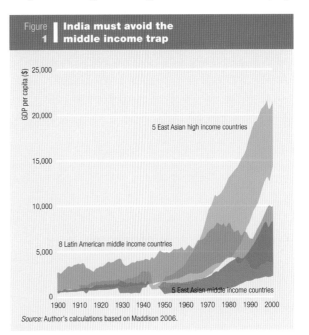

Figure 1 | **India must avoid the middle income trap**

GDP per capita ($)

5 East Asian high income countries

8 Latin American middle income countries

5 East Asian middle income countries

Source: Author's calculations based on Maddison 2006.

> 💬 The growth process from middle income
> to affluent country status is associated
> with specialising, moving up the value chain
> and innovating in selected products

Box 1 | **What is the middle income trap, and how did some East Asian countries avoid it?**

The middle income trap refers to countries stagnating and not growing to advanced country levels. This is illustrated in the figure, which plots the income per capita of three middle income countries between 1975 and 2005. In a steadily growing country, the line would be continuously rising over time (positive growth), that is toward higher income levels. That is the experience of South Korea.

But many middle income countries do not follow this pattern. Instead, they have short periods of growth offset by periods of decline. Rather than steadily moving up over time, their GDP per capita simply moves up and down. That is the middle income trap—unable to compete with low income, low wage economies in manufacturing exports and unable to compete with advanced economies in high skill innovations. World Bank 2009.

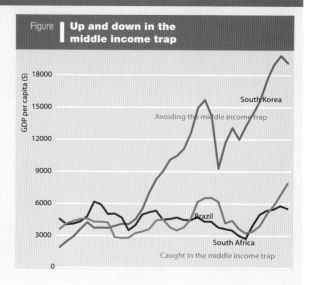

Figure | **Up and down in the middle income trap**

for highly skilled workers, and shortages can emerge. The traditional low-wage manufacturing for export model does not work well for middle income countries. They seem to become trapped, unless they change strategies and move up the value chain. Cost advantages in labour-intensive sectors, such as the manufactured exports that once drove growth, start to decline in comparison with lower wage poor country producers. At the same time, they do not have the property rights, contract enforcement, capital markets, track record of successful venture capital and invention, or critical mass of highly skilled people to grow through major innovations, like affluent countries.[2] Caught between these two groups, middle income countries can become trapped without a viable high-growth strategy (see box 1).

Way out of the middle income trap

Some recent work argues that the way out of the middle income trap is for developing countries to specialize.[3] This builds on the empirical observation that middle income countries have much more diversified economies than poor countries, but affluent countries tend not

to be more diversified than middle income economies. In other words, the growth process from middle income to affluent country status is associated with specialising, moving up the value chain and innovating in selected products.

Within affluent countries the production of certain goods tends to be highly concentrated in specific geographic areas. In the new growth theory, the forces driving specialization and agglomeration are closely linked to the ability to generate economies of scale. Affluent countries withdraw from products with constant returns to scale, in which they gradually lose competitiveness to lower wage countries.

Over the course of development, policymakers' role must change. The Commission on Growth and Development emphasizes that for poor countries there are clear advantages to backwardness. When a country lags behind in every sector, it can be organized like an army to advance on all fronts. The critical growth driver is to employ all factors productively in a market setting. But once productivity gaps have been narrowed and

> **Fast-growing countries have kept a single-minded focus on results and the long-term transformation of their economies**

resources become scarce, the efficient use of factors becomes more important for growth.

The first priority for policymakers is to anticipate the new role expected of them. There are several transitions that a middle income country or region will experience. The diversification of production will slow and then reverse, leading to a prolonged period of rising specialisation.[4] Physical capital investment will become less important and innovation must accelerate. Education systems need to produce advanced knowledge workers who can shape new products and processes and drive the speed of domestic innovations. Each of these areas has policy implications.

The second priority, less discussed, is to shift away from earlier policies, even when they had been proven successes. Many poor countries have used special economic zones to overcome the lack of adequate infrastructure for business, when it could not be addressed on a national scale. But such approaches become outdated. As the economy develops, other locational issues aside from good infrastructure become important. And when the general environment improves, the opportunity costs of locating outside a specified zone fall. A better approach then is to have incentives broadly available and to allow firms to determine where to locate on the basis of local land markets and other business considerations.

Sequencing these two priorities—what to do and what to stop doing—is an art, not a science. Not letting go of strategies to promote labour-intensive growth once wages have started to rise can be damaging. But attempts to transition too rapidly to the new economy of knowledge workers can also fail if the preconditions are not right. Premature shifts in strategy can make some workers unproductive, lacking the skills to add value in knowledge-intensive sectors. This can cause its own social and economic problems.

The middle income trap is a matter of country policy, not a structural phenomenon. That is, all countries are capable of emulating the high-income East Asian economies and can grow rapidly from middle income to advanced economies if they develop and implement the right strategies. Indeed, institutional depth is required for policies to be effectively implemented, and achieving that institutional depth requires considerable lead time. Avoiding the middle income trap requires policymakers to be foresighted and to adapt the growth strategy as new challenges arise. If there is already a societal consensus on the importance of long-term growth, the incentives improve for policymakers to make such changes.

Country growth experiences, policies and institutions are quite different from each other. So it is difficult to generalize about the exact policies that lead to success in avoiding the middle income trap—or to pin-point policies that lead to failure. But some features of success seem to be consistent across countries.

Fast-growing countries have kept a single-minded focus on results and the long-term transformation of their economies. They consistently adapt strategies in the light of changing global conditions, building on their competitive strengths. A caricature of the difference between successful East Asian countries and slower growing Latin American countries is that the former keep a focus on growth and let the policies emerge, while the latter focus on predetermined policy orthodoxy and hope that growth will follow.[5]

Sometimes this requires embarking on programmes that take many years to mature. For example, the South Korean strategy of building a knowledge economy started in 1998 and was initially envisaged as a three-year exercise. It evolved into a decade-long effort, with massive transformation. The detail that underpinned success was impressive: 83 associated action plans in the five main strategic areas of information infrastructure, human resource development, development of knowledge-based industry, science and technology, and elimination of the digital divide. The plan was led by five working groups and involved 19 ministries and 17 research institutes, all to be tracked by the Ministry of Finance and Economy and reported on to the president by the private committee of the National Economic Advisory Council.[6]

> " Leadership, public-private partnerships,
> the ability to sustain long-term changes,
> a focus on results ... are lessons from
> successful fast-growing countries

The scale and pace of programmes were tremendous. For example, the Maeil Business Newspaper offered a million free Internet connections. A special Informatization Promotion Fund supported information and communications technology training classes for housewives, elderly people, farmers and other groups—many conducted in stadiums, no less. When the initial plan showed results of a widening technological gap between small and medium enterprises and large firms, it was fine-tuned. Importantly, the plan combined supply-side policies—such as distributing low-priced personal computers to disadvantaged groups, building a high-speed Internet infrastructure and supporting venture start-ups and e-business—with demand-side policies—such as massive awareness and computer training programmes and a new approach to public procurement.

This example highlights what is required to escape the middle income trap. India does not have to embark on a knowledge economy strategy, but it does need to think through major transformations in its approach to basic health and education services, infrastructure, urbanization, energy, environment, the judiciary and other areas. Each such programme is likely to be multi-faceted, with long-term implementation challenges. Like South Korea, it will be important to avoid a process of marginal and piecemeal reforms.

Also like South Korea and other East Asian economies, it will be important to engage the private sector. As the economy becomes more complex, an interchange of views with the private sector is essential to be sure that policies are based on proper information about what is actually going on and to ensure that there is a feedback loop during implementation to permit policies to be fine-tuned.

In that process of consultation, the media have been critical in crafting, implementing and monitoring long-term reform programmes. Indeed, a media group, the Maeil Business Newspaper, was the original inspiration for South Korea's knowledge economy programme, based on its independent review of the threats and opportunities in 1998.

Leadership, public-private partnership, the ability to sustain long-term changes, a focus on results and outcomes and priority-setting with detailed implementation targets are lessons from successful fast-growing countries.

Costs of getting stuck in the middle income trap

In the midst of the world's worst economic crisis in perhaps 70 years, it may appear odd to be discussing long-term institutional issues that India may have to confront to grow rapidly in a sustained fashion. The immediate priority was to protect India from the global recession, and that requires aggressive fiscal stimulus and monetary easing. After a better than expected growth of 7.2 percent in 2008/09 at mid-year, most analysts forecast growth in 2009/10 of between 5–7.5 percent, compared to negative growth of the global economy as a whole. Economic indicators suggest that the current downturn may have bottomed out in the first half of 2009.

Perhaps the most remarkable aspect of these short-term forecasts is that few analysts are predicting a major slowdown to growth below 6 percent. That augurs well for the future. If indeed the deepest low-growth point is above 6 percent, the likelihood of attaining sustained, rapid, long-term growth of 9.5 percent is boosted.

This analysis suggests there is no a priori reason why India should not grow rapidly in the long term. It goes further and suggests that India's potential growth can indeed accelerate further. But there are also many examples where fast growing countries suddenly found themselves in the growth doldrums, unable to move forward at the speed they were used to. These countries have seen income stagnate.

Consider Brazil, which grew at almost 6 percent for almost a century. In 1965 it was one of the wealthier developing countries with a per capita income of $1,400 (in 2007 dollars). It continued to grow until 1978, when it reached $4,500 per capita, with average growth of almost 9.6 percent a year. But it then entered a long period of decline and stagnation. It did not regain its 1978 per capita income until 1995 and then only briefly in the burst of activity that followed the end of hyper-inflation and the beginning of stabilization. Within four years Brazil was again wracked by macroeconomic instability as it struggled to manage the aftermath of the East Asian crisis. It was only with the commodity boom in 2005 that Brazil again surpassed its 1978 income. In other words, after a century of growth, Brazil spent nearly 30 years without further improvement in its average living standards. Although recent growth has been better, Brazil has still not demonstrated a track record of sustained fast growth that would allow it to converge rapidly with advanced economies.

Imagine that India were caught in the same middle income trap. It might reach the $4,500 per capita income that Brazil attained in 1978 by 2023, in 15 years. But if it then followed Brazil's trajectory, it would still have a per capita income of around $5,000 by 2039. Instead of a $36 trillion economy, it would be an $8 trillion economy.

Put another way, if India can develop along the scenario indicated here, it can eliminate poverty within 15 years, under the World Bank poverty figure of 456 million poor in 2005 (or the Indian government figure of 310 million). If it sustains rapid growth at 8.5 percent, some 30 million people a year could be lifted out of poverty. Moreover, because so many of India's poor still live with expenditures below $2 a day—a number estimated by the World Bank at almost 850 million in 2005—sustained growth over the long term is required to make a substantial dent in that broader concept of poverty.

**INDIA
2039**

Part I

Chapter

3

Realizing the potential: Managing multiple transformations simultaneously

Realizing the potential: Managing multiple transformations simultaneously

Harinder S. Kohli

Managing the transformation of any economy, especially a giant like India's, is a daunting task. Over the next 30 years, India will almost certainly see an initial worsening of its income distribution, as parts of its economy benefit from integration with the global economy while other parts are left behind. It will also face pressures from other developing economies for a share of world exports. Its service exports have rapidly grown to global scale, but it has been much less successful in its manufacturing exports. Unlike China, Japan and South Korea in the past, India's march to prosperity must take place in a different world. And its sheer size makes its evolution different from the path of other emerging economies except China (box 1).

First and foremost, this will require a fundamental change in the focus and basic mindset of the polity, the policy makers, the civil service,,

and the private sector. In other words, all key players in the market must fully recognize their respective roles and responsibilities and undergo a corresponding change in mindset and behaviour.

If India is to be a growth marathoner, it must also manage three simultaneous transformations. First is becoming a more cohesive society. Second is becoming a globally competitive economy. Third is becoming a responsible global citizen. The challenge of managing these transformations is compounded by the:

- Fast-evolving expectations of a younger, richer, more urban, and more demanding Indian populace.
- Needs of a more visible and more critically examined changing Indian economy as it continues to climb up the global competitiveness ladder.

Box 1 | Historic nature of India's promising rise

The forthcoming rise of India will make history in at least four aspects:

1. *Size and speed.* The Indian economy's share of global GDP (at market exchange rates) would jump from about 2 percent in 2007 to almost 18 percent in 2039. This compares with the hundred years it took Europe to its increase share of GDP to 20.5 percent before the Industrial Revolution to 1900, and the United States, 93 years to go from about 1.8 percent of global GDP in 1820 to 18.9 percent in 1913. Japan went from 3.0 percent in 1950 to 8.6 percent in 1990.

2. *A continental economy—and a diverse and democratic society.* There is validity to the argument that the challenges facing India cannot be compared with the experiences of Hong Kong, Singapore, Taiwan or even South Korea. Europe's rise occurred when it comprised a large number of individual and independent nations. Indeed, India can be compared with only two continental nations—China and the United States. And in the diversity of its people and democratic political system, only the United States is comparable.

3. *No traditional levers of power.* India cannot rely on military power or a particular ideology to expand its global footprint. Historically, western countries expanded their global economic and political footprints either through military might or by leading an ideology. They often secured access to cheap resources needed by their home economies through dominant military power or through political alliances. India must manage its expansion in the global marketplace without these traditional levers of power. It must play by the rules of the global economy and become more competitive than others.

4. *A more competitive and global economy.* The international economic environment facing India during the next 30 years will be much more competitive, and natural resources much more scarce, than even for Germany and Japan after World War II. Indeed, India will be striving to increase its share of the global economy not only in competition with other large emerging markets such as China but also as large western economies become much more concerned about their own jobs and prosperity.

> **The country—all players—must simultaneously meet the challenges of becoming a more cohesive society, a globally competitive economy, and a responsible global citizen**

- Obligations arising from India's expanding global footprint on its interactions and relationships with the rest of the world—and the opportunity to take advantage of related opportunities.

Managing the three transformations simultaneously will require India to anticipate and adapt to the changes wrought by each of these transformations individually and collectively.

Required change in mindset

Until now, the Indian polity and economic policymaking have paid primary attention to the needs of society (figure 1): how to reduce mass poverty and maintain social and political stability. Whenever there was a (real or perceived) tradeoff with the economy or India's relations with the world, the policy choices were most often populist, intended to favour the common person. The repeated inability or perhaps unwillingness of successive governments of all political configurations to eliminate subsidies, open the economy faster or reform outdated labour laws are clear examples of these political compulsions and the populist policies adopted to win electoral votes. While this may have been the appropriate approach to decision-making when the country was still fighting mass poverty and

trying to keep itself together, such a uni-dimensional and doctrinaire mindset is no longer sufficient for India to become a much more prosperous society.

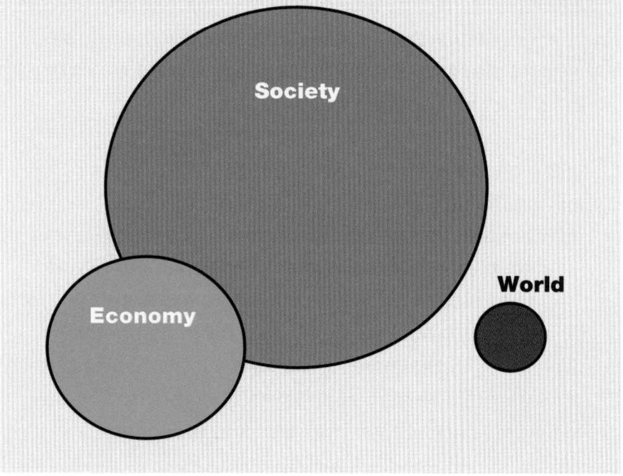

While societal considerations will obviously always remain important in India—large, diverse and democratic—the economic and global considerations will steadily become more important. Without taking account of the broader long-term economic considerations of its policies, India risks falling into the middle trap that has plagued many other developing nations. In light of its rapidly expanding global footprint, India will increasingly need to concern itself with the impact of its policies on the rest of the world; it will increasingly have to bear the responsibilities of preserving the global economic commons—whether for climate change, free trade or stable international capital movements.

All three considerations—societal, economic, and global—will also become more intertwined as the Indian economy advances. As a result, India's long-term prospects and growth will depend on its ability to balance all three dimensions as it makes policy decisions on almost every important issue.

The country—all players—has to strike a balance among all three dimensions if it is to stay on the marathoner route. It must also strive to simultaneously meet the challenges of becoming a more cohesive society, a globally competitive economy, and a responsible global citizen (figure 2). The effectiveness of institutions in shaping and implementing policies across the cross-cutting issues will be fundamental to becoming a marathoner.

The private sector also has a significant responsibility to fulfill—for adopting and adhering to more ethical behaviour. Accordingly, the business community must take steps to inculcate a new sense of ethics, morality, and self-discipline and to consider innovative business ideas that are profitable and, at the same time, would help solve some of the issues India must face in the future. In addition, it should support efforts by progressive political leaders to snap the country out of the current state of affairs as well as efforts by civic society and the media to act as honest watchdogs of the system.

Figure 1 | **Societal considerations have so far trumped the economic and the global**

> **Removal of structural inequities must be addressed aggressively, and will remain a challenge even after mass poverty has been eradicated**

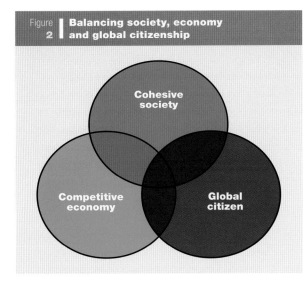

Figure 2 | Balancing society, economy and global citizenship

boom. As a result, India has an enormous backlog of poverty manifested in hunger, lack of education, high infant and child mortality, and limited access to clean water, sanitation, power, and health services. As incomes rise, demands for quality services in each of these areas will also rise, perhaps faster than incomes, given India's open democracy and the communications revolution.

In many countries, initial development brings with it greater equality as labour moves from low to high productivity occupations. But once middle income status is achieved, the drivers of development change and inequality can rise. Further, even as the per capita income of the country rises significantly and mass poverty is eradicated, disparities in incomes and access to public services and economic opportunities will need attention to maintain social cohesion. India also faces deep and persistent structural inequities (box 2). Removal of structural inequities must be addressed aggressively, and will remain a challenge even after mass poverty has been eradicated.

To become affluent in the next 30 years, India will have to solve the problems of rural society and deliver services to a massive population. This task will be made slightly easier by the fact that India's population will be on the move to cities. An unprecedented migration from rural to urban areas is under way. It will put a tremendous premium on the speed and effectiveness of local city governments in delivering adequate (and quality)

Moving from a poor society to a more cohesive, affluent society

As the country moves towards being affluent, it will need to change the focus of its social policy from alleviating poverty to maintaining social cohesion. Within one generation, India could be transformed from a poor and mainly rural society to an upper middle income and urban society, as its per capita income rises rapidly and millions of people move from villages to urban centres. Today, a large number of people still depend on traditional agriculture—not integrated into the mainstream economy and not participating in the current economic

Box 2 | Tackling structural inequalities

Inclusive growth has become a leitmotif of the policy discourse in the past few years. The focus is on how can government policy, directly and indirectly, bring the benefits of growth to all. Tackling disparities and achieving inclusive growth remain of great importance for India's longer term development prospects.

Structural inequalities in India are not only deep and persistent, they are also intimately linked with institutional structures in the political, social and economic domains—and they are likely to impede the transformations necessary for long-term growth. Institutional and policy change to affect genuine social cohesion is necessary if India is to avoid the "middle income trap" and reach the status of an affluent society.

> **The quality of the environment enjoyed by India's citizens—in its cities and villages—falls far short of the standard befitting an affluent society**

| Box 3 | **Creating functioning cities** |

For citizens, perhaps the biggest difference between a poor (developing) society and an affluent (developed) society is the quality of life—especially the access, quality and reliability of public services. In this context, the quality of public services available throughout the country is abysmal, and most cities in India have the look and feel of a poor country.

Indian cities suffer from inadequate resources, poor management, and corruption, that is believed to be

widespread. These considerations have ostensibly led most states to keep a tight grip on city administrations, leaving little room for local initiatives to improve the provision of services and the quality of life in cities. The efficient functioning of cities also influences labour costs and has a direct bearing on competitiveness and growth and thus must be urgently addressed.

---

services (box 3). Rural development and mass service delivery in both rural areas and cities will be crucial for achieving and maintaining social cohesion in order for India to transform itself into a more cohesive society.

The quality of the environment enjoyed by India's citizens—in its cities and villages—falls far short of the standard befitting an affluent society. India's policy stance appears driven by geopolitical considerations and is crowding out the urgently needed focus on actions to improve the well being and health of over a billion Indians living today. This policy is not in India's self-interest and, if sustained, would not only inflict great harm on India but also exacerbate problems making them much more expensive to remedy in the future

(box 4). A related issue that merits urgent attention is India's scarce and rapidly depleting water resources.

Three key inter-generational issues that India must address are, tackling structural inequities, creating functioning cities, and improving the environment. These are discussed in greater depth in Part II of this book.

Moving from a domestically oriented economy to a globally competitive economy

For India to continue converging with technologically more advanced economies, it must continue to enhance its global competitiveness. India's current growth is mainly based on productivity gains from a shift in the labour force from low to higher productivity

---

| Box 4 | **Improving the environment** |

One of the most visible improvements in the quality of life, as India moves from a poor society to an affluent society, must be in the quality of the environment. The citizens of an affluent India will deserve and expect to have high-quality water and sanitation, clean air and clean streets along the lines of Madrid, Seoul and Singapore today. This transformation in the quality of life will not occur

overnight. Its seeds must be planted now and nurtured over the years.

India's current policy is driven mainly by its geopolitical negotiating stance rather than by what is good for Indian citizens and what is in India's long-term self-interest. This basic mindset of public officials and citizens alike must change.

> **India also has to broaden its skills base beyond a few centres of excellence and foster innovation on a national scale**

Box 5 | **Overcoming infrastructure bottlenecks and creating a competitive edge**

Infrastructure is a classic intergenerational issue, which needs to be addressed immediately. Solutions to which need to be found starting immediately.

Since 1991 many far-reaching reforms have been announced, related laws passed by the Parliament, and a number of institutional changes implemented. Yet, infrastructure bottlenecks continue to hamper economic performance and that India. These bottlenecks have persisted and indeed worsened, despite the above efforts, because of the accelerating economic growth, sharp increases in (foreign and domestic) trade and rising consumer demand. The explosive growth in demand for infrastructure has far outstripped the increases in capacity that successive governments have managed to achieve. This has a tremendous economic cost. In addition, without basic infrastructure in rural India where some 70 millions live today, India's efforts to achieve inclusive growth are not likely to yield the expected outcomes.

This state of affairs cannot continue for long politically, socially or economically. It certainly is also not conducive to India either sustaining high growth rates or social cohesion required during the next thirty years for the country to become affluent.

Given the urgency to resolve the existing infrastructure bottlenecks but also the importance of making a start on developing infrastructure facilities that provide the foundations for meeting the longer term needs of an affluent society and globally competitive economy, India needs to adopt a two pronged strategy. The first prong would focus on the immediate future, while the second prong would anticipate and start to address longer-term—inter generational—needs.

activities, as people move from farms to service firms. Despite rapid growth, India has not built a foundation for a modern advanced economy. Its enterprise sector is highly fragmented, and the share of medium and large firms is very small by international standards, crimping the creation of formal sector jobs and the adoption of new technologies. This strategy helped India move from a low income to a middle income economy. But it will not sustain the long-term growth that will permit India to become affluent.

India's infrastructure deficiencies are well known and must be resolved to create and enhance its globally competitive edge. There has been a widespread consensus in India for some years that Infrastructure is crucial to India's competitiveness, to growth and to economic development. Since 1991, many far-reaching reforms have been announced, related laws passed and institutional changes implemented. Yet, with notable exceptions in civil aviation and telecommunications, severe infrastructure bottlenecks hamper economic performance. Infrastructure needs urgent attention—with a long-term and inter-generational perspective—to meet the needs of both an affluent society and a globally competitive economy (box 5).

India also has to broaden its skills base beyond a few centres of excellence and foster innovation on a national scale. To do that requires support for a highly skilled workforce, innovation, technological upgrading, and ultimately new technology development to continue the climb up the global technology ladder, as Japan and South Korea have done in the past 50 years. For this to happen, quality and merit-based education for the entire population will be a must (box 6).

Finally, India has to launch a revolution in energy. It must appreciate the consequences of its actions on the international community and it needs to act as a responsible global player (box 7).

> " Intergenerational issues underlying India's transformation to a more competitive economy—an aggressive programme to revolutionize infrastructure; renewed focus on education, technological development, and innovation; and launching an energy revolution

---

Box 6 | **Renewing the focus on education, technological development and innovation**

The recent growth in India's economy has come mainly from productivity gains as workers move from farms to services. But to sustain long-term growth and become an affluent nation without falling into the middle income trap, India will need continual improvements in competitiveness and productivity. It will have to replicate its success from information technology to other sectors, laying the foundation for perpetual gains from a workforce that consistently creates, acquires and uses knowledge, and making full use of existing technologies to raise productivity to the best possible domestic and global benchmarks.

In the new global economy a nation's wealth lies not in its land or capital but in its skilled people, who generate new knowledge and convert it into useful ideas, goods and services. With plenty of smart, young and competent workers, the challenge for India is to deploy its resources to produce the highest possible return through a massive increase in the capacity and quality of higher education and in the amount and scope of investments in technology and innovation.

The solutions in all these areas require making choices that have long-term consequences: rail or road transport, coastal or inland development, coal or renewable (including nuclear) energy, and whether or not to develop Mumbai into a well-functioning modern city capable of hosting a global financial centre.

These intergenerational issues underlying India's transformation to a more competitive economy—an aggressive programme to revolutionize infrastructure; renewed focus on education, technological development, and innovation; and launching an energy revolution—are discussed in greater depth in Part III of this book.

Finally, as demonstrated by recent events, availability of a well functioning and stable financial sector and an open global trade regime are key global and national public goods, essential for the real economy to develop and prosper. Pressing ahead with and indeed speeding up reforms in these areas along with restoring fiscal balance are still of paramount importance. Hence the need to widen the focus of economic policies from achieving and maintaining high growth to enhancing global competitiveness and closing the gap with global best practices.

Moving from a small player to a responsible global citizen

In 2008, India's $1.2 trillion economy represented 2 percent of global GDP. It was the world's 12th largest economy. The latest IMF projections suggest that in 2009, India will leapfrog over Russia to become the 11th largest (IMF 2009).

In many respects, until now, India has been small in global terms, able to take advantage of global economic growth, but without having to worry about how its own actions might affect the global economy. It has benefited from being a global price-taker in its exports. And even rapid growth in foreign direct investment, nonresident deposits, remittances, and other capital flows does not make India a major player in global economic imbalances. Nor is India central to the current discussions on the global response to the financial crisis and the need to revive global growth.

This absence of global scrutiny has allowed Indian policymakers considerable freedom and flexibility to pursue economic policies in the short-term national interest, without having to worry about the impact on the rest of the world. That will soon change.

> **India could be the world's third largest economy by 2030, and conceivably overtake the United States by 2037**

India's aspirations to become an affluent society within one generation must be pursued in a global context of scarce, unreliable and expensive energy supplies, with rising pressures to reduce carbon emissions to preserve the global climate. India's long-term competitiveness will depend also on its ability to use natural resources efficiently. In this context, the efficiency of energy use and the fuel mix will be most important. It is thus in India's interest to base its growth path on an energy and carbon scenario that emphasizes efficiency, minimizes the use of fossil fuels, and is thus sustainable for India and for the world.

In the model scenario here, India's footprint in the global economy and resource base would expand dramatically, by a factor of nine, as its share of the global economy jumps from 2 percent now to almost 18 percent by 2039. India's sheer global size implies that it must take a different path to sustain development. Its use of water and energy is wasteful, and it seems clear that India must develop a competitive economy that is much less resource intensive than today. The size of India's economy also means it must concern itself with global economic citizenship—in the G-20, in the World Trade Organization, in its relations with China and Japan, in the Association of Southeast Asian Nations and in other global groupings.

India could be the world's third largest economy by 2030, and conceivably overtake the United States by 2037. The dates are not important: what is clear is that India is on track to be one of the three largest economies that among them will account for about half of global output. India could be larger than the Euro zone.

There are significant implications of this change in how the global economy is managed and the responsibilities of major economic powers. For a start, the largest global economies—China and India—would not be the most advanced economies in technology and per capita income. The institutional development of their financial and trade sectors would likely not match those of the most advanced countries. India's needs in some aspects, such as pursuing access to rural finance and protecting poor farmers, may not be consistent with global rules of the game.

India will also become a major consumer of the world's natural resources. Not only will this affect its approach towards economic security and its relationships with other countries, it also implies that the world will have an interest in ensuring that India becomes more efficient in its use of resources. In some instances, that could redound to India's advantage. For example, if clean technologies are made available at low cost or if global schemes are adopted to accelerate faster introduction of efficient technologies through subsidies that promote the global commons, India stands to benefit handsomely. But in other instances, there will be no such schemes, and India will have to demonstrate to the rest of the world that it is taking its global economic responsibilities seriously. Ultimately, India will have to launch a revolution in energy in order to earn its place as a globally responsible player (box 7). This issue is discussed in greater depth in chapter 10.

Recent events suggest six critical areas where India will be called on to play a leading global role: trade, finance, oil, food, climate change, and water. In each there are examples where what may be good for India may not be good for the rest of the world. Until now, that has not become a serious issue for India's global relations, but as it becomes a larger part of the world economy, such tensions will ramp up. India is already being invited to the world's major stages to discuss these issues. But its current positions are narrowly defined by its short-term interests. It is time to think more broadly about the long-term implications of such approaches.

With respect to its immediate economic neighbourhood, India is simultaneously advantaged and disadvantaged. The rapidly growing Asian economy, led by East Asia, positions India close to the dominant source of global growth for the next three decades. As the example of India's explosive growth of trade with China shows, proximity to rapidly growing markets is a major growth driver.

The World Bank's World Development Report 2009 shows two sources of neighbourhood externalities.[1] First, there is the direct market linkage source. For every percentage point increase in the growth of a "neighbour", defined as a country or a region with which there is a regional trade agreement, growth in the home country rises by 0.14 percent. In other words, India's regional trade agreement with the Association of Southeast Asian Nations (ASEAN) could add a full percentage point to India's growth, if Asian countries grow by 7 percent. Yet India has been slow to recognize these advantages.

At the same time, regional externalities can work to accentuate the growth effect of domestic policies through another channel. In East Asia and Europe, where regional integration has been strong, the effectiveness of domestic policies on home-country growth was raised by 14–18 percent because of the spillover onto neighbouring countries that then reinforced the initial growth impulses at home. There is a spatial multiplier to economic policies when local economies are integrated with each other.

India misses out on such spatial multipliers because South Asia is the least integrated region in the world. Despite considerable progress in most other economic areas, South Asia remains dead last in regional cooperation.

There is a limit on how far India and the other South Asian economies can go without cooperating as other world regions have done. For example, the countries share many regional public commons that cannot be effectively tackled in isolation—such as environmental degradation and climate change, water resource management, and security and terrorism.

South Asia is also home to six countries—Afghanistan, Bangladesh, Myanmar, Nepal, Pakistan and Sri Lanka—that have suffered serious internal conflict and violence to a greater or lesser degree. Most conflict in the modern world is intrastate. It is increasingly recognized that even such localized conflicts have very large economic costs, amounting to an average of 105 percent of pre-conflict GDP in net present value terms, according to Paul Collier, the pre-eminent scholar on conflict.

For these and other reasons, none of India's immediate neighbours, except China, is in the group of converging countries. Their prospects for sustained development are uncertain. A rapidly growing India would therefore stand in sharp contrast to its neighbours.

"Fortress India"—the strategy of major border restrictions and minimal economic interactions with neighbours—is India's current approach to minimize negative spillovers from its failed state neighbours. But that strategy will become harder to implement over time.

Today, India's per capita income is only slightly higher than Pakistan's, half of Sri Lanka's and less than twice that of Bangladesh. By 2039, in one model scenario, India's per capita income could be as much as 7 times higher than Sri Lanka's, 10 times higher than Pakistan's and 20 times higher than Bangladesh's. The latter two countries would have half a billion people combined.

Such a scenario, though highly unlikely to materialize, points to obvious fragilities. The pressures for migration and access to the affluent Indian neighbour would become enormous, almost matching those between Europe and North Africa, or the United States and Central America. India could face similar debates on how to manage illegal immigration while ensuring domestic security without disrupting an overall outward orientation in economic policies.

❝❝ India's mindset and the goal of foreign policy must shift from protecting India's narrow interests to becoming a responsible global citizen, and a good and trusted neighbour

Both Europe and the United States have used foreign aid and regional cooperation as instruments for balancing such tensions with neighbours. They recognize the self-interest in having growing, stable economies in their neighbourhoods. China is adopting the same approach in South-East Asia.

In the not-too-distant future, India too will need to consider how it can best ensure that the whole South Asian subcontinent develops. The fledgling efforts at regional trade liberalization and bilateral agreements between India and some of its neighbours have been half-hearted and nowhere near as comprehensive as other regional integration initiatives among developing countries. Indian foreign aid has not been developed with a coherent regional or international approach. Regional infrastructure arrangements are poor. Existing regional institutions have a legacy of failed initiatives suggesting that they may not be the best vehicles for a new approach. In short, neither the institutions nor the policies for regional cooperation are adequate to

the task at hand. Given the enormous complexity and deeply political nature of the problem, India needs to start now to build think tanks and research programmes to develop a coherent strategy towards the rest of the region.

Given the magnitude and speed of the expansion of India's global economic footprint, it will be in its self-interest to improve relations with its neighbours, to take responsibility for preserving a stable and well functioning global financial system and an open global trade and investment system, to use energy and natural resources carefully, to accept appropriate global standards for efficiency, and to care for the environment and minimize its carbon footprint. Can India learn from China's recent strategy to "extend" its growing economic prosperity to its neighbours and nurture closer relations with them despite past tensions? India's mindset and the goal of its foreign policy must shift from protecting India's narrow interests to becoming a responsible global citizen, and a good and trusted neighbour.

INDIA
2039

Part I

Chapter

4

Realizing the
potential:
Overarching
imperative—
Improving
governance

Realizing the potential: Overarching Imperative— Improving governance

Harinder S. Kohli

What is striking and common across the basic inter-generational issues is that their solutions are invariably rooted in the issue of governance. Seven facets of governance must change to transform the Indian economy and society:

- Make the government smarter, more focused, agile and more credible.
- Retool the civil service to meet the needs of today and tomorrow.
- Focus on the long term and open the public-private dialogue.
- Support competitive markets and prevent capture of state organs.
- Inculcate a code of self-discipline and ethical behaviour within the business community.
- Implement priorities, monitor results, ensure transparency and enforce accountability.
- Reverse the deterioration in political governance.

Identifying practical solutions requires appreciation of all these facets that are closely intertwined like the pieces of a jigsaw puzzle.

Consider a simple example. If delivery of quality basic education to all Indians is the stated national objective, one facet is making sure that the state and local governments actually give education the requisite priority and resources. Another is that mechanisms are in place to recruit enough fully qualified teachers—and post them to schools serving all segments of the society. Another is that teachers turn up at school every single day. And yet another is that someone monitors actual results and that individuals and units are held accountable for addressing shortcomings and delivering results. All are facets of governance.

Governance of the education system thus comprises clarifying the role of governments at all three levels—centre, state and local—and executing agreed policies by various parties, setting incentives for the behaviour of teachers (civil servants), focusing the system on the long-term implications of quality basic education and monitoring outcomes against agreed objectives.

India can certainly make do in the short term without fundamental changes in governance. And the needed change—painful, contentious and certain to be resisted by the entrenched powers and vested interests—will require political courage. It will be thus very tempting to leave such actions to successive governments.

There is, however, a very long gestation period for such fundamental changes in the system. It will take at least a decade, if not longer, before the requisite changes are fully realized. By that time India may be exactly in the trough where most countries get mired in the "middle income trap". So, despite the hurdles and the temptation to put it off to another day, procrastination is just not a responsible option; in fact the lead times required to make the cultural and institutional transitions permit little leeway.

Immediate actions on each of the facets could be regarded as a down payment and visible demonstration of the Indian leadership's commitment to build the foundations of an affluent nation.

Make the government smarter, more focused, agile and more credible

Through the first generation of macroeconomic reforms launched around 1990, India has been able to jumpstart growth. But it still relies on the mindsets, institutional structures and practices inherited from the British Raj. While the values and attitudes of people and the private sector have changed dramatically since the 1990 reforms, the government's reach, structures, processes and centre-state-local relations as well as the basic mindset have remained essentially unchanged.

Today's highly centralized government is over-stretched and ineffective. The current model cannot be expected to work in one of the world's largest and most complex economies—1.1 billion people now (up from 350 million at Independence) and 26 states (about double the number in 1950), some larger than a majority of the world's countries:

- The government is still trying to do too much, well beyond its capacity and capability. As a result, almost everything done by the

> **A refocused government is thus essential to facilitating dramatic transformations in the Indian economy and society. There is a need to rethink not only what the government does but also how it does it**

government is inadequate and inefficient, while many aspects critical for long-term success are being overlooked (such as the state of the education system, the imminent large-scale shift from rural to urban areas, the plight of cities, international economic diplomacy to enhance energy security, threats from climate change and India's role in global governance).

- The central government still performs functions better handled by state or local authorities, despite the federal structure anticipated in the constitution (central government programmes to provide basic education, improve urban management and provide power to rural areas).
- The role of the Indian civil service—with highly intelligent generalists—in both policymaking and public service delivery was a major strength during colonial times and immediately after Independence. But the system has become outdated and a barrier to change (see also next section on retooling the civil service).
- Until administrative fiat is significantly curtailed at the central, state and local levels, crony capitalism and petty corruption will continue to be a drag on the economy (for example, through the ongoing capture of regulatory organs and the access to public land and concessions by business houses and politicians).
- The continuation of a combination of weak and ineffective state and more powerful and creative big business houses will inevitably lead to large-scale misuse of market power and invite a massive backlash against a market-based economic system. While scaling back many current government activities, India urgently needs more self-regulation by industry as well as stronger and more vigilant independent state organs to ensure more ethical and transparent behaviour by the private sector.

A refocused government is thus essential to facilitating dramatic transformations in the Indian economy and society. There is a need to rethink not only what the government does but also how it does it. Refocusing and curtailing some of the current functions will make more room for performing the remaining government functions well. It will also release space and senior leadership time to focus more on the new functions and activities of modern governments (periodic assessment and reformulation of broader economic strategy, stronger supervision of the markets—including financial markets—and an active and more coordinated role in various international fora).

India needs to fundamentally rethink and refocus the role of government at all three levels—centre, state and local—and create honest and well functioning institutions in all spheres of life. Tinkering at the margins will not do. Three interrelated changes are required:

- Rethink the role of the public sector relative to a growing role for the private sector and civic society in all aspects of the economy and society.
- Decentralize authority from the central government to state, municipal and local (panchayat) levels. Consistent application of the principle of subsidiarity—tested and proven worldwide (European Union, United States) and enshrined in India's constitution—is the only long-term solution.
- Build high-quality and credible institutions across the public and private sectors accountable for delivering quality services and for overseeing private market players.

The primary role of government has to be to inspire, lead, coach and oversee the private sector and civil society, instead of being the primary decisionmaker and controller of the main economic and social activities. The shift will give greater space to the private sector to innovate, take risks and compete with others. At the same time, India must create room for strengthening government capacity for performing its basic functions and in addressing new areas critical for long-term success.

> **"** Another priority is simplifying administrative procedures and reducing the number of agencies, at different levels, providing clearances for undertaking any activity

Another priority is simplifying administrative procedures and reducing the number of agencies, at different levels, providing clearances for undertaking any activity. For example, at least 30 clearances involving several agencies at the centre and the states are required for setting up even a modest-sized industrial factory. Except in selected areas (such as provision of power and water), it is desirable to cut through the elaborate red tape and rely primarily on self-certification. The government can lay down standards and norms (say, for environmental impact or safety), and the entity concerned may be required to self-certify at the highest levels of management that the notified procedures have been complied with. Government agencies can make random checks and if there are violations, appropriate penal action can be taken. Similarly, the complexity in regulations should be reduced drastically, as has been tried with success in some areas (for example, foreign exchange transactions). (See box 1 for immediate steps.)

Box 1 | Immediate steps to transform the role, focus and effectiveness of government

The required transformation in the role, focus and effectiveness of the government—and at all three levels—is a huge undertaking and will take a decade or more to bring about. But that is no reason to delay action. Instead, it demands an immediate start with strong support from top political and business leaders alike.

We propose two major first steps as a demonstration of the change in mindset and the resolve of national leaders to build the foundations of an affluent India within one generation (a closely related proposal on the retooling of the civil service follows):

- Refocus central government ministries. To be credible, the move towards a smarter and more focused government has to be led by the central government reforming its own role and functions. A basic principle should be to fully separate strategy and policy functions from the execution of operational activities. Central ministries should focus on strategy, policy and monitoring, and delegate policy implementation to the states, independent public enterprises and the private sector. Enterprises retained under state ownership, currently under the purview of sector ministries, should become fully autonomous, with an independent state organ exercising normal ownership rights (including oversight). This will eliminate the current conflicts and duplication in policymaking, create a more level playing field for all competitors (public or private), severely reduce the workload on the line ministries (allowing them to focus on their core functions and perform them much better) and permit a major consolidation of the ministries.

- Give full autonomy, with clear accountability, to cities over 1 million in population within the next 10 years. This can be done by implementing the intent of 74th Constitutional Amendment, which acknowledges cities as a "third sphere" of government. As Gujarat and Kerala have demonstrated, delegating full autonomy to cities and having fully empowered elected mayors is feasible under current Indian laws and can dramatically improve the quality of city management and public life. The three main obstacles—none of them legal—are: the reluctance of state authorities to cede power, the perceived risks of increased corruption and the low institutional capacity at local levels. To overcome the first obstacle, the central government can deploy its considerable power of suasion and use financial incentives by modifying the Jawaharlal Nehru Urban Renewal Mission. The other two obstacles can be addressed by using public scorecards that measure service delivery, designing appropriate financial incentives, building capacity and "professionalizing" local administrative services. Colombia turned its cities around—Bogota is widely regarded as a model—through a local financial accountability act.

> ❝ An integral part of creating a smarter and a more credible government is a retooled bureaucracy aligned with the future needs of a large, complex economy

Case studies of international experience in managing public services show that the objective of such programmes can be achieved better, and at less cost, if a distinction is made between the financing of these services (by the government) and, the delivery of such services (by nongovernmental organizations and local enterprises). In such cases, the public authorities retain the responsibility for regulating and monitoring the activities, providing subsidies where necessary and laying down distribution guidelines. In India, two noteworthy examples of public-private collaboration in public services are the public call offices, which revolutionized the availability of telephone services all over the country in the 1990s, and the Sulabh Shauchalayas which, despite some problems, are estimated to have provided sanitation facilities to 10 million people at very low cost.

The functions of government thus carefully defined once should be periodically updated to eliminate those that are no longer needed or that are beyond its capabilities. Periodic functional reviews should identify areas from which the government should withdraw from through downward decentralization, privatization, outsourcing or simple elimination. At the same time, core functions such as the judiciary, police and other internal security institutions should be strengthened (see box 2).

Retool the civil service to meet the needs of today and tomorrow

Effective, professional and credible bureaucracies are a hallmark of all successful Asian economies and the United States. At Independence, they were also a major strength of the Indian state. An integral part of creating a smarter and a more credible government is a retooled bureaucracy aligned with the future needs of a large, complex economy, with the expectations of a more demanding affluent society and with the changing values and capacity of a dynamic private sector. Unfortunately, the Indian bureaucracy, despite its illustrious past, is far removed from meeting these criteria, and there is a major hurdle in implementing the government's strategy and policies.

Numerous administrative reform commissions have recommended fundamental change—but there has been no follow-through. We do not need to go further than the recent report of the Second Administrative Reform Commission, which stated quite categorically: "It is ironical that there has been no sincere attempt to restructure the civil service although more than six hundred committees and commissions have looked into different aspects of public administration in the country." The report went on to conclude: "Civil service has to change, not in the incrementalist manner that barely

---

Box 2 | Judiciary, police and other internal security institutions

A strong, independent, efficient and credible judicial system as well as law enforcement machinery is critical to any nation's well being. This is even more the case for India given its vast size and huge religious and cultural diversity. An aspiring affluent Indian nation needs (and its citizens will demand) these institutions to be functioning well.

The problems in the Indian judiciary, police and internal security apparatus are well known. The judicial system is plagued with vast under capacity resulting in huge backlogs of cases and very long delays in resolving cases as well as elements of corruption, especially at lower levels (but also in higher courts).

At the same time, the judiciary is increasingly getting involved in certain aspects that are clearly in the domain of the executive branch of the government. The police apparatus also has its own problems: poor equipment, facilities and training; lack of full integrity and transparency in the recruitment at Thana levels; corruption; and poor accountability, to name a few. The November 2008 events in Mumbai have also highlighted the nation's vulnerability to such attacks and exposed weaknesses in its internal security.

These deficiencies have persisted despite continuous pronouncements by successive governments. A crash programme is required to overcome them.

> **This focus on the long term involves forging a shared long-term vision and goals for the country, and then using all available tools to achieve that vision**

Box 3 | **Immediate steps to retool the civil service**

Accountability to the people should become the guiding principle of the civil service at all levels. This would require a major attitudinal shift among the civil servants, too few of whom see themselves as serving the people. It would also require a new structure for the civil service, consistent with the general thrust of decentralization. This should be the starting point for a retooled civil service.

The first major step would be to replace the current national Indian Administrative Service, comprising generalists, with officials specialized at state and functional level. The Indian Administrative Service as a national civil service should be replaced by general civil service recruitment unique to central and state levels of government. Selection should continue to be competitive and transparent. All professional employees should be recruited through the civil service at the relevant level of government, with competitive progression from one level to the next based on merit, not pre-ordained for an elite group of officers. Top managers should be allowed to select key members of their teams, based on merit and a transparent selection process.

The insularity of the senior civil service should be broken by recruiting senior professionals with an outstanding record in business, science or academia for the top 15–30 percent of positions, while encouraging promising young civil servants to obtain experience outside the government. The current system of perks, particularly housing, reinforces the image of civil servants as "rulers" and should be abolished, with its value monetized in the salaries. The key here would be to inculcate the spirit of public service, re-create integrity and introduce accountability. The new national service could be named the "Indian Public Service".

Permanent civil services in Japan and the United States are structured along these lines, with some variance to reflect their political systems.

Another powerful instrument for improving the transparency, responsiveness and credibility of all branches of government is strong support by the top political and civil service leadership.

---

touches the basic structure. It has to be a total change, a thorough transformation, a metamorphosis."[1] (See box 3 for immediate steps.)

Focus on the long term and open the public-private dialogue

A major distinguishing feature between the success of East Asian economies in raising incomes and the difficulties Brazil and Mexico have had in going beyond middle income status—is a sustained long-term focus in all policy deliberations, to anticipate change, to constantly rethink strategy and to make timely strategic and institutional changes.

This focus on the long term differs fundamentally from the traditional concept of central planning. It involves forging a shared long-term vision and goals for the country, and then using all available tools to achieve that vision. It requires motivating all economic agents, developing a concrete and realistic strategy that is periodically refreshed to reflect changed circumstances, forging strong partnership between public and private sectors, creating appropriate policies and incentives and constantly reinventing the related institutions. The basic challenge is to maintain a long-term focus within a country's political and social setting.

Indian democracy precludes single-party dominance, as in China, Malaysia and Singapore. India's weakened bureaucracy precludes following the French (or Japanese) model. And given the recent era of coalition governments and India's size, it is not realistic to expect a single national leader to emulate Malaysia or Singapore.

> **" India needs to learn from East Asia, recognizing the mistakes in earlier years and not allowing powerful business interests to capture the state**

In this respect, other distinguishing features in East Asia were the close interactions and partnerships between government and private sector. Their absence has been a negative factor in Latin America. Hong Kong, Japan, South Korea and the United States have forged a consensus among policymakers, academia and business on major economic policy and strategy issues as a result of regular interactions (formal and informal), mutual respect and recognition of joint interests.

In India having closer and more open interactions between the three, while equally important, will be a much bigger challenge. As in many former British colonies, the basic mindset is still mutual distrust. The Indian Administrative Service disdains the "impurity and vulgarity" of the private sector and the "ivory tower" mentality of academia, so there is little basis for them to talk to each other. Yet in today's world they must.

India needs to learn from East Asia, recognizing the mistakes in earlier years and not allowing powerful business interests to capture the state (see next section). The private sector and public leaders have to work hard to eliminate widespread suspicion and distrust of the business community among many intellectuals and the bureaucracy, a remnant from the British Raj.

The United States, while not a perfect match, comes closest to India in its diversity, its politics and its intellectual capacity. Like the United States, India must find ways to maintain a long-term focus beyond the term of individual governments. In our view, in the absence of any obvious alternatives, India should look to the U.S. think tank model. Across several administrations of both parties, the Council for Foreign Relations has shaped foreign policymaking and long-term strategy formulation, the Rand Corporation defence policy, and the Centre for Strategic International Studies international security. While it will take much time and effort to replicate the United States model in India, we believe this is the best, if not the only practical, way to go.

The think tanks would also promote public-private sector dialogue by following the example of how the United States forges consensus through the interchange between academia, business and the civil service, so that there is a constant flow of ideas and exchange of expertise and experience between the three. In the U.K. model, there is less of this, but certainly much more porosity than the current colonial models in the Commonwealth. So, building think tanks that bridge all three is the key to "selling" the national vision. Such think tanks will inevitably move towards different party affiliations due to different points of view.

India already has numerous think tanks. Under our proposal, however, there will be three major differences: much less reliance on government funding and on government-sponsored projects; much greater specialization, combined with a critical mass of specialized professionals; and leadership by recognized professional experts in the field of specialization of the think tank. (See box 4 for immediate steps.)

Support competitive markets and prevent capture of state organs

Effective competition policy combined with significant self-regulation is the hallmark of the United States and the successful Asian economies.

Corporate wealth in India has soared in the past two decades. By early 2008 India had almost 50 billionaires. The ratio of their net worth to GDP was over 20 percent, way above Latin American countries such as Brazil or Mexico, and even Russia. A handful of Indians reportedly own more than 80 percent of stock market capitalization. While the expansion of corporate wealth resulted in part from the pro-business policies that helped support growth, there is now a growing risk that parts of the corporate sector will wield excessive influence over the state. Indeed, some of the biggest fortunes have been earned in "rent-thick" activities that offer opportunities from privileged access to land, natural resources and government contracts. This concentration of wealth and influence could be a hidden time bomb under India's social fabric.

The emergence (or consolidation) of oligarchic capitalism can slow long-term development through

> ❝❝ Laying the institutional bases for competitive and effectively regulated markets will thus be an essential ingredient of India's long-term social cohesion and economic competitiveness

---

Box 4 | Immediate steps to focus on the long term

India should create a network of independent think tanks—independent of government, individual parties, advocacy groups and business houses—focusing on and specializing in longer term issues of great national interest. These think tanks should avoid becoming all-purpose general research houses. Instead, they should each focus on one major critical issue and seek to become the very best source of ideas and national strategies on that issue.

The issues identified in this report could provide the starting point for the selection of the issues to be covered by the network of think tanks. In addition to domestic issues such as education, energy and cities, an early priority would be to facilitate work on two topics not yet

on the government's core agenda. First is India's role in the long-term political stability and economic prosperity of its immediate neighbourhood in South Asia. Second is India's long-term relationship with the global economic community and the major multilateral institutions.

The effectiveness of the think tanks will be highly dependent on their having a critical mass of dedicated and well qualified staff led by highly respected leaders with demonstrated track records and widespread credibility in their functional area. To ensure quality, independence and professionalism, their core financing must be long term, preferably in endowments. Relations with the government in office should be at arms-length.

---

its adverse impact on incentives for structural change and through the reduced autonomy of the state (box 5). Laying the institutional bases for competitive and effectively regulated markets will thus be an essential ingredient of India's long-term social cohesion and economic competitiveness. (See box 6 for immediate steps.)

Inculcate a code of self-discipline and ethical behaviour within the business community

While stronger, more effective and independent regulatory bodies are a must in a market economy, they neither are nor can be a substitute for market discipline. The business community must accept its responsibility for adopting and adhering to more ethical behaviour and self-discipline.

The dangers posed by the continuations over the longer term of today's combination of weak state organs and a more powerful, assertive and at times unethical business community are enormous. Already, there are mounting concerns about the regulatory capture by big business and politicians (witness the failure of state electric regulatory commissions to carry out their fundamental responsibilities to protect consumer interests) and the

state capture by large business houses on public policy (undue influence of policy, access to scarce land and mineral resources, award of large government contracts).

Recent events in developed countries have highlighted the enormous economic cost of privatizing profits and socializing losses. In many respects India's chronic fiscal deficits are part of this syndrome. Populist policies designed to win votes over the short term not only use public funds for gains by individual political parties or leaders, but also give priority to consumption today over investment in the future.

The private sector must recognize that many current practices that allow a few powerful business houses to thrive are ultimately against the long-term interests of the business community as a whole. Not only is the current model not sustainable, it is potentially disastrous, as it could bring into disrepute the entire system and launch a popular backlash that will be difficult to contain.

Accordingly, the business community must take steps to inculcate a new sense of ethics, morality and self-discipline and to consider innovative business ideas that are profitable and that would help solve some of the intergenerational issues discussed here. In addition, it

Box 5 | Oligarchic or competitive capitalism?

India's corporate sector has been a major source of dynamism in the period of rapid growth. Many Indian firms now have global recognition and reach. This has led to a large-scale expansion in productive capacity—and also generated massive increases in wealth amongst India's corporate billionaires. A common narrative is that India's capitalism is in good shape, and it is only the creaking Indian state that is holding back long-term development and inclusion.

There is a large element of truth in this story. But there is a risk that India will evolve towards a condition of oligarchic capitalism, in which the market and political power of major corporations will become a drag on long-term growth and a source of distortion in policy design. India is vulnerable precisely because parts of the state are weak and so susceptible to influence, whether via political finance, the political need to get investment or outright corruption.

India's development dynamic is not unusual. Many countries have experienced periods of rapid growth thanks to family-based corporations and then had to deal (or failed to deal) with the risk of oligarchic capitalism. U.S. dynamism in the late 19th century involved highly successful investors such as J.D. Rockefeller—known as "robber barons" by some—who formed immense conglomerates or "trusts". Japan and South Korea also relied on family-based conglomerates. But all these countries then developed policies and institutions to check their power. Mexico's recent history provides a warning. The development of corporations, controlled by wealthy business families, has in many sectors led to high-cost structures that are hurting growth prospects—and this despite an external opening that is deeper and broader than India's. In Mexico's case the problem is closely linked to the weakness of the judicial and

regulatory system, and a poorly informed legislature. The consolidation of oligarchic capitalism would lead India into the middle income trap.

Fostering competitive rather than oligarchic capitalism is a major issue of institutional design for India. This does not mean a return to a controlling state, but it does require a more effective and autonomous state in many areas. Specific domains for action include the effective implementation of the long-delayed new competition law assuring transparent and competitive mechanisms for award of concessions and independent regulation of public private partnership in infrastructure and getting greater transparency and openness into land allocation processes.

These will involve tackling the broader problem of links of power and money between politicians, the state and the private sector. The Right to Information Act and social watchdogs will be a necessary complement to accountability mechanisms within the state. Also central to competitive capitalism over the long run is the continued broadening of the financial system and the big issue of an effective judiciary. Policy design is not a once-off affair, but an ongoing challenge, as illustrated by the more recent experience of the United States, from Enron to the subprime crisis.

Equally important is the behaviour of the business sector itself: there is scope for establishing codes of conduct over independent directors and procurement behaviour. Established firms can work the system. But the business sector as a whole—especially actual and potential new entrants—has an interest in pressing for stronger checks and balances, working with the state and societal groups. Whether the business sector can organize itself to support such changes is one of the big questions India now faces.

should support efforts by progressive political leaders to snap the country out of the current state of affairs as well as efforts by civic society and media to act as honest watchdogs of the system. (See box 7 for immediate steps.)

Implement priorities, monitor results, ensure transparency and enforce accountability

Another distinguishing feature of successful East Asia countries and China—and perhaps their biggest difference with India today—has been their single-minded focus on results. Consistent with this basic mindset, these countries set and agreed on specific

> **"** The country must build upon transparent markets to enable the easy exit and entry of the private sector in all aspects of the economy—including infrastructure

Box 6 | Immediate steps to support competitive markets and prevent capture of state organs

The country must build open transparent markets to enable the easy exit and entry of the private sector in all aspects of the economy—including infrastructure—to generate economic growth and serve the needs of society.

The public sector should give the highest priority to making the long dormant Competition Commission effective and credible. And it should focus on creating genuinely independent regulatory bodies to eliminate the ongoing "capture" of regulatory bodies by big business and politicians. Political leaders and policymakers should not only allow the regulators but also encourage them to use whatever authority they have to maximize competition and protect consumer interests.

---

and time-bound outcome targets, put great emphasis on monitoring results in real time and enforced accountability.

It is widely accepted that the biggest difference between China and India is China's far superior (political and administrative) ability to produce results on the ground, by effectively implementing agreed policies and programmes. A major reason for the difference is implementation and structural coherence in China because of the single party system. But that coherence comes also from a consistent vision, a pragmatic approach to implementation and clear accountability.

The fundamental governance problem everywhere is how to align the vision (which the layman associates with globally sophisticated elite) with ground-level local politics. In this sense, how Meiji was able to forge

Box 7 | Immediate steps by business community to inculcate a code of self-discipline and efficient behaviour

The major business associations and chambers—including the Bombay Chamber—should voluntarily promulgate a strong code of ethics and full disclosure, putting in place measures to ensure that their members adhere to it. The private sector should develop new business models that facilitate inclusive growth and are good long-term business propositions: models for affordable housing, higher environmental standards and green projects, and low-cost delivery of quality health and education services.

Two important groups must accept and carry out special responsibilities. The professional service entities—for example, the chartered accountants, auditors, corporate lawyers and credit rating agencies—must accept their special role and responsibilities in ensuring that their reports and activities are indeed independent, meet the highest ethical standards and fully adhere to the standards set by their professional bodies. This is essential to avoid repetition of episodes like Satyam and Enron. Second, independent directors of listed companies must recognize and perform the special role expected of them in corporate governance in market-based economies. The relevant professional bodies must impose severe and public penalties, without exception, on members who violate their standards.

In other words, all key players in the markets must fully recognize their respective roles and responsibilities and undergo a fundamental change in the mindset, just as we recommend for policymakers and the civil service.

I/4

> 66 The country has already adopted the appropriate policies and laudable—publicly announced—targets. But the country almost uniformly falls short in delivering on its intentions

---

Box 8 **| Accountable government**

The functioning of the Indian state lies at the centre of current concerns about political, social and economic outcomes. Its future performance will have a determining influence on whether India succeeds in the long transition to higher income or gets stalled in a middle income trap.

Currently the state displays a perplexing mix of characteristics. There is a tradition based on the principle of an autonomous, even Weberian, bureaucracy, epitomized by national services, such as the Indian Administrative Service. But many parts of the state are stuck in a low-level equilibrium—with dismal service quality, low levels of effort, widespread corruption and extensive politicization. All this is clearly problematic for the complex and responsive functions the state needs to carry out—now and increasingly more so in the long transition. But there are also problems with the many parts of the state where the Indian Administrative Service is dominant; for all their collective talent, the service has become a force for inertia, for resisting change in favour of just keeping the existing system and privileges.

The poor performance of the state is vividly manifest in a wide range of functions, from teaching to the judiciary. But the larger problem is that the state does not appear to be on a path of transformation to being more responsive and effective. And this is in large part because a weak state can facilitate political and economic decisions through corruption or political influence (as opposed to the highly desirable political influence that flows from an effective democratic process).

How can change occur? The challenge is to make the government genuinely accountable—to citizens, business and politicians—but through transparent processes. Such accountability works best when external societal pressures complement internal accountability structures within the state to provide incentives for responsiveness and checks and balances against corruption, discrimination or abuse. Among the catalysts for change, the most promising developments in India today probably flow from external, societal pressures, facilitated by important state-created processes. Examples include the Right to Information Act and the social audits as a legal requirement for government programmes. Potentially of equal importance would be pressure from business associations for a better state—working as a collective force, rather than seeking individual favour.

Also of great potential influence is the deepening of local democracy, with evidence of change in rural areas through the Panchayati Raj system. But a major gap in the existing structure of formal democratic accountability is the weakness of local democracy in urban areas, which will be the primary motor of change.

The transformation of the state is of fundamental importance for any transition to prosperity: there are no silver bullets, but change can occur through societal (and business) pressure and the deepening of democracy, complemented by internal administrative reforms.

---

a consensus among not just the intellectuals, but more broadly across Japan is a telling lesson. Deng's Southern Sojourn had a historical precedent in the 18th century, when Kangxi made the same journey to signal the commitment to reform.

Our review of India's policy framework—be it in education, rural electrification, power generation, administrative reforms, or subsidies—reveals that, overall, the country has already adopted the appropriate policies and laudable—publicly announced—targets. But the country

almost uniformly falls short in delivering on its intentions. This is partly due to the government's overstretched reach and the lack of institutional capacity to deliver on most promises. But the underlying problem is that the basic mindset of the leadership does not put a premium on results, or on holding people accountable for implementing agreed policies and programmes (box 8).

The power sector is a prime example. At the centre, the Ministry of Power and enterprises under it have repeatedly failed to meet accepted targets amply

> **The country must set measurable outcome targets, monitor actual results and enforce clear accountabilities**

funded by the government. The state governments have routinely failed to cut power subsidies or make state electricity boards genuinely viable despite repeated agreements at many national summits. State-owned distribution companies routinely fail to reduce distribution losses required under various centrally funded schemes. Even though successive governments have assigned the highest priority to resolving the power shortages, reducing subsidies and connecting all rural areas, the shortages continue to mount, subsidies continue unabated and millions of rural users remain without grid-supplied

power. Yet, no state has been deprived of funds, no fundamental changes have been made by the power ministry, and no senior officials or political leaders are known to have been held accountable.

Within this pernicious environment there are promising examples, albeit too few, showing that the "system" is still capable of responding quickly to changes in the mindset and priorities of the top leadership. Consider improvements in the overall quality of life, air quality and road transport in Delhi. Also look at the metro system in Delhi, the utilities and urban

| Box 9 | **Immediate steps to improve implementation and enforce accountability** |

What is necessary is a massive nationwide replication and scaling up of isolated successes. And that calls for a basic change in the mindset of the entire political and administrative as well as business leadership. The country must set measurable outcome targets, monitor actual results and enforce clear accountabilities. Again, the starting point has to be at the central government level (until the decentralization and refocusing of government recommended above is fully in place).

Specifically, we propose that a high-level monitoring unit be created in the office of the Prime Minister. It should have an unambiguous mandate to agree with the responsible parties and consolidate a timetable for policy implementation and for the outcome targets for all major government programmes, initiatives and projects. It would report quarterly and publicly on the progress relative to the agreed outcomes. It would identify issues needing cabinet attention and propose remedial actions. And it would pinpoint responsibility and accountability for success and for any major shortfalls.

In China similar functions are carried out by the State Council, with analysis by the State Economic Reforms Commission. In the United States, the Office of Management and Budget in the White House and the Government Accountability Office in the Congress have

similar responsibilities. In both countries a critical success factor is their direct access and reporting to the head of national government as well as a strong professional staff (that transcends the term of the government in power).

The proposed monitoring unit should be in the Prime Minister's office, professionally led by a person of stature with no stake in a career in the general civil service, and have a permanent statutory role (to transcend terms of individual governments and to give it the necessary clout over the bureaucracy). Similar monitoring capacity should be tried for state and local governments.

A related area is transparency in decisionmaking within the government. A major step in this respect has been the enactment of the Right to Information Act in 2005. The beneficial impact of this legislation in making government accountable and citizen-friendly is already visible. A further step in this direction is to require all ministries and departments of the government to proactively make information on their decisions available to the public (excluding security-related subjects). The information should be released by the ministries without the need for any member of the public to ask for it. If this is done, the free media and civil society institutions will be better placed to promote accountability in the decision-making process.

> **The Indian electorate in the recent elections ... has unequivocally demanded a government that can function and deliver**

management in Gujarat and the recent strides made in primary education in Bihar, a state often dismissed in the past as "ungovernable". (See box 9 for immediate steps.)

Reverse the deterioration in political governance

There is almost universal agreement amongst everyone we consulted that almost all problems concerning the mentioned facets of governance and their solutions are rooted in India's political governance. There also appears a strong consensus that India's democracy and political governance—a major strength and reason for India's survival during the period immediately after Independence—have deteriorated alarmingly during the past two decades, making it extremely difficult to govern the country, irrespective of which party is in power.

Our team was initially reluctant to comment on this central issue, since solutions can be devised only through an open and candid debate and agreement between the leaders of major political parties and experts much more knowledgeable than we are.

However, the Indian electorate in the recent elections has probably shown a greater recognition of the issue than the political power brokers and has unequivocally demanded a government that can function and deliver without having to drop to the lowest common denominator in order to mollycoddle its coalition partners who share neither a national aspiration nor perspective.

This clarion call of the voters in May 2009, in our view, presents a historic opportunity for bold and decisive action. While clearly the government needs to develop a strategy and a plan of action first to generate a consensus around end outcomes and then the means, the momentum provided by the recent verdict of the electorate should not be allowed to dissipate.

The smaller regional parties have a vital role in their states, where they often form the state governments. Even with an effective national government at the centre, state leadership has to grasp control and act in

---

Box 10 | Immediate steps to reform political governance

The central government should lay out clear targets for where the country should be on the intergenerational issues. These should be debated in a public-private dialogue that engages the political sphere, civil society and the private sector. Based on the outcome of these discussions, the government should then refine these targets, establish clear yardsticks and milestones and spell out the accountability and the "how" of achieving them. These should then go through the formal federal and state legislative approval processes. The high-level unit recommended to be set up in the Prime Minister's office (see earlier section) should be charged with monitoring and periodically reporting on progress.

Such an agenda should be supplemented by measures to enable and empower state and local governments to carry greater responsibility and accountability for meeting day-to-day needs of the public, including most essential public services (basic education, health, water, sanitation, power and public safety).

These suggestions for reforming political governance are by no means exhaustive. But if implemented, they would set the stage for India to seize the opportunities that lie ahead and make it one of the strongest economies in the world by 2039. Widespread poverty, illiteracy and disease would also be correspondingly reduced. The universally lauded democratic system of government would then have given all Indians their just rewards.

a number of the areas mentioned in this report. A confident and committed central government that provides leadership and facilitates the states' ability to act would clearly accelerate the process. (See box 10 for immediate steps.)

A concluding note: A unique window of opportunity for the new government

India can be a growth marathoner, but to do that it must understand the world in which it is operating and the changing shape of its economic footprint. It must start to put in place the governance of institutions and policy frameworks that will be consistent with a move from poverty to affluence in one generation. Few countries have achieved this, so the challenge is enormous. And no country has achieved this without serious deliberations over the ingredients for future growth.

Many important changes for India require a long-term perspective. Reforms in the civil service, judiciary, education, health, sustainable energy, water and natural resource use, climate proofing, land use and zoning, decentralization and urbanization take decades to initiate, pilot, adapt on the basis of lessons learned and ultimately to scale up. If they are not started early, such reform programmes will not be mature enough to deliver results at the time they become binding constraints to continuing growth. Marathoners initiate programmes to permit analysis and solutions to emerge over time.

At the same time, the deeper social and political economy institutions must be reformed to ensure

transparent debate, consensus building and continuity of policy (or at least in the direction of its change) over the long term. When presented with the McKinsey report on how to boost growth in India to 10 percent, Prime Minister Atal Bihari Vajpayee is said to have remarked, "but how is all this to be put through our polity?" Indian democracy is called upon to manage complex regional, social, religious and economic divisions. Rapid economic growth can accentuate these divisions, in a way that leads politicians to prefer a stalemate or the status quo to what they may perceive as an unfair outcome. Deep institutional changes are needed to ensure that the polity indeed has the ability to respond to the challenges of long-term growth.

India is already being called on by the international community to start taking on its global responsibilities. In 2009, major efforts are underway to restart the Doha round of trade negotiations (ongoing), the G-20 discussions on reform of global finance (April), the Food and Agriculture Organization of the United Nations discussion on how the world can feed itself (November) and the post-Kyoto negotiations on climate change in Copenhagen (December). India needs a coherent approach to these events, consistent with its long-term strategic aspirations.

As India plays a stronger role in global affairs, it must not neglect its neighbourhood. Regional cooperation can be an important ingredient in stabilizing smaller regional economies. Only Indian leadership at the highest level can lead these efforts.

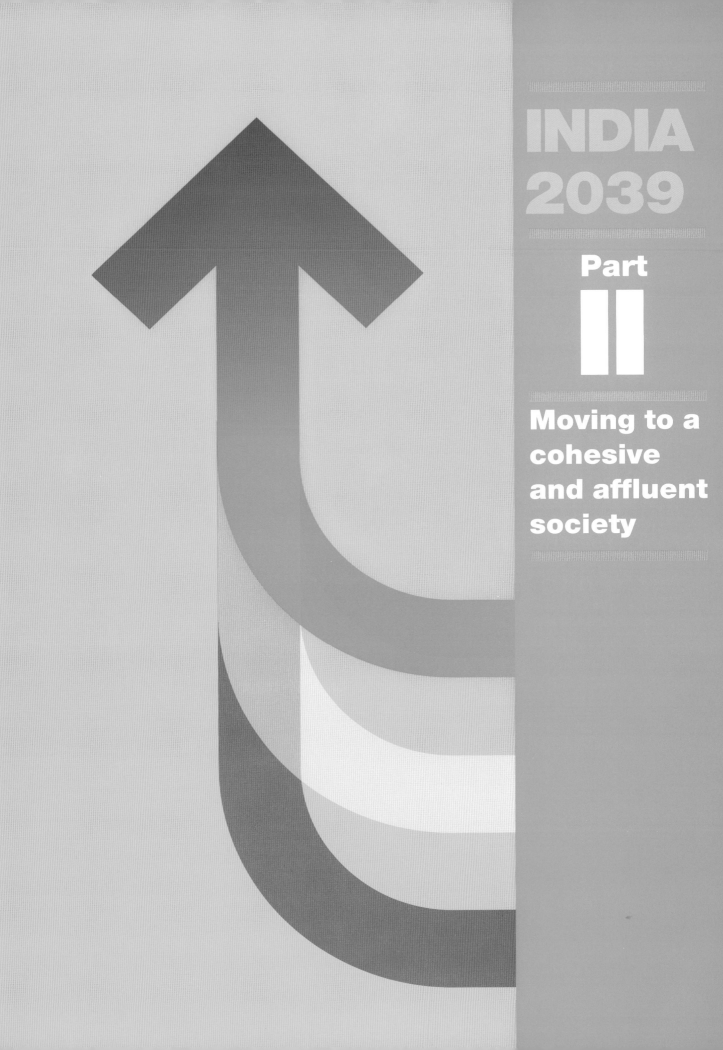

INDIA
2039

Part

II

Moving to a
cohesive
and affluent
society

INDIA
2039

Part II

Chapter
5

Inequities
and India's
long-term
growth

Inequities and India's long-term growth: Tackling structural inequities

Michael Walton

Does inequality matter for long-run development in India? With the extraordinary acceleration in growth of the past 25 years, can't troublesome arguments over distribution be put aside? Rapid growth is indeed the most effective way of improving the incomes of the poor and generating government revenues for service provision in the long term. But is this story incomplete?

Questions over inequality are usually framed in terms of whether all Indians are adequately sharing in this extraordinary burst in aggregate economic performance. Incomes of the poor have increased significantly, but at a slower pace than overall growth in incomes per capita. Malnutrition in rural areas has failed to go down, especially worrying because this can hurt the long-term development of children, reducing their future opportunities. Basic education services have expanded, but remain of dismal quality. Basic health services are even worse. Urban slums continue to be a major feature of the urban landscape—millions of urban dwellers live in awful conditions. There are truly massive contrasts between the overall quality of life in areas such as rural Bihar, Chattisgarh, Orissa and Uttar Pradesh and the emerging gated suburbs around the major cities.

In this narrative, distribution matters, but the issue is how to organize policies and institutions in ways that ensure the poor get a larger share of aggregate economic advance—in jobs, markets and services. This is hugely important. But the central framing of the question here is different. This chapter explores the following view: Failing to tackle a variety of social cleavages in Indian society will impede the transformations that are necessary for long-term progress. The issue is not one of adding inclusion to growth, but of achieving inclusion for growth.

The starting point for this analysis is that the current medium- to long-term conjuncture in India is characterized by a range of economic pressures for either further disequalization or continuing inequality (of incomes, risks, human capital, social status) across four axes:

- In the returns to corporate ownership, as evidenced in the surge in billionaire wealth.
- Across identity-based groups, with slow progress on differences with scheduled castes, widening differentials with adivasis and continuing divisions along religion and language lines.
- Across spatial areas, as seen in rising interstate and rural–urban differentials of income.
- By skill category, with sharp rises in returns to highly skilled workers.

These combine with political pressures for redistribution that are either already present or latent in all four axes of inequality and that will rise only with the process of growth, urbanization and mass education.

What does this mean for the future? Earlier chapters have developed the idea of a middle income trap—that a common pattern is for countries to lose their growth momentum, as Brazil and Mexico did, and that often leads to failed transitions beyond middle income status.[1] Also argued is that failures to tackle problems of governance form a central part of the story around such a trap.[2] This chapter fills out this argument by showing how institutional processes are integrally linked to the longstanding structural inequalities. The evolution and management of inequalities in power, wealth, status and influence lie at the heart of the success or failure of this institutional transformation.

These issues are framed in terms of two illustrative scenarios.

The first can be thought of as the "Latin Americanization" of India, since it has parallels with countries such as Brazil and Mexico. Under this scenario structural inequalities interact with political, social and economic institutions in ways that entrench these inequalities, alongside a variety of rent-sharing policies, to assure a minimum level of political support from

> **Social institutions include not only core services to all ... but also the effective management of group-based differences**

middle and poorer groups. This will be bad for long-term growth. Business dynamism could become a form of consolidated oligarchic capitalism, undercutting the creative–destructive process, and further weakening the autonomy of the state. Identity-based differences could become even sharper and lead to heightened distributional conflict and populist backlash. Spatial differences could continue to slow gains for large numbers of Indians, and could also be a source of national political conflict and inefficient national policies. Failures in the education system could lead to skill differences perpetuating inequalities and hurting growth.

An alternative scenario is termed "transformational" and involves the institutional change to support the transition to genuine prosperity. It is intended to be broadly consistent with the rapid growth path presented in Kharas (2009). This involves change in economic, social and political institutions. In the economic realm this would include effective competition policy, a broad-based financial system and a property rights system, with implications for the effectiveness of the judiciary and police services. Social institutions include not only core services to all—notably in education, health, water and sanitation, and urban services—but also the effective management of group-based differences, by providing economic and political opportunities across groups, managing conflict and ensuring group-based dignity and respect. Political institutions include the maturation of the party system, political finance, the information available to voters and the accountability, quality and information base of legislators. Cutting across all of these is an evolving and changing role of the state: rapid long-run transformation requires a state that is effective and accountable, with incentives for, and a culture of, delivery and responsiveness, both to political leaders (in overall policy direction) and to citizens.

The chapter is divided into three parts: the first covers trends in inequality, the second turns to interpretation of the interaction of inequalities with rents and political processes, and the third explores questions of change, framing them around the alternative qualitative scenarios.

Patterns and trends in inequality

This section summarizes patterns in the traditional presentation of overall trends in income/expenditure poverty and inequality across households and then turns to the "structural" inequalities, along the four dimensions of corporate wealth, group-based identity, spatial differences and education.

Overall poverty and inequality

Start from a specific, and in many respects, narrow dimension of welfare and inequality—outcomes in household incomes and expenditures. It is narrow in three respects. It is about outcomes rather than opportunities. It does not include important dimensions of well-being, such as health, education, insecurity and dignity. And it refers to individual households. But it is the most commonly used measure of economic welfare, and there is great interest in its relationship with aggregate economic growth.

The most common definition of the income poverty of individuals in India is based on per capita household expenditure and a poverty line based on expenditures required to meet basic caloric food requirements. This is extreme deprivation. On this measure there was a substantial, if less than spectacular, decline between the early 1980s and the mid-2000s: 46 percent of the Indian population lived below this line in 1983; 27 percent in 2004/05 (figure 1).[3] There is nothing magical about the particular poverty line. A large proportion of the population lives above it, but in conditions that would be considered very poor in middle income countries. For example, in 2005 some three-quarters of India's total population lived on less than $2 a day (in 2005 purchasing power parity terms), down from more than 85 percent in the early 2000s. In Mexico the extreme poverty line is about $2 a day in purchasing power parity terms; the moderate poverty line is above $3 a day. As India's income rises, what is considered a

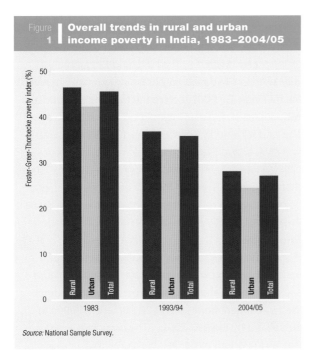

Figure 1 | Overall trends in rural and urban income poverty in India, 1983–2004/05

Foster-Greer-Thorbecke poverty index (%)

Rural Urban Total — 1983
Rural Urban Total — 1993/94
Rural Urban Total — 2004/05

Source: National Sample Survey.

minimum level of income or expenditure to live a decent life will also rise.

There is controversy over the level and trends in inequality in India. For inequality, the dominant prevailing view is that India's measured household income or expenditure inequality is modest by international standards. This is true for measures based on the National Sample Survey, though there is considerable debate over whether this effectively captures a lot of what is going on.

Using the Gini index—the most common aggregate index of the level of inequality between individuals in a population—the inequality captured in the National Sample Survey is indeed moderate. It has shown a modest increase since the early 1990s, after an earlier modest decline from the early 1980s. More specifically, between 1993/94 and 2004/05 there was somewhat faster average growth in urban than rural per capita expenditure (about 1.4 percent annual growth, compared with 1 percent in rural areas), and significantly faster growth at the top, especially in the top 10 percent

of individuals. This is primarily driven by unequal growth within urban areas: richer urban dwellers experienced relatively rapid growth, while the bottom 40 percent experienced growth at or below that of their rural counterparts (consistent with similar urban and rural poverty rates). This pattern is quite different from what occurred in the preceding decade, between 1984 and 1993/94, when the fastest growth was among poorer rural households, with no significant variation in growth across the distribution in urban areas.

This is where the controversy starts. As extensively discussed in the literature on poverty and inequality in India, the National Sample Survey covers a fairly low and declining share of measured private consumption.[4] There is not space to review this here, except for a summary assessment:

- Both the National Sample Survey and the national accounts have imperfections, but it is clear that the National Sample Survey fails to capture all private consumption.
- It is highly likely that underreporting is greater at the top of the distribution, especially for the rich. Conversely the National Sample Survey expenditure module is probably the best measure of spending of the poor.
- Rising overall inequality—especially at the top— is consistent with other sources, including tax returns[5] and initial analysis of the labour earnings module of the National Sample Survey.[6]

While important differences in per capita spending are important, this analysis focuses on the four axes of inequality, to capture inequalities not covered in the National Sample Survey and to focus on dimensions of inequality that may be more salient than others, in terms of societal concerns, behaviour and political influence.

Corporate wealth

Start at the top of the distribution, with the truly wealthy. There are no comprehensive data for this group, but what exists suggests a major increase in reported wealth accumulation. Take the net worth of Indian billionaires as reported on Forbes.com.[7] There has been a spectacular increase in their wealth over the past decade, driven both by rising numbers of billionaires and by rising wealth for existing billionaires. The sources of wealth come primarily from the business sector, with a wide range of activities listed, including mining, energy, petrochemicals, pharmaceuticals, information technology, construction, real estate and finance. In the short run there was a big impact of the rise and fall of the stock market. There were large falls in billionaire wealth between February and November 2008, when the market had fallen some 60 percent off its highs. This large rise and partial fall is shown in the ratio of net worth to total GDP (figure 2).[8]

This indicator is still way above levels prevailing in the early 2000s and 1990s. It is, of course, an imperfect indicator: apart from probable measurement problems, it captures only those among the wealthy who cross the level into reporting a billion dollars of net worth. Below this are a much larger number of millionaires.

How does this compare internationally? In the mid-1990s India hardly appears. East Asian countries such as Indonesia, Malaysia, Thailand, and Singapore—all with large family-based corporate structures—are high in the rankings. By 2007 (before the further surge and subsequent fall in net worth in India in 2008) Indonesia and Thailand fell sharply, reflecting the 1997/98 crisis. India had risen above Brazil, Chile, Colombia and Mexico—all highly unequal Latin American countries—and the United States (figure 3). Three of the four countries with higher billionaire wealth relative to national income were Kuwait, Russia and Saudi Arabia—all with high concentrations of resource wealth.

The increase in billionaire wealth occurred in a period of rapid growth in corporate investment (figure 4) and a rise in the share of the corporate sector in total fixed investment from around 20 percent in 1990s to 30 percent by the mid-2000s. The corporate sector was an important player in India's growth acceleration,

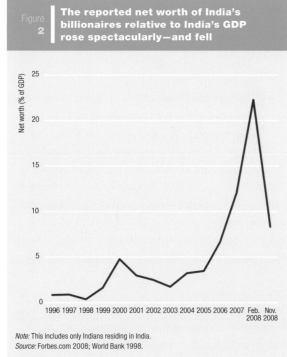

Figure 2

The reported net worth of India's billionaires relative to India's GDP rose spectacularly—and fell

Note: This includes only Indians residing in India.
Source: Forbes.com 2008; World Bank 1998.

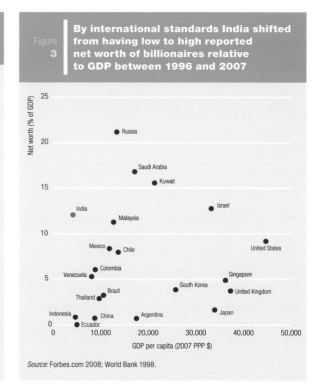

Figure 3

By international standards India shifted from having low to high reported net worth of billionaires relative to GDP between 1996 and 2007

Source: Forbes.com 2008; World Bank 1998.

There has been a broader entry of individuals into successful business— including those from castes traditionally not associated with business

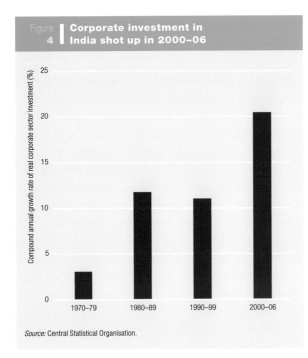

Figure 4 | **Corporate investment in India shot up in 2000–06**

Source: Central Statistical Organisation.

especially in technological innovation and catch-up. Particularly notable is the surge in investment in the 2000s: this occurred in the context of a long-term boom in the stock market and a large step-increase in the private investment rate that contributed to the rise in the aggregate investment rate to East Asian levels of nearly 40 percent as a share of GDP. This was financed to a significant extent by rising corporate savings—fuelled by rapid growth in profits—as well as by substantial capital inflows of portfolio and foreign direct investment.

Many of the billionaires are established household names in India, and many come from long-standing business families, often from groups associated with business, such as Jains, Marwaris and Parsis. India's genuinely long-term business capabilities have truly come into play in this period. But there have also been new entrants to the large-scale business community, most famously Dhirubai Ambani, whose two sons became the two richest individuals in India, according to Forbes. This has been complemented by a broader entry of individuals into successful business—including those from castes

traditionally not associated with business, among Hindus especially from Brahmin and Other Backward Classes.[9] The interpretation and implications of rising corporate wealth is discussed in the next section.

Identity-based differences

Some of the most socially and politically salient inequalities in India are linked to identity-based differences of various types. Some flow from a history of vertical social differentiation, reflected in the (primarily Hindu) caste structure. Others, in principle horizontal, are nevertheless associated with differences in socioeconomic status, as with adivasi groups, and along lines of religion, language and regional origin. Identity-based differences have also frequently been sources of conflict and violence, related to caste, religion, language and region. A further, and fundamental, identity-based difference is that of gender, of immense importance in India, with long histories of subordinate status of women, but it is not covered in any detail in this chapter.

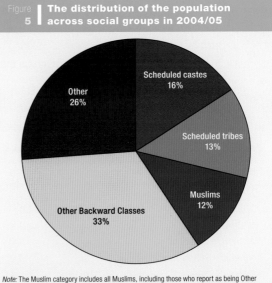

Figure 5 | **The distribution of the population across social groups in 2004/05**

Note: The Muslim category includes all Muslims, including those who report as being Other Backward Classes and very small numbers reporting as scheduled tribe or scheduled caste. Scheduled tribe, scheduled caste, and Other Backward Classes thus refer to the non-Muslim population in these categories. Scheduled tribe in particular includes significant numbers of both Hindus and Christians.
Source: National Sample Survey.

The historically most deprived groups, scheduled castes (or dalits) and scheduled tribes (or adivasis), are minorities, as are Muslims (figure 5). The largest single groups are in middle caste categories, predominantly Hindu. These became known as the Other Backward Classes and account for a third of the population. The historically "forward" castes, and various other religious groups, including non-scheduled tribe Christians, Jains and Sikhs, are in "others," together making up a quarter of the population.

Even this simple population distribution is of immediate political interest. The most striking aspect is the numerical importance of Other Backward Classes—and to the extent that they are in the middle with respect to socioeconomic status and voting preferences, they are of special political salience. Add to this a further consideration emphasized by political scientists: India's social history has led to weak underlying social solidarity between middle groups and either dalits or adivasis.[10] Furthermore, the complexity of the relationship between Hindus and Muslims is a central part of India's history. Political alliances are formed all the time, but this is quite different from, say, the broad lower class alliances typical of European history. There is a closer resemblance to societies with subordinate ethnic minorities, such as the

United States (Afro-Americans) and Latin American societies (Afro-Latinos in Brazil and Colombia, indigenous groups in Mexico and Peru).

Now look at relative well-being. The first big result is the continuity in the relative position of most groups over more than two decades—broadly encompassing the major reforms. The relative position of Hindu scheduled tribes rose between the early 1980s and early 1990s and then fell substantially by the mid-2000s (table 1). By contrast, Christian scheduled tribes experienced large relative gains. Other Hindus enjoyed modest gains. Muslims continued to be disadvantaged relative to Hindus on average, but less so than scheduled tribes or scheduled castes. Note that all distributions overlap— for example, better-off households among scheduled castes have higher per capita spending than poorer other backward classes.

That's about relative spending. Since average spending per person rose almost 30 percent in real terms between 1983 and 2004/05, all groups experienced some absolute real gains. With respect to deprivation, the overall poverty incidence fell some 18 percentage points on average, 19 percentage points for Hindu scheduled tribes, 21 percentage points for scheduled castes and 17 percentage points for Muslims

Table 1 | **Household expenditure per capita of groups as a share of the national average (percent)**

Groups	1983	1993/94	2004/05
Hindu: Scheduled tribe	70	75	67
Hindu: Scheduled caste	79	78	78
Hindu: Others	109	110	111
Hindu (all)	99	100	97
Muslim	90	89	89
Christian: Scheduled tribe	92	95	103
Christian: Others	128	131	158
Other religion	139	128	132
All	100	100	100

Source: National Sample Survey, various rounds.

> **Hindu scheduled tribes, Hindu scheduled castes and Muslims continued to have the highest poverty incidence in 2004/2005**

(table 2). All three of these groups continue to have higher poverty incidence than average in 2004/05: Hindu scheduled tribes continued to have the highest incidence in the most recent survey, at 47 percent, and experienced smaller gains in the 1993/94 to 2004/05 period.

A similar story comes from information on human development indicators. Scheduled tribes and scheduled castes experienced significant absolute gains, but scheduled tribes' progress was relatively slow.[11] A related finding from analysis of information from the censuses of 1990 is that areas with high proportions of scheduled castes enjoyed relative advances, but this did not apply to areas with more scheduled tribes.[12] On average, Muslims suffered relative deprivation on a wide range of indicators—literacy, access to education, public employment, access to bank loans and (as seen here) household per capita expenditures (Sachar Committee 2006).

What about the top of the distribution?

Disadvantaged groups were also significantly underrepresented among households with relatively high levels of spending in the survey data. Take the top 5 percent of the overall distribution. Only 1 percent of Hindu scheduled tribes, 1.8 percent of scheduled castes and 2.9

percent of Muslims were in this group, but if they had the same share as the population average, this would have been 5 percent.

In light of the reservation policies on tertiary education and public employment for scheduled tribes and scheduled castes, another interesting angle is access to high-level jobs. There were almost no adivasis or dalits in professional or technical jobs at Independence, except for a few outstanding individuals. By 1983 this had changed significantly, with further gains by the mid-2000s, when 4 percent of professional and technical jobs were held by individuals from scheduled tribes, and 11 percent by scheduled castes, compared with shares in the total population of 13 percent for scheduled tribes and 16 percent for scheduled castes (table 3). This again shows scheduled castes enjoying faster gains than scheduled tribes. But these "elite" groups represented only around 2 percent of their groups: for most people the real action lies elsewhere.

As discussed further below, competition for state-mediated preferences can also be a source of conflict. The Gujjiar group has been campaigning for scheduled tribe status for some years, and was promised it by the previous Rajasthani government. But the government did not deliver, in part because this would lead to direct

| Table 2 | Poverty incidence amongst scheduled tribes, scheduled castes and others |

Groups	Incidence (percent)			Change (percentage points)	
	1983	1993/94	2004/05	1983–1994	1994–2005
Hindu: Scheduled tribe	65.3	51.3	46.5	−13.9	−4.9
Hindu: Scheduled caste	59.0	49.2	38.5	−9.8	−10.7
Hindu: Others	39.0	28.6	20.6	−10.4	−8.0
Hindu (all)	45.2	35.1	26.9	−10.1	−8.2
Muslim	53.0	45.9	35.5	−7.1	−10.4
Christian: Scheduled tribe	41.7	32.8	20.2	−8.9	−12.7
Christian: Others	31.7	25.0	11.2	−6.7	−13.8
Other religion	25.3	23.7	17.6	−1.6	−6.1
All	45.2	35.9	27.5	−9.4	−8.4

Source: National Sample Survey, various rounds.

> **Identity-based differences remain central to social and political interactions, and will continue to be a core feature of distributional struggles in India in the coming years**

Table 3 | The share of scheduled tribes and scheduled castes in professional and technical work

Year	Scheduled tribes	Scheduled castes	Other	Total
As a share of the total number of professional and technical jobs				
1983	3.8	7.8	88.4	100
1993/94	3.9	7.7	88.4	100
2004/05	4.2	11.1	84.7	100
As a share of the population in each group				
1983	1.0	1.2	3.5	2.8
1993/94	1.2	1.3	4.0	3.2
2004/05	1.6	2.1	4.6	3.8

Source: National Sample Survey, various rounds.

competition for reservations with another group that already has scheduled tribe status. "Rajasthan could become another Kashmir if the Meenas get more reservations in 2010," says one Gujjiar representative.

Overall there has been some progress, if slow, on severe deprivation of disadvantaged groups, and possibly relative gains for scheduled castes. The picture looks much more like a situation of the reproduction of inequalities than the reproduction of poverty. With respect to the bottom of the distribution, there is no evidence of poverty traps at the level of these aggregate groups. At the top of the distribution a small proportion of disadvantaged groups have experienced gains, but this has not had a significant impact on relative positions on average. Identity-based differences remain central to social and political interactions, and will continue to be a core feature of distributional struggles in India in the coming years.

Spatial inequalities

Both rural–urban and interregional differences in incomes have risen. Focus on interstate differences, and use of the per capita net state domestic product, for which an annual series is calculated. There has been a substantial rise in an overall measure of dispersion, with a particularly large increase in the decade after 1990. Richer states seem to have benefited more from the

economic liberalization. The scale of the change can be illustrated by comparison with Bihar, the poorest state in this period. Both Gujarat and Tamil Nadu had average state incomes around twice that of Bihar for the 20 years from 1970 to 1990. But since then, the ratio has risen to between three-and-a-half and four times, due entirely to

Figure 6 | Tamil Nadu's and Gujarat's income per capita climbed relative to Bihar, 1970/71 to 2006/07

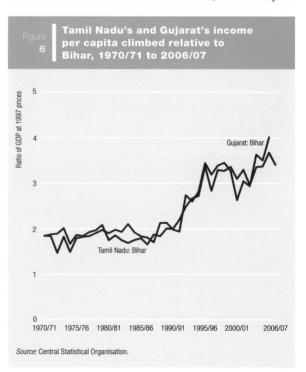

Source: Central Statistical Organisation.

> **The interaction between the relative demand and relative supply of skills is a central force in inequality dynamics, both in rich and poor countries**

the growth acceleration, since Bihar continued to grow slowly (figure 6).

Extensive work on economic geography in developing countries explains why activities concentrate there.[13] For India, on the basis of detailed empirical work, Chakrovorty and Lall (2007) attribute this to a mix of the economics of agglomeration—especially the benefits to firms of the wide range of services available in urban economic concentrations—and the persistent effects of institutional divergence.

This has two implications. First, the attraction of locating in established centres of urban industrial and service activity is, and will continue to be, a central and rising feature of India's modern growth path. This only heightens the importance of access to urban land and infrastructure as a central domain of rent-seeking and contestation. There may well be opportunities for some relocation to smaller towns (as is beginning to happen in the business process outsourcing and information technology sectors), but this will only create new locales for rent-management. Second, the benefits of agglomeration make it harder for economically lagging and institutionally weak states or districts to make the big push needed to catch up: the evidence of either infrastructure-led catch-up or benefits from fiscal subsidies is very weak for India, as for most countries.[14] Moreover, many of these "backward" areas are also stuck in a more "extractive" private rent-sharing equilibrium between business and state, making the challenge of an institutional big push even greater. In particular, where there is a confluence of mining resources, forests, adivasis population and weaker state traditions, the forces will tend to support more unequal and corrupt resolution that will continue to weaken institutions.

Skill-based differences

Part of the rise in per capita household expenditure inequality, especially for urban areas, is associated with rising differences in earnings with respect to skills. A theme in the interpretation of India's growth acceleration has been that the pool of highly skilled graduates, especially

in engineering, was an important initial condition and shaped the pattern of growth. Rapid growth occurred in relatively skill-intensive industrial and service activities.

However, with the further growth acceleration of the 2000s, the main concern in the market has been shortages of highly skilled labour, with rapid rises in salaries for highly qualified people. By 2007/08 there were anecdotes of information technology companies reversing their locational decisions back to Silicon Valley.

As one measure, take the average starting salaries of graduates of the Delhi School of Economics. They now go mainly to the private corporate sector because of a tough selection process to get into the school and the quantitative training they get. Between 2001 and 2008 the average starting salary rose from less than 300,000 rupees to over 800,000 rupees (around $21,000).

The interaction between the relative demand and relative supply of skills is a central force in inequality dynamics, both in rich and poor countries. On the demand side, many economists believe that opening would favour the returns to unskilled workers in labour-abundant economies. This seemed to be consistent with the first set of East Asian countries as they entered their periods of rapid growth. But things are more complicated in practice, both in general and in India. On the demand side, a dominant influence on returns to labour is agriculture, the most important labour-intensive sector, and rural productivity growth has been sluggish. A second demand-side influence, as already noted, has been the fact that India has followed a relatively skill-intensive path in industrial growth—under most interpretations a product of both its comparative advantage in the associated skills and the high cost of labour in formal manufacturing.[15] More broadly, there is considerable international evidence, especially from Latin America, that opening up to trade and foreign investment leads to skill-biased technical change, as companies shift to new techniques.

On the supply side, there are major institutional issues, both at the level of basic and tertiary education. This is overlaid on the intrinsically slow impact of changes in the flow of education on the stock of

> **For both secondary and tertiary education, India is clearly now lagging, in contrast to its earlier reputation of having invested in higher education**

workers: India has to live with the heritage of poor education for some decades.

For basic education, while there has been much growth in enrolments in India in the past decade, the quality remains dismal, and this is intimately tied up with how the state functions in the education system.[16] The central and state governments have been increasing public resources—not least in poor northern Indian states such as Bihar. But deep questions remain around teacher motivation and organizational incentives.[17]

For both secondary and tertiary education, India is clearly now lagging, in contrast to its earlier reputation of having invested in higher education. Tertiary enrolments were around half those of China in 2006, and substantially below Indonesia (figure 7). The state system is again bedeviled by organizational problems and low quality, outside the few islands of excellence. It is not at all clear that the big plans for expansion will be successful without major reforms.

The underlying dynamics of relative demand and relative supply would suggest that India is in for an

extended period of pressure on skill differentials, and institutional weaknesses reinforce this. Offsetting this pressure would require a major shift towards unskilled and semi-skilled labour on the demand side.

India as a rent-sharing equilibrium

How are the inequalities surveyed in the previous section related to the long-term development process? This is based on an interpretation of the relationship between society (including business), state and political processes.

Rent-sharing and growth

It is useful to think of India (and states within India) in a "rent-sharing equilibrium", with political support exchanged for the provision of economic rents by the state and politicians. This creates incentives for the perpetuation of institutions that create rents. The reforms of the 1980s and 1990s affected the nature of rents, but only partially, with the corporate sector shifting, to some degree, from "static" to "dynamic" rent-sharing. There was no major shift in the rent-sharing relationship between the state and social groups, though there were some shifts in patterns of rent distribution and, in some areas, further politicization of group-based identities. India's unequal structures have a strong tendency to support and sustain the rent-sharing processes, including a "patronage democracy" and a state that does a bad job at delivering many public goods. There are also likely to be periodic conflicts over rents, between business and social groups, between different social groups and between the various states of the federal system.

There is no guarantee that the rent-creating and rent-sharing processes will automatically disappear with economic growth and likely political developments. While the rent-sharing equilibrium (or series of equilibria) has been consistent with the current growth acceleration, over the long term it is more likely to undercut it, especially through weak public good provision, periodic distributional conflict and undermining of the development of the state.

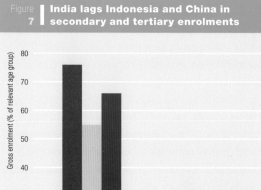

Figure 7 | **India lags Indonesia and China in secondary and tertiary enrolments**

Source: World Bank 1998.

> **An economic and political system has structured mechanisms for shring economic rents across competing groups that lead to a stable, self-sustaining path for the economy and society**

In a rent-sharing equilibrium, an economic and political system has structured mechanisms for sharing economic rents across competing groups that lead to a stable, self-sustaining path for the economy and society. Economic rents can be thought of as returns to factors that exceed their opportunity cost in other uses. In the economic literature these are classically created through restrictions on economic competition (more on "bad" and "good" rents below).

A rent-sharing equilibrium is "static" not because there is no growth, but because the primary effort of actors involves competition for rents that have been established under the existing economic and political system. This may include rents that will actually be received in the future, such as government commitments to long-term access to jobs, reservations on education or support for policies and institutions that restrict competition now and in the future. But this does not involve creation of new products or processes.

A rent-sharing equilibrium is "dynamic" in the sense that some of the rents, and associated rent-sharing arrangements, provide incentives for growth-related processes by economic actors, such as innovation, accumulation of human or physical capital, resource shifts into new activities and so on—by individuals, households, firms or the state.

This distinction is related to different kinds of rents. Consider a heuristic distinction between "bad" and "good" rents, based on whether they tend to spur or inhibit growth-related processes (table 4).

"Bad" rents are traditionally considered to be those created by restrictions on competition or access. They can flow from the exploitation of market power by a monopolist or a group of oligopolists, or through the creation of market restrictions by a government, through licences on production on investment or a protective trade regime. These are bad for growth because individuals and firms have incentives to put their energy into getting access to these rents, rather than into investment and innovation. Beneficiaries have an incentive to maintain the institutional structures that are the source of the rents. But the very existence of differential access to rents sharpens the possibility of distributional fights, which can also undercut growth processes, through increased risks of instability and loss in the benefits of investments. And rents can form part of a political system based on patronage rather than providing public goods.

Not all rents are bad for growth, with some integral to core growth-related processes. Schumpeterian rents, named after Joseph Schumpeter's classic account of the creative-destruction process, are the rewards to

Table 4	On "bad" and "good" rents	
	Sources	**Effects**
"Bad" rents	• Restrictions on economic competition • Political or administrative biases or exclusions • Politicized social differences	• Divert effort into creation and capture of rents via economic, political and social processes. • Encourage distributional fights • Can amplify biases against public good provision
"Good" rents	• Schumpeterian rents from newly created profitable activities • Learning rents for early movers • Natural resource rents • Rents from agglomeration economies	• Provide incentives for innovation, restructuring and learning • Integral to resource exploitation • Typically intrinsic to efficient spatial location

II/5

innovation in new products or lower cost processes, over and above the post-innovation cost of production. In the absence of such rents there can be suboptimal effort in innovation, since innovators face costs of exploration and risks of low returns. In a variant of this argument, there are costs to "discovery" of whether it is profitable to produce a new product in the specific conditions prevailing in a country.

So rents can occur either because an innovator has a first-mover advantage or because policy supports protection through patents or subsidies. Learning rents have a similar structure. Costs of production can decline as firms learn new techniques, labour processes and markets. At initial cost structures they may be uncompetitive (say, at international prices) and so have to receive protection or subsidies until the learning occurs.

Rents can also be linked to other economic development processes. Natural resource rents are intrinsic to resource extraction and will exist even with efficient production that fully incorporates externalities on the

environment or social conditions. Of course their existence can also lead to incentives to extract favourable (and thus inefficient) deals from politicians. Similarly, there are powerful agglomeration economies in many types of industrial and service production, and this can also lead to economic rents to those closer to "centres" of economic production.

A broad-brush indication of the absence of any simple relationship between rents and economic growth is shown by a plot of an index of corruption in the 1980s, as a proxy for rents, with subsequent economic growth in the 1990s (figure 8). Now many people might have the intuition that corruption is a better proxy for "bad" than "good" rents. Even so, there is effectively no relationship in the data! China, India, Malaysia and South Korea grew fast relative to other countries with similar levels of corruption; Brazil and Mexico grew relatively slowly. A more complex account is needed.

To start to explore this, the actors are organized into three groups: large-scale business; middle and lower

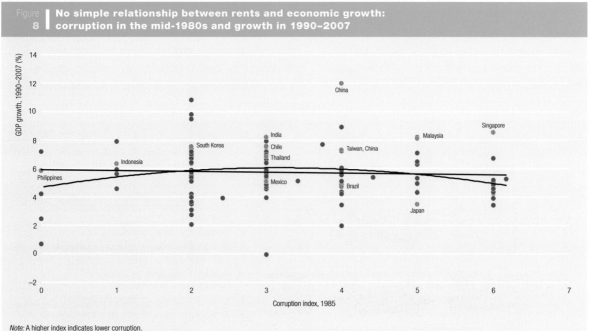

Figure 8 | **No simple relationship between rents and economic growth: corruption in the mid-1980s and growth in 1990–2007**

Note: A higher index indicates lower corruption.
Source: International Country Risk Guide 2008, World Bank 1998.

> **While there was significant new entry, there is no clear trend in market concentration across industries between 1993/94 and 2002/03**

social groups, including both households and small-scale business (which more often than not overlap in the farming and the informal sector, in the form of household enterprises); and the state, which here includes politicians, the bureaucracy, legislature, regulatory agencies and the judiciary (figure 9). There are then two categories of interaction.

- First, large-scale business needs various kinds of "permissions" to undertake investment or business activity. This could include an approval, or a specific complementary public good. Politicians and other state actors dispense them, under a mix of legal and illegal decisions and regulations.
- Second, social groups receive various kinds of benefits from the state, in the form of services, jobs, local public goods or affirmations of dignity in line with their preferences in return for political support for state actors. These can occur through formal voting or other means of providing political loyalty.

These two circuits of reciprocal interaction have a direct relationship to the first two categories of structural inequalities surveyed in the previous section—corporate wealth and group-based differences. The other two categories of inequality, spatial and education differences, are also embedded within this system. Each area is briefly reviewed here.

The corporate sector, rents and the state

For the corporate sector the License Raj system was a functioning, rent-sharing system that worked, with reasonable levels of credibility between the state and business, but at a low-growth equilibrium, thus the characterization as "static" rent-sharing. Restricted permissions held back investment. Successful businesses learned how to work the system, through contacts or bribes. The 1980 reforms have been described as either pro-business or pro-market.[18] Both have some truth, but it is more useful to think of them as shifting to a credible, more "dynamic" rent-sharing system for large-scale business. Important areas of permissions were liberalized in the 1980s and 1990s. There was an implicit deal with business to open to external competition in return for the internal.[19] While periods of inconsistent macroeconomic policy held back growth, the long-term impact was a major rise in investment, creative restructuring and business profits, which supported first two accelerations in growth—in the 1980s and then the 2000s. While there was significant new entry, there is no clear trend in market concentration across industries between 1993/94 and 2002/03.[20]

However, the post-reform system is not rent-free. Not only are there dynamic Schumpeterian and learning rents, but also many areas for state-business relations to involve rents. This applies whether the focus is on the national state's interaction with the corporate sector as

Figure 9 | A schematic representation of the relations between social and economic interests and the state

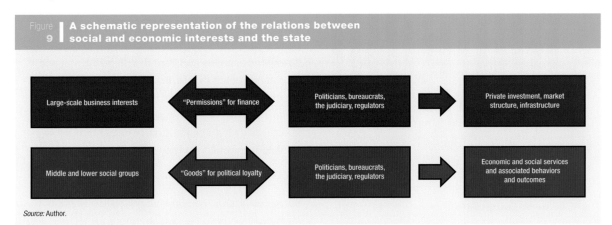

Source: Author.

> **India's business sector may be consolidating an oligarchic form of capitalism, in which large, family-controlled business empires play a powerful role vis-à-vis a relatively weak, and corruptible, state and potential competitors**

a whole, or local interactions, such as Bangalore's focus on supporting the expansion of the information technology sector through land allocations and tax breaks. In similar fashion, it applies to regional state-level efforts to attract private investors, as illustrated by the competition for Tata's investment in its greenfield investment for the Nano car in 2008, which West Bengal lost because of local social and political conflicts, and which Gujarat subsequently won.

It is noteworthy that many of the billionaires had sectors still thick with rents as primary sources of the corporate fortunes (figure 10).

There was a period from the late 1990s to early 2000s when billionaires from sectors such as information technology and pharmaceuticals accounted for a high fraction of the total, but this shifted back to dominance of those from rent-thick sectors in the second half of the 2000s.

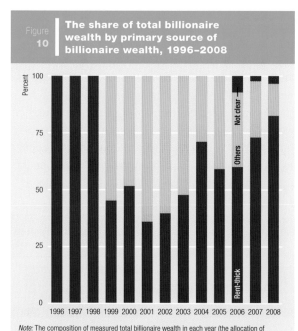

Figure 10

The share of total billionaire wealth by primary source of billionaire wealth, 1996–2008

Note: The composition of measured total billionaire wealth in each year (the allocation of billionaires weighted by wealth) is according to whether Forbes listed their main source of wealth in areas that are more likely to be thick with rent than others. Natural resources, land, and sectors involving government contracts were classified as "rent-thick." Others, such as information technology and pharmaceuticals, were classified as "other" (though, as just noted, even the information technology sector, seemingly an iconic example of Schumpeterian creation, benefited from favorable land deals.)
Source: Forbes.com 2008 and author's calculations.

Links can come through legal negotiations, informal relations, bribes or political finance. Political finance is murky, and inadequately documented because it is murky.[21] Political parties—and individual politicians—need finance to run for elections, with rising financial stakes as the political system has become more embroiled with money, both legal and illegal. Finance is needed to run the campaigns, even when the core voting blocks come from middle and poor groups. This can form part of a circle of interactions between business, politics and voting block.[22]

The pattern raises the possibility that India's business sector is consolidating an oligarchic form of capitalism, in which large, family-controlled business empires play a powerful role vis-à-vis a relatively weak, and corruptible, state and potential competitors. This is entirely consistent with major business houses playing a central role in past (and future) dynamism: for family-controlled conglomerates have important advantages in solving market failures, in providing finance and indeed in dealing with a slow and inefficient state. But this can come at a cost, especially over the long term, and especially if associated with an equilibrium in which a weak state functions to the interests of large business.

There are two conflicting forces: from the consolidation of market power by established business groups, and from substantial new entry by new firms, as well as competition from the international marketplace.[23] History—from India and elsewhere—suggests that both processes will play out. Entrenched business groups benefit from their established industrial and organizational capabilities and from their large internal and external resource mobilization capabilities—especially important in light of the major capital market failures in India. They also have the advantage of greater wealth and connections with the state, whether through legal influence, corruption or grey political finance.

Social groups, rents and the state

For social groups the rent-sharing relation with the state is distilled into the phrase "goods for loyalty". The

> **" The state and social groups have had two main thrusts to deal with deprivation and inequality: universal provision of basic social and economic services, and affirmative policies for scheduled castes and scheduled tribes**

"goods" can involve material benefits, including private goods, such as government jobs (or even goods such as televisions, as are now periodically offered in elections), club goods that benefit particular groups and public goods that benefit all. They also include symbolic goods of respect or dignity, of particular relevance in light of India's history of humiliation of subordinate castes and tensions over religion. Loyalty can literally mean votes in an election but can also extend to other forms of political support for local or national elites. These interactions lead to particular patterns of provisioning economic and social services, the responses of individuals and groups and the social and economic outcomes that are the final concern of development.

The relationship between the state and social groups since Independence has had two main thrusts to deal with a history of deprivation and inequality: universal provision of basic social and economic services, and affirmative policies for the two main deprived groups, scheduled castes and scheduled tribes, through reservations of public sector jobs, places in tertiary education, establishment and political seats, plus targeted support for tribal areas.

In practice, this policy mix ran up against three obstacles: the continued power of the group-based differences that make alliances between the poor and middle groups difficult,[24] the consolidation of a patronage democracy[25] and a state that is "weak" in the sense of being stuck in an equilibrium that is pervasive, but also corruptible and unresponsive to citizens.[26] The weakness of lower group alliances has tended to keep political movements embedded in a patronage-based system, and both have reduced external pressure on improving state functioning, sharpening the tendencies for the state to deliver private and club (group-specific) goods.

At one level, reservations have been successful in fostering a small professional elite from scheduled castes and tribes, as seen earlier. And there is evidence that political reservations that increased scheduled caste seats were associated with more job reservations, while increased scheduled tribe seats increased scheduled tribe-related welfare spending—but neither increased education spending.[27] But both the centrality of patronage and the workings of reservations have led to "static" rent distributions. They have also politicized identity, leading to the "demand for disadvantage," for groups being classified as deserving of state-mediated transfers to compensate for the disadvantaged status.[28] The most sweeping effect of this was the extension of (some) reservations to Other Backward Classes in the wake of the Mandal Commission.

Rent-sharing has led to gains, albeit often via patronage-based mechanisms, for other backward classes, probably increasingly to scheduled castes and least to scheduled tribes. Other Backward Classes and scheduled castes have become central to the general functioning of the polity in most if not all states. Many states have important Other Backward Class-based parties and leaders. Uttar Pradesh now is under the scheduled caste-based BSP and has a scheduled caste chief minister; and a small minority from all groups have risen into the professional elite (table 3), with a parallel emergence of business elites, especially from Other Backward Classes.[29] There has been a major, long-term shift in the political dominance of upper castes, with the transitions in the southern states substantially ahead of northern states. The measures to support smallholder agriculture—from the Green Revolution, to rural banking and to water, fertilizer and electricity subsidies—have been driven by the political salience of the Other Backward Classes in particular.

However, there has not been any dramatic movement in the relative position of different social groups, and there has been a long-term failure in provisioning public goods that would be good for growth and human development for all. A patronage-based system is likely to undermine elements of state capacity that are oriented towards collective welfare and associated with an independent bureaucracy, since it intrinsically involves discretionary action linked to political support rather than either need or efficiency.

> **While there are pockets of real excellence, the government university system seems to be stuck in a low-effort, high-inertia equilibrium**

influenced by the history of access to primary and secondary schooling. At tertiary levels the reservation system for scheduled castes and scheduled tribes is overlaid on this underlying inequality in access. As noted earlier, this has indeed brought benefits to a minority from these historically deprived groups, but it is generally from households that are substantially better off than the average within scheduled castes and scheduled tribes.[34] This is not necessarily a bad thing: part of the intent of the reservation policy was to create an elite among these groups. But they, like others, are effectively recipients of rents.

There are also large rents on the supply side. This is first of all true among teachers: while by no means well-off by international standards, teachers in government schools have incomes higher than they would otherwise have obtained in the market given their qualifications.[35] Teachers in private schools generally earn much less. Less well documented is the presence of rents in the supply side of tertiary education. While there are pockets of real excellence, the government university system seems to be stuck in a low-effort, high-inertia equilibrium. Yes, teaching faculty tend to receive very low salaries (if somewhat less so after the 2008 adjustment), but they do receive job security, weak incentives for high effort in teaching (again outside the elite institutions) and sometimes housing. On the private side, there are anecdotal reports of favours in the permissions to open new colleges, a potentially lucrative source of income, given the surging demand for skills.

Cutting across these conditions are two truly large changes: the expansion in government education, and the entry of private schooling, in the form of education establishments and tuition. While important, it is unclear how these changes will reduce the inequality of opportunity. Poor children go to poor schools and end up with poorer jobs and lower incomes; their children also have worse schooling. The growing access of poorer children to basic and increasingly beyond-basic education is an immensely good thing, but will not necessarily produce greater equality. The mechanisms for sustaining inequality in education could shift to differential access to (quality) private education and consequentially differential

access to higher education. Latin American countries have had major educational expansions in the past—with a further push in the wake of the 1980s democratization—but without a major impact on inequality. Instead, access to tertiary education has become the primary locus for the perpetuation of inequalities.[36]

Education is also a growth issue. Some commentators have argued that India's unusual pattern of growth acceleration was shaped by its unusual education endowment: poor basic education and tertiary centres of excellence producing large absolute numbers of engineers at low international prices.[37] This also explains the relatively slow take-off of labour-intensive manufacturing by East Asian standards, and impressive growth in services, such as outsourcing. But the absorption of the stock of highly skilled workers is the reason why high-level salaries have taken off. So the big growth question is whether the supply response of basic-to-secondary and tertiary skills will be sufficient. If not, skills could become a constraint on growth.

Future dynamics will depend on two questions. Will the beneficiaries of existing rents preserve the existing system with its inertia and strong tendency to low quality? What will be the medium and long-term response by the private sector? The answers will shape growth and inequality dynamics in the coming decades.

Is the Indian state weak?

A cross-cutting issue in much of the interpretation here has been the apparent failing of the Indian state. A recurrent theme has been that rent-creation and rent-sharing may be suboptimal relative to some ideal of limited government, including Weberian bureaucracies enthusiastically following rules of behaviour driven by goals set by democratic processes. But such an ideal is unrealistic, and rent-based systems can be a good-enough second best—for growth dynamics, for social peace and for service delivery. But when this is also combined with an ineffective state, the outcomes can be really bad.

So is the Indian state ineffective? And is this a necessary consequence of rent-based systems?

> **The Indian state is typically characterized as being active and pervasive but "weak" in its implementation of public action**

The Indian state is typically characterized as being active and pervasive but "weak" in its implementation of public action. Pritchett (2008) refers to India as having a "flailing" state. However, an account of generalized weakness is unsatisfactory. At a cross-country level, indicators of "government effectiveness", based mainly on subjective assessments by investors and citizens, show a strong positive relationship, but lots of variation at any given income (figure 11).[38] India performs reasonably well for its current income level, comparable to China and Mexico, but significantly below Chile, Malaysia and South Korea, as well as rich countries. There are always questions of comparable data, but this must be capturing perceptions of at least some groups who deal with the state.

There is also substantial variation within India. Elections, a clear public good and a huge organizational challenge, are implemented effectively. Macroeconomic policy is generally well managed, or more precisely, while there is room for disagreement of choices over interest

rate and fiscal policy, the macroeconomic managers, especially in the Reserve Bank of India, effectively implement what they judge to be desirable. And take Indian Railways, one of the largest companies in the world, with more than 1.5 million employees, and a natural vehicle for patronage. Trains are not always on time, but it is a system that works—perhaps remarkably well relative to its size. By contrast, the state health and education systems generally perform dismally—with problems even in getting nurses and teachers to attend their clinics and schools. Similarly, most observers agree that there are large differences in performance across states—a standard comparison is between the southern states of Andhra Pradesh, Karnataka, Kerala and Tamil Nadu and such northern and eastern states as Bihar, Orissa and Uttar Pradesh.

As noted, India's performance in child malnutrition is awful—with respect to other countries at a similar or lower incomes, and with little progress over time, even in a period of rapid aggregate growth. This, despite the fact that India has for decades had a large program oriented towards child development—the Integrated Child Development Services. There is little or no evidence that this programme has had a positive impact in the aggregate. According to the FOCUS report (2006), this was associated with a classic mixture of weak incentives for effort and disempowered front-line workers in the anganwadis (village-level child development centres).

The general assessment seems even worse than for basic education. It was suggested earlier that this is linked to the importance of both public good provision and coordination across agencies for effectiveness, making it poorly aligned with political incentives to deliver to supporters. But this does not seem to be inevitable. Even within this programme, the FOCUS report found markedly different performance in Tamil Nadu, with well supplied and attractive anganwadis managed by motivated staff. This state, with a longer history of developing an initially distinct programme, had apparently maintained an equilibrium in which the organizational culture and individual incentives supported reasonably effective state performance.

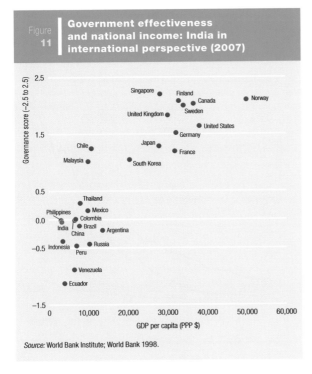

| Figure 11 | **Government effectiveness and national income: India in international perspective (2007)** |

Source: World Bank Institute; World Bank 1998.

Alongside this variation across agencies and space, a central narrative of the Indian state in the post-Independence period is the transition from a significantly autonomous state to a pervasive but constrained state. In the initial period the political leadership—especially that of Jawarhalal Nehru—used the state as an instrument of change for the modernization and socialist project. This was facilitated by the decision to take over the core structures of the colonial civil service and put them to use to this end. But in the decades after Nehru's death, societal embeddedness has risen through processes of politicization, patronage and the institutionalization of corruption. While the state is not fully embedded, it has become substantially constrained by societal and political influences.[39]

So how can this be interpreted? This is one of the major questions for India's future. Rent-based systems can undercut the performance of the state, through diverting effort into preservation of public sector rents, the pursuit of corruption and channelling goods and services to favoured groups. Furthermore, there is an argument that the very ineffectiveness of the state in areas of public goods delivery helps sustain an equilibrium in which politicians rationally choose to provide short-run benefits—either to specific groups or, in populist vein, to all—since the state cannot be relied on to deliver on promises on real public goods of quality education or better nutrition.

But the areas of relative success—the railways, malnutrition in Tamil Nadu and indeed the broader reputation of the state getting things done in Gujarat and Tamil Nadu—suggest there is no necessary link with rent-seeking and rent-sharing processes. It is not because Gujarat and Tamil Nadu are innocent of rents. The Weberian ideal of an independent, rules-based bureaucracy is not only unrealistic, but may not be the best means of getting high levels of commitment and effort from public sector workers.[40] The issue is not how to move "weaker" parts of the Indian state to a Weberian or other ideal, but how to get shifts in the existing, rent-thick system, to an equilibrium that is consistent with the overall political and social conditions, but that supports both more effective state action, and action that is more likely to deliver on public goods. That is one of the big questions for the future.

Alternative scenarios and the process of transformation

This section now sketches a qualitative account of the relationship between potential trajectories of institutional change and long-term development, flowing directly from the interpretation of the nexus of unequal structures and institutions developed in the preceding sections. While speculative, it provides a useful way of framing the issues.

Start with a comparison of long-term growth of GDP per capita in India, Indonesia, Mexico and South Korea (figure 12).

- First, Mexico had a growth "miracle," lasting almost three decades until the early 1980s. The

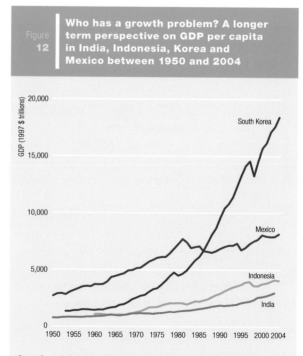

Figure 12 | **Who has a growth problem? A longer term perspective on GDP per capita in India, Indonesia, Korea and Mexico between 1950 and 2004**

Source: Center for International Comparisons of Production, Income and Prices, 2008.

last few years were driven by unsustainable fiscal deficits and external borrowing, but the longer term picture is of a major increase in economic capacity.

- Second, Mexico then got stuck, with little advance in the past 25 years, and this despite a highly favourable geographic location, next door to the most productive rich economy in the world, and a radical opening to trade and foreign investment under the North American Free Trade Agreement at the beginning of 2005.
- Third, even after adding the additional growth since 2004 (not included here to ensure consistency of data sources), India's per capita GDP in 2008 is still only at the level prevailing in Mexico in the mid-1950s!
- Fourth, the blazingly obvious message is that South Korea did something that Mexico did not, and went a very long way towards high income.

This is only one (illustrative) comparison. A similar comparison could have been undertaken with Brazil, which had miraculous growth that took it to upper middle income status and then stalled.[41]

India could follow a qualitative scenario involving the entrenchment of old and new inequalities or one of transformation (figure 13).

The first scenario is termed the (further) "Latin Americanization" of India. This is a metaphor. It may not work for everyone, but it is a useful metaphor, because it captures the mix of structural inequalities and the middle income trap that have typified countries such as Brazil and Mexico. It has become even more apt in the past two decades since most of Latin America returned to democracy in the 1980s. Its key features are:

- Consolidation of oligarchic capitalism, with major business groups wielding disproportionate influence over markets and the state.
- Intensification of group-based conflicts, in legal and extralegal arenas.
- Continuation or deepening of spatial disparities in economic, social and institutional conditions.

Figure 13 | Alternative long-term institutional scenarios for India

Institutional design

"Latin Americanization"
- Oligarchic capitalism
- Heightened group-based conflict
- Spatial polarization
- Persistent educational inequality

→ Middle income trap

"Transformational"
- Competitive capitalism
- Intergroup equity and programmatic politics
- Upward spatial convergence
- Meritocratic education

→ High income society in a generation

Source: Author.

- Both basic and tertiary education continuing to be sites for the reproduction of inequality, despite expansion in overall access.

The second scenario is termed "transformational" because a major institutional evolution in the political, social and economic domains fosters greater equality of influence and citizenship in ways that support dynamic growth. This is the counterpart of sustained rapid growth comparable to Japan, South Korea or Taiwan in their high-growth periods. This could lead to India becoming a high income society in a generation—by around 2039. This scenario contrasts with the first along all four dimensions:[42]

- Consolidation of competitive capitalism, with the dynamism of large and small businesses depending on innovation rather than influence.
- Genuine group-based equity, but effected by increasingly programmatic politics, with reduced politicization of group-based identities.
- Upward economic and social convergence of poorer regions, affected by institutional convergence in poorer states and districts.
- An increasingly meritocratic education system, in which all children have access to similar educational possibilities.

There are connections between the varying elements of these scenarios, with the functioning of the polity

> **In India vertical and horizontal group-based conflicts are more open and explicit; and there has been concerted public action and legislation**

Figure 14 | A contemporary view of Standard Oil's role in the United States circa 1900

Source: Publicly available archival cartoons, via Robinson (2009).

Add to this the interests of the business sector itself. The business community as a whole has a strong interest in pushing for institutional structures that provide both checks on opportunistic, corrupt or exploitative behaviour of individual businesses and develop a more effective state, alongside greater societal pressure for competitive capitalism. Fundamentally a collective action issue, this displays the classic problems of collective action: beneficiaries of the current system can make it work for their private business interests; moving to a better system is uncertain and could involve forsaking such individual interests. Yet the business community as a whole has to be a central player in any change. Debate within the community and development of a code of ethics can play an important role. But it is difficult to imagine creating the checks and balances on business without an effective state and designing and implementing the institutional design outlined earlier. Business also

has a role here, in using its political capital and skills to push for state reform.

Identity-based differences

The dynamics and associated risks of identity-based differences, distributional fights and implications for patronage were discussed earlier. Here again, India has parallels with Latin America, where cleavages between groups of European, indigenous and African origin have been salient for a long time—and remain so despite extensive mixing. India is arguably "ahead" of much of Latin America in two respects: both vertical and horizontal group-based conflicts are more open and explicit; and there has been concerted public action and legislation along at least some of the dimensions. But it is also easy to be pessimistic, along several lines:

- Hindu–Muslim differences show few signs of abating, along with the continued salience of

> **Reservations will receive too much weight within a strategy oriented towards the pursuit of equity if the political classes have incentives to mobilize support around group-based identity and if universalist principles of citizenship fail**

Hindutva political movements. Moreover, they interact with an inauspicious regional context, especially for tensions with Pakistan.

- While the rise in the dalit-based political movements is an important and in many ways desirable phenomenon, it is unclear what they will mean for provisioning public goods and development dynamics.
- Conversely, adivasi groups suffer from much weaker organization and are particularly caught in the destructive interaction between Naxalites and the state.
- Other axes of group-based conflict continue to be salient—in 2008/09 this included Hindu-Christian violence in Karnataka and Orissa and violence against Northern Indians in Mumbai.
- Identity-based politics could continue to hold back the development of programmatic parties.

International experience only confirms that these are tough issues to manage in a heterogeneous society. Identity-based differences are extraordinarily persistent, and can lead to either sustained deprivation and stigma, or open conflict. The United States is a partial model, with its history of incorporating immigrant groups. With a black president, it is currently a symbolically potent one. But that should not hide the continued relative deprivation and stigma attached to African Americans.[54] The United Kingdom experienced decades of violent conflict in the troubles between Catholics and Protestants in Northern Ireland. South Africa is struggling with policies that foster black empowerment, that may be creating a small rent-sharing black elite rather than genuine equality of opportunity for all.

Affirmative action will clearly continue to be part of the story, and there is a particular challenge in escaping from the trap of the "demand for disadvantage" and the fights over static rents that have become integral to the reservation approach.[55] There is some creative thinking on how to pursue the end of affirmative action through alternative means that seek to escape this trap: for example, through a "diversity index" in organizations

affected by reservation policy, as opposed to quotas, and through stronger antidiscrimination legislation.

Making affirmative action work better is important, but reservations will continue to receive too much weight within a strategy oriented towards the pursuit of equity if the political classes continue to have incentives to mobilize support around group-based identity and if universalist principles of citizenship continue to fail. These have counterparts in public action that are outlined here.

Reducing political incentives for group-based mobilization. The second interpretive section discussed the reinforcing links between group-based political mobilization and a patronage democracy, drawing on Chandra (2004). So what could make a difference? Here are three areas:

- *A more effective state.* One of the reasons politicians have little incentive to follow political strategies promising public goods that benefit all groups is precisely the ineffectiveness of the state. If they cannot rely on actors in the executive branch to deliver, their promises will not be credible. Strategies that emphasize conflicts with "other" groups can then be more reliable, in an extreme making a politics of hate a means of sustaining support. Conversely, a more effective state will shift the relative incentives towards political strategies that favour public goods provision, or at least cross-group appeals.
- *Greater intra party competition.* The lack of internal competition within parties means aspiring politicians have incentives to please the party hierarchies rather than be accountable to their constituents. As noted above, this was an important reason for emerging dalit elites to pursue a strategy of leaving the Congress to set up the Bahujan Samaj Party. Democratization within parties is intrinsically desirable, especially if linked to stronger links between individual politicians and constituencies.

> **There has been significant creativity in India in changing incentives for the behaviour of state actors, with the complementary strengthening of specific rights with social mobilization**

- *Deepening local democracy.* The development of local fora for social and political debate in the panchayati raj system provides an arena for deliberative processes between different groups. Evidence from the functioning of deliberation now finds that the form of interaction often remains embedded in sociocultural differences linked to group-based status. But there is potential for the very process of deliberation to shape the identities and agency of subordinate groups.[56] If successful, this would be a different process from those that occur through reservations, and one that could foster a move towards genuine equality of agency. There appear to be parallels with the political and sociocultural transitions in sites with deep participatory processes, notably Porto Alegre in Brazil.

Universalism and citizenship. As frequently emphasized here, the post-Independence vision for dealing with historically shaped deprivation involved two tracks: creation of political and intellectual-managerial elites via the reservation policy; and universal provision of services for all. Probably the bigger failure was on the second part of this.

Deepening universalist policies is both intrinsically desirable and could gradually offset harmful aspects of identity-based conflicts. Some of the action falls within the realm of making established policies work—provision of basic education for all, water and sanitation for all and so on. But the issue goes beyond the adoption of policies; Indian governments have been good at that. The real issue lies in changing incentives for the behaviour of state actors, for which changes in the nature of state-society interaction are central, with the complementary strengthening of specific rights with social mobilization. There has been significant creativity in India in this area in the past decade or so. The Right to Information Act is a central example of a policy that can empower citizens, though the capacity of different citizens to access it could continue to be unequal.

Of equal interest is the design of the National Rural Employment Guarantee Act (NREGA), because of its incorporation of a right of all citizens to a given number of days of work, the prohibition of private contractors and complementary requirements on social audits. The social and economic rationale is to provide a safety net in the context of highly imperfect private and informal insurance markets (especially when communities suffer common shocks.) But these institutional designs are centrally concerned with breaking through the pre-existing political equilibrium around provisioning of local works, which involved discretionary action by politicians or other state actors. This intrinsically involved provisioning rents to both recipients and contractors, creating incentives for bribes and patronage. NREGA's institutional form—when it can be made to work— removes these incentives. Implementation appears to be highly varied, with resistance to the new mechanisms in parts of the country, including violence against some involved in social audits. These important issues could undermine NREGA's effectiveness. But they can be seen as evidence that the institutional change is indeed challenging the existing distorted system.

History suggests that resolving group-based conflicts is a long and complex process. The suggestions here are not intended to deny or dissolve sociocultural differences, which will continue to evolve and form a central part of India's society. Differences are a source of societal wealth. What is problematic, in the short term and for development in the long term, is the politicization of group-based identity and the associated heightening of conflict, especially over static rents. The proposal here is that it will be important to develop and pursue of a complementary mix of continuing (and potentially reforming) affirmative action, political reforms that reduce incentives for political classes to use group-based identities and broader pursuit of universal citizenship.

Tackling spatial inequalities

For spatial inequalities, Latin Americanization remains a relevant comparator—all large Latin American countries

> **Underurbanized now, India will go through massive urbanization in the coming decades. Yet it already has immense urban problems and weak urban governance**

have regions that have experienced long-term relative deprivation, with political, economic and social institutions intertwined in the nexus. The southern states of Mexico and the northeast of Brazil are examples. But such spatial inequalities, not a Latin American preserve, are also a feature of almost all large countries: recent examples from Asia include China's inner provinces and Indonesia's eastern islands.

There are several reasons why current forces could perpetuate inequalities and have adverse aggregate development effects:

- The interaction between agglomeration forces and institutional divergence tends to lead to persistence, and this can be magnified by differential benefits from global integration—a feature of divergence across (and sometimes within) India's states, which was also experienced by Mexico when it joined the North American Free Trade Agreement.

- The evidence on successes from proactive national pushes for regional catch-up, say pushing infrastructure, are weak. In a recent review of the potential for this strategy for India, Chakrovorty and Lall (2007) were pessimistic. The northeast of Brazil has experienced decades of regional policies but still suffers relative deprivation. Indeed, such regional policies often become new domains for the distribution of rents.

- Urbanization is a huge and unruly domain of action. Underurbanized now, India will go through massive urbanization in the coming decades. Yet it already has immense urban problems and weak urban governance—an area where many Latin American countries and cities are way ahead.

- There is plenty of scope for adverse effects from continued lagging regions, precisely because they are so populous, through two pathways. First is the potential electoral and political pressures for populist national policies from poorer states (further pursuit of static rent-sharing with

a short-term horizon). Second is the interaction with identity-based conflicts in migration-receiving areas, as seen in 2008 in the Marathi–North India conflicts in Mumbai.

What might an alternative path look like?

- In the medium term the most hopeful scenario is for institutional changes within lagging states, perhaps spurred by democratic deepening and interstate competition. An optimistic interpretation of the rise of the BSP in Uttar Pradesh is that this is part of a long-term resolution of caste-based conflicts, analogous to what occurred in southern states some decades earlier. The current government in Bihar came in on a development platform. It has pursued a dramatic expansion of education efforts, with a threefold increase in teachers, a push on roads and (according to initial reports) a more effective response to relief after the catastrophic flooding with the breaching of the Kosi embankment in 2008. The big question is whether this indicates an underlying shift in the political equilibrium to a more pro-development stance, with a realignment in the incentives for politicians and other state actors.

- In urban areas, as discussed in chapter on urbanization, it is possible to envisage systemic changes in urban governance, with decentralization and democracy likely to be core components.[57] Here, there are salutary lessons from Latin America: yes, such democratizing reforms have brought changes through diverse pathways (Bogotá in Colombia, Porto Alegre in Brazil). But many cities with a similar legal context have not effected a transformation. Devolution is central.

- If long-run development to high income status is successful, the United States is an example of long-term interregional convergence; but this occurred in an unusually mobile society, with migration as an important factor.

> **" India is moving quite fast, if belatedly, to massifying access to basic education, but has not worked out how to get decent quality in state education systems**

Skill-based differences

For the inequality-skills-growth nexus, Latin Americanization is already fully present in India.

- Liberalization and globalization will be pressures for rising skill-based differences, with the bottom of the wage ladder set by the Bihari labour market, and the top converging to levels in New York and San Francisco.
- India is moving quite fast, if belatedly (like most of Latin America), to massifying access to basic education, but has not worked out how to get decent quality in state education systems. Middle class flight to private education will rise; "middle class" used ambiguously to refer to elite shifts to top schools in urban areas and to shifts of rural children, disproportionately from the middle and top half of the distribution, to better rural private schools.
- Tertiary education will become an even more important source of the reproduction of inequalities, especially if the quantity and quality problems are not resolved at this level, with continuing growth in the premium from the high quality institutions.

Is there an alternative? This is an area where it is fairly easy for an education specialist to describe the contours of broad-based, high quality basic education and meritocratic tertiary education. But the really hard issues concern institutional reform, reshaping teachers' incentives, organizational functioning and the local political economy.

For basic (primary and secondary) education there will be a large and growing role for the private sector, in schools and tuition. But this has to be complemented by a major improvement in the quality of the state sector: experiments are under way in many states. One important example is in the work of the nongovernmental organization Pratham, and its sister organization, the ASER Institute. This group developed the organizational capacity to test a statistically representative sample of children in basic reading and maths skills in almost every district in India. This has already revealed the potential for information to spur action by state governments, through the evidence it provides on (severe) learning deficits. It is now being complemented by the Read India campaign, in which Pratham develops teaching materials and works with the state school system to support teachers in basic, and beyond basic, skills development. It is too early to assess its impact, but this kind of initiative is an essential complement to the expansion of private education if all children are to have access to decent education. Options for a major change in the tertiary education system are discussed in the chapter on education and technology.[58]

Governance, accountability and the state

A recurrent theme of this analysis has been that a central element of any transformation—good or bad—is the performance of the state. It is again fairly easy to describe what would be desirable: a state accountable to citizens, with sufficient internal and external checks and balances to minimize capture by particular groups, whether this is over a specific judicial decision, the design of policy or the local allocation of public resources. It also means a state that has an effective organizational structure, with a balance of financial incentive systems, hierarchy and organizational cultures that support reasonable, high intrinsic motivation.

Effecting change is harder, precisely because the state is to a significant extent endogenous, and will co-evolve with the structure of inequality described here. Large businesses can have an interest in a weaker state, which is more susceptible to its influence. Similarly, a more effective and more universalistic state is critical to more effective management of identity-based conflicts. Yet identity-based structures have also been a source of continuing patronage, with dangers that parts of the state become more sharply aligned with communal forces. In every domain, transforming the state will be central to success. All is not bleak now—the state is heterogeneous in its performance across sectors and across space. Future change is likely to involve social

> **"** Institutional structures that encourage, share and manage "dynamic" rents are necessary for growth and change. But they need to be sharply distinguished from the "static" rent-sharing so central to India's polity

pressure—from businesses with longer term interests, from the growing middle class and from civil society groups—and internal reforms around governance. Issues of governance reform are discussed further in the chapter on governance.[59]

Conclusion: The need for and possibility of change

In the coming decades India will experience major social, economic and political transformations. Structures of inequality will co-evolve with changes in the economy, the functioning of the state, and delivery of services. This co-evolution will involve processes of mutual causation, which are imperfectly understood. While quantitative scenarios have been avoided, the interpretation here suggests a substantial probability of the continuing entrenchment of some inequalities, combined with inefficient redistributive efforts. This is deeply connected with the way in which the Indian political system functions and the nature of the Indian state. A metaphor for this is the Latin Americanization of India. As figure 12 shows, Mexico did achieve upper middle income status—and this would bring truly significant benefits to Indians. But this occurred in the context of substantial state capture by vested interests, inadequate mechanisms for managing distributional conflict, rising violence and real difficulties in effecting the transition to high income.

The creation and sharing of economic rents is pervasive and central to the current political equilibrium in India. Economic liberalization, while necessary for India's long-term transformation, has tended to heighten structural inequalities. It has shifted the locus of rent creation and distribution, rather than fundamentally changing this. In some areas, rents—associated with innovation, the Schumpeterian process of creation and destruction, and agglomeration—are intrinsic to long-term economic transformation. Institutional structures that encourage, share and manage these "dynamic" rents are necessary for growth and change. But they need to be sharply

distinguished from the "static" rent-sharing so central to India's polity, distorting the functioning of the state and diverting it from the essential tasks of delivering a range of public goods and assuring genuine equity for all citizens.

Long-run development will require transformation in social, economic and political institutions. Effecting change is complex and poorly understood. It is especially challenging when desirable changes conflict with endogenous political forces and patterns of influence. Historical experiences suggest change can occur, even though no country experience provides a blueprint for India. Three interconnected areas have been systematically emphasized throughout this chapter: the need to develop a competitive corporate sector with checks and balances against excessive market or political influence; tackling group-based inequalities but with more emphasis on reducing the politicization of such differences and the pursuit of universal citizenship, to complement explicit affirmative action; and the development of a more accountable state.

Many issues are not on this shorter list, issues clearly important to the joint evolution of inequality and growth—the deep problems in basic and tertiary education, spatial differences, rural productivity, inequalities in urban areas and so on. There is uncertainty over which will matter most. This returns to the centrality of the state and overall governance. Technical design questions are crucial in all of these areas. But whether the most important issues for change are identified—and whether the political process and public decisionmaking lead to institutional changes in the right direction for growth and equity—will depend fundamentally on the relationship between government and society over the coming decades.

INDIA
2039

Part II

Chapter

6

Urbanization
and public
sevices

Urbanization and public services: Creating functioning cities for sustaining growth

Inder Sud

Within a generation, India will be transformed from a largely rural to an urban economy. According to UN projections, about half the total population of nearly 1.6 billion will be living in cities by 2039; others believe the share could be as high as 60 percent. The absolute numbers are even more staggering. There will be at least 400–500 million more urban dwellers by 2039.

Almost all cities can be expected to grow. The current big cities will become still bigger, and many medium-size towns will become large cities (figure 1). This shift in population to cities is an inevitable consequence of economic growth driven largely by industry and services, sectors that attract job seekers from rural areas and need urban agglomerations for their labour and skills.

Yet, as the demand for highly skilled labour rises, businesses are likely to face stiff global competition over the quality of life they can offer Indian professionals. The efficient functioning of the cities will influence labour costs and social conditions, which bear directly on India's competitiveness and growth prospects. In a global world, Indian businesses will need to compete globally for highly skilled Indian professionals, who will increasingly consider the quality of life as a factor in their own location decisions.

But most Indian cities are dysfunctional, suffering from serious deficiencies in the quality and quantity of infrastructure. Most suffer from poor roads, uncollected garbage, regular flooding, stagnant storm and waste water, and unreliable supplies of drinking water. Major investments are needed not only to overcome the backlog of services but also to keep pace with population growth. Operations and maintenance are entirely inadequate. The ranks of those in slum and squatter settlements continue to grow. In short, the quality of life in Indian cities compares unfavourably with that in other lower-middle income countries, and is far from the level India should aspire to as an affluent country.

Most Indian city administrators point to a lack of resources as the underlying cause of poor quality of infrastructure services. This is indeed true. On average, an Indian city spends less than $50 a year per capita on infrastructure and services. Estimates for what would be an adequate level vary widely, but it is generally recognized that the current level of expenditures needs to increase several-fold. Needs remain great, even though the Indian government provided significant additional resources to some larger cities during the past two plan periods, and states are sharing more of their resources with cities (and other local bodies) following the direction of the 12th Finance Commission.

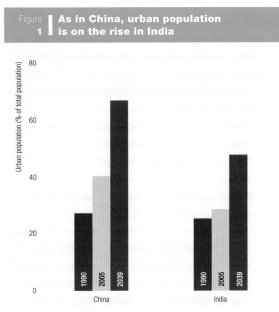

Figure 1 As in China, urban population is on the rise in India

Source: National Sample Survey Organization 1990–2005; United Nations Population Division 2009.

> **More than a third of all urban dwellers— some 110 million people—live in slums; the proportion is much higher in some larger cities**

semiprivate schools. Poor governance is widely recognized as the heart of the problem.

- Public hospitals and health centres suffer from chronic shortages of medicines and supplies; the available supplies are often pilfered and sold illegally. Without an adequate public health system, far too many poor people continue to die from simple and curable diseases. Without a safety net against catastrophic health events, both the poor and non-poor are highly vulnerable to the economic shock of extraordinary medical expenses.

Unaffordable land prices

The growing urban population exerts ever greater pressure on land prices, pushing ownership beyond the reach of many urban dwellers. Low income and poor families are forced into marginal, often illegal, settlements. More than a third of all urban dwellers—some 110 million people—live in slums; the proportion is much higher in some larger cities.[4] Government housing and land development programs have mostly failed to reach low income families. In addition, archaic urban planning methods and housing standards are further barriers to affordable housing. The resulting flurry of land use violations has paralyzed many municipal governments and created conflicts with courts that insist on enforcing the land use plans, no matter how unrealistic. Land speculation and the power to grant variations in land use without a proper framework present enormous opportunities for corruption.

Getting to the root of poor service

The first reason any city official will cite for the dismal state of affairs in the city is the lack of adequate resources, and indeed urban expenditure data tend to confirm this view. But money is only a part of the story. Most cities also suffer from weak capacity and poor governance, which are amongst the first reasons cited by state officials for their unwillingness to vest the cities with powers to raise and spend additional resources.

Causes of dysfunction

So there is a vicious cycle of insufficient resources, weak capacity, and lack of autonomy that holds back any meaningful change. Corruption, too, takes a toll. Action in all four areas is needed concurrently.

Insufficient resources

Urban government finances are not tracked systematically in India, so any assessment of resources has to be based on secondary sources or data collected sporadically for other purposes (as for the 12th Finance Commission and the current 13th Finance Commission). This haphazard accounting needs to be rectified, both because it reveals a basic information gap and because it indicates a broader lack of policy attention. Nonetheless, although the reported numbers should be treated with caution, they do confirm the prevailing view of acute shortages of funds.

Data collected by the World Bank for selected cities in three states—Karnataka, Maharashtra and Tamil Nadu— and published in 2004, indicate that the larger urban bodies classified as corporations spent between 944 rupees (Karnataka, 2000/01) and 2,300 rupees (Maharashtra, 1999/2000) per capita annually on infrastructure services.[5]

Assuming average annual growth of 10 percent since then, these municipal corporations may now be spending in the range of 1,700–4,000 rupees (or \$35–\$80) per capita annually. The numbers for Maharashtra are larger because it is one state where education and health functions are municipal responsibilities. For most of the larger municipalities, then, total per capita expenditure on infrastructure services may be \$35–\$50 a year. For the smaller municipalities in these states, based on the World Bank estimates, the number may be 35–60 percent lower. The First State Finance Commission for Punjab (1995) estimated annual expenditures of less than \$10 per capita for the cities in that state. Estimates (by the National Institute for Public Finance and Policy and the 12th Finance Commission)

> **International comparisons, even with the caveats about data and comparability, confirm that expenditure on services in Indian cities is grossly inadequate**

for all urban areas in 2001/02 are in the range of $15–$20 per capita annually.[6]

Of course, it is difficult to know what level of expenditures would be needed to provide adequate urban services. While international comparisons can be misleading given the widely varying nature of urban governments and their responsibilities in different countries, they can still be illustrative (table 1). International comparisons, even with the caveats about data and comparability, confirm that expenditure on services in Indian cities is grossly inadequate.

Moreover, the share of public spending going to urban expenditures has declined steadily from nearly 8 percent in 1960/61 to 4.5 percent in 1977/78 and about 2 percent in 1991/92, even though the share of the population living in cities has increased.[7] One reason for the low expenditures is the poor job most Indian cities do at mobilizing their own resources. Self-generated revenues cover only 70–85 percent of current expenditures,[8] and cities must rely on resource-constrained state governments for the balance. Since salaries and wages alone account for more than half—and as much as 80 percent—of cities' current expenditures,[9] the resulting tight budgets mean that maintenance is neglected.

Table 1	**Urban government expenditures and revenues per capita in India and comparable countries**

Country	Year	Expenditures per capita ($)	Revenues ($)
India	2008	<50	<40
Brazil	1994	149	140
Brazil	2004	210	195
Mexico	1997	51	50
South Africa	1998	125	125
Poland	1998	358	355
Russia	1995	349	347

Source: Author's estimates based on World Bank (2004, 2005) and the International Monetary Fund (various years).

Cities depend largely on financing from the central government for capital investments. Resources are either transferred directly in the form of centrally sponsored urban development schemes or they are granted to states to be passed on to urban local governments. The Eleventh Finance Commission provided additional funds (20 billion rupees) earmarked for urban bodies in the Tenth Plan as an impetus to the implementation of the 74th Amendment. Nonetheless, these central initiatives have not improved the quality of services in most cities.[10] Despite increased emphasis on urban development, the central resources are still meagre compared with the needs. Central transfers and centrally sponsored urban development schemes amounted to less than 100 billion rupees in the Tenth Plan,[11] which translates to an average of less than $2 per capita. Although some cities benefited more than others from central resources, the overall level of central support is quite inadequate. Urban expenditures may need to be tripled, if not quadrupled, from their current levels on a sustained basis—which means an annual commitment of $100–$200 per capita—to see a discernible difference in the quality of life.

Such a leap in requested financing is not out of line with recent experience. The cities eligible for the Jawaharlal Nehru National Urban Renewal Mission (see box 1) submitted requests for new investments alone of $500 per capita on average over the five-year program. It is simply not conceivable, however, that central and state governments can provide such resources, given other development priorities and their own fiscal constraints. Cities will need to generate much of the needed resources themselves.

Currently, revenue generated by cities in India is a mere 0.75 percent of GDP, in contrast to 4.5 percent in Brazil and 6.0 percent in South Africa.[12] Numerous studies over the past two decades have pointed out the potential of property taxes as a source of revenue for cities.[13] Property tax is estimated to account for 0.2 percent of GDP in India, compared with an average of 0.5 percent for all developing countries and about 2 percent for industrialized countries.[14] The cities will need to tap their own local revenue sources and reduce their dependence on national and state governments, which are themselves strained for resources.

Cities have other reasons as well to reduce their reliance on national and state governments. First, most funds from higher levels flow through state agencies or are earmarked for specific programs, leaving cities little discretion on expenditures. These flows are often underutilized and inefficient. Second, state transfers are generally not timely, stable or predictable, because of fiscal problems at the state level and because transfers may be intercepted to cover arrears in local payments.

Third, reliance on transfers from higher levels reinforces cities' lack of initiative. City functionaries see their job as advocating for more "projects" rather than assuming any real responsibility for managing their affairs. Local politicians also prefer to have funds flow from higher levels, so they are absolved of the responsibility of convincing voters about the need for taxes.

Fourth, the availability of resources weakens the accountability of local officials to citizens. Politicians define success as mobilizing more *sarkari* (government) money rather than demonstrating that they have been good guardians of citizens' money. This issue of governance pervades all levels in India, but it is most serious at the local level, where accountability should be the strongest.

Weak capacity

The ranks of most city governments are filled with large numbers of low-level staff and unqualified or underqualified technical and managerial staff, while senior positions are often filled as itinerant appointments for state government officials. The result is a lack of administrative capacity that most city officials readily acknowledge.

The Ministry of Urban Development has, over the years, tried to upgrade skills through various schemes of staff training. Some states (such as Karnataka) have also set up specific training programs for urban management as a part of their administrative staff training institutes. No amount of training or capacity building will be effective, however, unless the issues of

autonomy and financing are addressed. City officials have little motivation to strengthen their staff capabilities so long as they have inadequate resources at their disposal and a tight control from the state over their functions.

Lack of autonomy

Since urban development is a state subject under the Constitution, the states must define how their cities are governed. States typically control virtually all city functions, often down to the smallest detail. Until the early 1990s when the 74th Amendment was passed, states could dissolve elected municipal councils. This power was frequently used in the 1970s and 1980s, ostensibly for malfeasance but often also for political considerations. States then kept the local bodies under their administrative control for long periods of time.

The 74th Amendment restrained this power by requiring that elections be held within six months of the dissolution of a council. Nevertheless, the states continue to hold many other powers including, for example, powers to review and approve:

- Any resolutions passed by the municipal council, with power to countermand.
- All budgets and expenditures, except for the most insignificant procurement decisions.
- Any proposals to levy local taxes.
- All city master plans and any subsequent modifications, as well as to review and approve individual decisions of land use modifications above a certain level.

Moreover, these review and approval powers rest with low- or mid-level state government bureaucrats in the designated supervising department (the Department of Local Government or equivalent), placing them in essence above the duly elected officials. As one mayor of a major city remarked: "The only power I have is to convene a meeting of the municipal council."

State control over local government is further strengthened by the power of the state to appoint most of the senior local government officials. The municipal

> **The Government of India recognizes the need to reform some critical urban policies and institutions**

commissioner, who is supposedly the manager of the city, is often selected from amongst the ranks of state administrative services. Similarly, many technical staff are seconded from various state departments. These officials are only notionally responsible to the mayor and other elected officials; their real allegiance is to their managers in the state cadre and the state-level politicians who hold sway on their service. The municipal commissioner essentially has the power to ignore decisions by local elected officials by referring such decisions to higher levels in the state, thus ensuring non-implementation or countermand.

In addition, the state sets the salary and service conditions of municipal employees, without any consideration of the local circumstances or the financial health of the city. The cities are also bound by the periodic salary adjustments awarded by national pay commissions, which wreak havoc on local government finances or any possibility of performance management.

Although the 74th Amendment has created some political stability and at least two municipal elections have been held since then in most states, the role and functions of the city administration remain largely subservient to state bureaucrats. It is difficult to see much prospect for improvement in urban management unless cities assume much more autonomy over local resource mobilization and service delivery.

Corruption

Concern for corruption is one of the reasons often cited by state officials and politicians for their reluctance to grant more autonomy to city governments. Although the experience of maladministration in many cities in the 1970s and 1980s gives some credence to this concern, it may also be an excuse for inaction.

While corruption no doubt exists in city administrations, it is not clear why corruption is lessened at all by shifting control to state officials and politicians. Many of the controls demanded by state officials and politicians are precisely so that they can enjoy the fruits of corruption. Controls on land-use planning are one example.

State officials are reluctant to cede to local officials lucrative opportunities to benefit personally or to confer benefits on others as a result of increases in land values or changes in land use.

The answer lies in instituting appropriate checks and balances at the local level, rather than simply adding more layers of review far removed from the citizens. The basic precepts of good governance apply: the closer the government to the citizens, the higher the chances that citizens will demand accountability.

Initiatives under way

Most states have begun to decentralize some functions to cities, as called for in the 74th Amendment, which talks only about the assignment of functions and not about autonomy in the broad sense used earlier. The degree of autonomy granted in expenditure management varies widely, with states continuing to exercise a fair degree of control. With the possible exception of Gujarat (see annex 2), no state has gone anywhere close to genuine managerial autonomy.

The government of India recognizes the need to reform some critical urban policies and institutions, as envisaged under the 74th Amendment, to make India's cities more livable. Even so, the central government cannot require the necessary reforms under the current constitutional division of powers. It can only encourage action through incentives (or disincentives).

In November 2005, the government of India launched a major initiative, the Jawahar Lal Nehru Urban Renewal Mission (JNURM), intended to improve the infrastructure in some 63 cities, while also requiring certain reforms in the cities' policies and governance as a condition for receiving funds. The reform agenda encourages more delegation of key responsibilities to urban local governments, greater resource mobilization, greater poverty focus, and various measures to improve governance (box 1). The program is still in an early stage of implementation, so no independent evaluation is available.[15] Nevertheless, some states (mostly western and

> **To enable cities to deliver better services and support economic growth, they should function as true corporate entities responsible for financing and managing the services under their jurisdiction**

Box 1 | **Jawaharlal Nehru National Urban Renewal Mission**

For urban local governments and parastatal agencies, this mandatory reform program requires:

- Adoption of a modern accrual-based double-entry system of accounting.
- Introduction of a system of e-governance that uses modern information technology, such as geographic or management information systems.
- Reform of property tax to increase buoyancy and transparency.
- Levy of reasonable user charges by urban local governments and parastatals.
- Earmarking, within local bodies, of budgets for basic services to the poor (including security of tenure at affordable prices, improved housing, water supply, and sanitation).

For states, the program requires:

- Implementation of decentralization measures as envisaged in the 74th Constitutional Amendment Act.
- Repeal of the Urban Land Ceiling and Regulation Act, except for schemes relating to water supply and sanitation.
- Reform of rent control laws to balance the interests of landlords and tenants, except for schemes relating to water supply and sanitation.
- Rationalization of the stamp duty to bring it down to no more than 5 percent.
- Enactment of a public disclosure law to ensure release of information periodically to stakeholders.
- Enactment of a community participation law in institutionalizing citizen's participation.
- Assignment of city planning functions to elected urban local governments or associating them with such functions.

southern ones) have successfully tapped the program to initiate some important infrastructure investments.

The extent of the reforms is still unclear. The most recent progress report of JNURM, as well as discussions with local government officials, indicate that effective decentralization is still lacking in most states. Even when on paper a function has been transferred to the city, the state still seems to retain significant powers of oversight that can dilute the intention of decentralization. The measures fall short of granting cities effective autonomy. Many important policy measures are simply promises of actions at future dates, rather than actions already completed. Experience with the ability of the government to enforce such conditions is not very encouraging. Furthermore, by passing funds as projects instead of budgetary grants for agreed expenditure priorities reflected in a medium-term plan for the city, the program may ultimately suffer from the well known implementation problems of other centrally sponsored schemes. Thus, although the JNURM is an important

initiative in the right direction, it will need to be monitored closely and kept on course, if it is extended in the next plan (as it should be).

Empowering cities to provide better service

If the cities are to provide better basic municipal services to their growing populations, three linked steps are needed: cities must be given full autonomy, cities must adopt modern management practices, and cities must take strong measures to improve governance.

Full autonomy

To enable cities to deliver better services and support economic growth, they should function as true corporate entities responsible for financing and managing the services under their jurisdiction. This aspiration resonates in the 74th Amendment and the recommendations of the Second Administrative Reform Commission.[16] Bold action is needed now to make the aspiration a reality.

> **India needs to view cities as the third sphere of government rather than as a third tier, which implies a hierarchy of control**

A start can be made with the 100 largest municipal corporations. These would cover all cities with populations over 500,000, today accounting for some 160 million people. Most of these cities, if not all, will have million-plus populations by 2039 (see annex 1). By focusing on these large cities first, policymakers would recognize that these cities have the potential to mobilize significant resources to meet their own needs and are more likely to have the active civil society organizations that are crucial to ensuring good governance. It would be a first step towards a phased introduction of autonomy for all cities.

The autonomy for cities should be defined under state law to encompass:

- *Functional autonomy* for all activities normally carried out within the city jurisdiction— including town planning, land use regulation, infrastructure and service provision, basic education, and public health. The state should not directly manage or oversee any of these functions. Instead, it should set policy in education, finance, basic education and public health through revenue sharing, and enforce environmental and labour regulations by industry.

- *Financial autonomy* to mobilize taxes and user fees consistent with the needs of the city— and to plan and implement budgets. The law could specify types of taxes that the cities are empowered to levy but not the levels. Property taxes, a grossly underused source in most Indian cities, should become the most significant source of revenues. The state governments have limited and well defined powers—for example, to prohibit taxes, such as Octroi, that hinder free movement of goods within the state.

- *Administrative autonomy* to permit cities to have their own system of staff selection. Professionalism in various aspects of city management should be promoted through competitive appointments, particularly for managerial positions. A city manager, accountable to the city council, should be the CEO of the city, as in many developed countries. Heads of other departments should report to the CEO. The state should have no role in any staff and managerial appointments.

- *All procurement* by relevant departments in the municipal corporation within a prescribed procurement law. That law would set out procedures for efficient and transparent procurement, without reference to the state government.

- *Land use planning entirely within the control of the city.* There is also a need to overhaul the land use planning process, which lacks any economic rationale and is subject to frequent litigation and court intervention. Current state laws mandate each city to prepare a town plan that is approved by the relevant department in the state. Any changes in these plans and almost all exemptions are also subject to approval by the state. The process has often been out of touch with realities on the ground, excessively rigid, subject to abuse and corruption, and paralyzed by extensive litigation. A modern concept of land use envisages the plan to be a living document that must be revised and updated with changing conditions. An open and transparent process encouraging debate among competing interests is much more appropriate than adherence to a rigidly prescribed plan.

Once state laws have laid out the power and responsibilities of the cities along these lines, enforcement against abuse of power or malfeasance should be through the normal judicial processes, not through the control of state functionaries. India needs to view cities as the third sphere of government rather than as a third tier, which implies a hierarchy of control.

Modern management practices

Amongst India's three tiers of government, cities have the longest distance to travel in delivering services that

> **Autonomy for cities needs to be accompanied by measures that ensure good governance**

affect people's lives most directly. That transformation would require the following:

- *A sharp focus on essential functions—without being burdened with peripheral activities that are wasteful.* There are far too many examples of half completed or dilapidated projects that city officials had envisaged as profit-making commercial ventures.

- *A commercial orientation in service delivery.* Water and sewage are invariably mismanaged by unwieldy municipal bureaucracies without any financial discipline. They must be run by corporate bodies responsible to the city government and operating under a transparent regulatory structure for tariffs and service expectations.

- *Contracting out under clear service expectations, as the norm, in as many activities as possible—including road maintenance, solid waste collection and disposal, and billing and collecting taxes and fees.* These services could then be monitored more efficiently by a small cadre of qualified city government staff.

- *Qualified staff, selected transparently and competitively at all levels, but most specifically for managerial positions.* City managers in the developed countries are in great demand and often move from smaller to larger cities based on their highly valued managerial experience.

These principles of modern management should be captured in letter and spirit in the governing law for the cities.

Good governance

Autonomy for cities needs to be accompanied by measures that ensure good governance. Without such measures, the effectiveness of decentralization will be severely limited, adding to public skepticism about government. Indeed, consistent with the experience of most developed countries, local government, as the government closest to citizens, should enjoy the highest level of confidence.

The main elements of good city governance include:

- *A municipal law that sets out the functions and responsibilities of the city government, the way in which it should perform the functions and its accountability to the citizens.* Full transparency and disclosure should be enshrined in the law.

- *Stronger accountability for results—of the city managers to elected officials, and of the elected officials to citizens.*

- *Elected municipal councils as the most important part of accountability to citizens.* Party-based elections and the large number of councillors needed for adequate representation make it difficult to assign clear accountability. Implementation of the recommendation of the Second Administrative Reform Commission for a directly elected mayor, with requisite powers, is necessary to pinpoint accountability more sharply. The council should have no executive implementation authority. Its functions should be defined under the law as setting policies and priorities and conducting oversight.

- *Transparent selection process for senior managers of the city, including the city manager, proposed by the mayor and approved by the council.* The mayor should also have the power to remove managers for cause, with approval by a majority of the council.

- *Appointment of an inspector-general with the power to investigate citizen complaints.* The inspector-general need not have any enforcement power. Any reports should be in the public domain and provide a basis for elected officials to initiate action against city officials and for the electorate to judge the performance of individual councillors.

- *Public information and disclosure of all aspects of the functioning of the municipal government—particularly in the areas of*

> **The funding under JNURM should be increased even further and made available to the 100 largest municipal corporations if the states pass laws that grant full autonomy to cities, in letter and spirit, and implement measures for good governance**

budget, expenditures, procurement, personnel, land use planning and modifications, building permits, property valuation and taxes, and all deliberations of the council. The Right to Information Act already requires the appointment of public information officers to respond to citizen requests for information. But the cities should be required to do more proactive disclosure. Jannagraha, a nongovernmental organization in Bengaluru, has prepared a useful model code for disclosure.

- *Monitoring of the performance of the city government by citizen organizations that act as watchdogs against malfeasance.* These organizations can pursue the requirement for disclosure, using the Right to Information Act, if needed. They can also issue citizen report cards on the effectiveness of various government functions (as has been done in Bengaluru with positive results). And they can act as advocates for the citizens, particularly the poor and disadvantaged. Such organizations are emerging in many cities, particularly in the large metropolitan cities. Indian business houses should support their efforts.

Implementing the new urban management paradigm

Only the state governments have the power under India's Constitution to implement the recommendations we have presented here. Vested interests at the state level are likely to be serious obstacles to implementation, regardless of the support for reform at the national or local levels.

Autonomy for city governments would diminish and redirect the state government's power. State bureaucrats are likely to resist changes to their turf, and state politicians are likely to want to maintain their control over municipal resources and their opportunities for patronage and aggrandizement, particularly in municipal personnel appointments, transfers, and land use regulation.

In the shifting allegiance and coalition politics of India, even sympathetic state chief ministers are likely to be reluctant to take stands that make the members of the legislative assemblies unhappy. Here unfortunately lies the crux of the problem. Most knowledgeable people in India consider this fundamental shift in city government as a mission impossible.

The only prospect for reform along the lines proposed is if an enlightened state chief minister decides to place personal and party interests behind the interest of the people. Whether this will happen is difficult to say, but some states show signs of such a change in the political climate.

Gujarat is one state that has made significant strides (see annex 2). But it also raises a question about the sustainability of reforms. Gujarat's success has relied on the strong personality and leadership of its chief minister, and the state government has not yet created leaders at the municipal level who might push for greater decentralization in the future.

The government of India can encourage these reforms from the centre. Some have suggested a new Constitutional amendment that strengthens the 74th Amendment (and the 73rd) by making them mandatory instead of just advisory. While being attractive for its expediency, such an amendment is not regarded as a wise choice by the balance of thoughtful observers in India, and in any event a strengthening amendment is perhaps beyond the capacity of the central government to push through and implement. Indeed, the debate at the time of the 73rd and 74th Amendments was precisely along these lines, with the final versions being much diluted from the initial intent.

So the central government's role must be one of persuasion, either moral or party-based, or through incentives. The Jawaharlal Nehru National Urban Renewal Mission provides a useful model to build on. The funding under JNURM should be increased even further and made available to the 100 largest municipal corporations if the states pass laws that grant full autonomy to cities, in letter and spirit, and implement measures for good governance.

These measures should be required as prior actions and not be promises of action before funding is released. The funding should be tied to the augmentation of self-generated revenues and be committed for a long period (say, 10 years) for budget support, not specific projects. Better governance and greater resource mobilization provide much better assurance of wise investment (and maintenance) decisions.

Such a system of requirements and conditions may well mean that not all 100 cities are able to participate in and benefit fully from the new urban paradigm. But a system that rewards the willing is much more likely to be effective than one that tries to pull along unwilling reformers in the states.

Table 2	**Distribution of Indian cities, by population size and share of the total urban population, 1970–2039**						
Size class	**1970**	**1980**	**1990**	**2000**	**2005**	**2025**	**2039**
More than 10 million							
Number of cities	—	—	2	3	3	4	5
Population (thousands)	—	—	23,197	41,585	47,537	79,572	95,000
Share of urban population (%)	—	—	11	14	15	15	
5–10 million							
Number of cities	2	3	2	3	4	5	6
Population (thousands)	12,737	23,247	13,544	17,365	24,621	39,047	50,000
Share of urban population (%)	12	15	6	6	8	7	
1–5 million							
Number of cities	7	7	19	26	33	56	70
Population (thousands)	14,000	16,513	32,729	43,858	55,029	105,587	135,000
Share of urban population (%)	13	10	15	15	17	20	
500,000–1 million							
Number of cities	10	29	30	39	46	70	85
Population (thousands)	6,523	19,728	20,741	28,336	31,923	49,858	60,000
Share of urban population (%)	6	12	9	10	10	9	
Less than 500,000							
Population (thousands)	75,286	99,558	129,546	158,294	166,453	263,991	225,000
Share of urban population (%)	69	63	59	55	51	49	

Note: Projections for 2039 are extrapolated from UN projections to 2025.

Source: United Nations 2008.

Population data for Indian cities

Table 3 | Population of Indian cities with more than 750,000 people in 2005, 1970–2039

City	1970	1980	1990	2000	2005	2025	2039
Agra	624	739	933	1,293	1,511	2,118	2,364
Ahmadabad	1,695	2,484	3,255	4,427	5,122	6,989	7,735
Aligarh	247	316	468	653	763	1,083	1,215
Allahabad	506	640	830	1,035	1,152	1,592	1,781
Amritsar	453	604	726	990	1,152	1,619	1,811
Asansol	235	356	727	1,065	1,258	1,776	1,985
Aurangabad	159	303	568	868	1,049	1,499	1,678
Bengaluru	1,615	2,812	4,036	5,567	6,465	8,795	9,719
Bareilly	322	440	604	722	787	1,087	1,219
Bhiwandi	77	112	362	603	745	1,081	1,212
Bhopal	370	655	1,046	1,426	1,644	2,288	2,553
Bhubaneswar	98	209	395	637	790	1,147	1,286
Chandigarh	219	406	564	791	928	1,314	1,472
Chennai (Madras)	3,057	4,203	5,338	6,353	6,918	9,170	10,129
Coimbatore	710	907	1,088	1,420	1,619	2,243	2,503
Delhi	3,531	5,558	8,206	12,441	15,053	20,484	22,498
Dhanbad	410	658	805	1,046	1,189	1,656	1,852
Durg-Bhilainagar	234	468	670	905	1,044	1,465	1,640
Faridabad	81	302	593	1,018	1,298	1,887	2,109
Ghaziabad	122	272	492	928	1,237	1,830	2,046
Guwahati (Gauhati)	195	329	564	797	932	1,318	1,477
Gwalior	397	544	706	855	940	1,298	1,455
Hubli-Dharwad	367	516	639	776	855	1,184	1,327
Hyderabad	1,748	2,487	4,193	5,445	6,117	8,224	9,092
Indore	546	808	1,088	1,597	1,914	2,696	3,005
Jabalpur	520	740	879	1,100	1,231	1,703	1,904
Jaipur	616	984	1,478	2,259	2,748	3,867	4,298
Jalandhar	290	400	502	694	811	1,150	1,290
Jammu	159	219	356	588	739	1,079	1,211
Jamshedpur	445	653	817	1,081	1,239	1,729	1,933
Jodhpur	310	491	654	842	951	1,327	1,486
Kanpur	1,250	1,612	2,001	2,641	3,019	4,141	4,601
Kochi (Cochin)	424	666	1,103	1,340	1,463	1,999	2,232
Kolkata (Calcutta)	6,926	9,030	10,890	13,058	14,282	18,707	20,560
Kota	204	346	523	692	789	1,108	1,243
Kozhikode (Calicut)	324	528	781	875	924	1,257	1,409

Table 3 **Population of Indian cities with more than 750,000 people in 2005, 1970–2039 (continued)**

City	1970	1980	1990	2000	2005	2025	2039
Lucknow	801	993	1,614	2,221	2,567	3,546	3,944
Ludhiana	387	590	1,006	1,368	1,572	2,186	2,440
Madurai	692	893	1,073	1,187	1,255	1,697	1,897
Meerut	361	523	824	1,143	1,328	1,862	2,080
Moradabad	266	340	436	626	743	1,062	1,192
Mumbai (Bombay)	5,811	8,658	12,308	16,086	18,202	24,051	26,385
Mysore	347	470	640	776	853	1,179	1,322
Nagpur	910	1,273	1,637	2,089	2,350	3,219	3,583
Nashik	267	416	700	1,117	1,381	1,981	2,213
Patna	480	881	1,087	1,658	2,029	2,879	3,207
Pune (Poona)	1,105	1,642	2,430	3,655	4,411	6,135	6,797
Raipur	200	327	453	680	824	1,184	1,327
Rajkot	291	434	638	974	1,186	1,696	1,896
Ranchi	244	480	607	844	990	1,400	1,567
Salem	404	511	574	736	834	1,168	1,309
Solapur	393	506	613	853	1,002	1,417	1,587
Srinagar	412	592	730	954	1,087	1,518	1,699
Surat	477	877	1,468	2,699	3,558	5,142	5,703
Thiruvananthapuram	394	512	801	885	927	1,256	1,408
Tiruchirappalli	454	599	705	837	916	1,262	1,414
Vadodara	453	722	1,096	1,465	1,675	2,324	2,592
Varanasi (Benares)	597	777	1,013	1,199	1,303	1,781	1,991
Vijayawada	335	527	821	999	1,094	1,505	1,684
Visakhapatnam	349	583	1,018	1,309	1,465	2,020	2,256
Total (60 cities)	**45,916**	**66,923**	**93,172**	**125,188**	**144,230**	**197,380**	**218,823**

Note: Projections for 2039 are extrapolated from UN projections to 2025.

Source: United Nations 2008.

Annex 2
The Gujarat approach to urban management

Gujarat is one of the few states to have granted significant autonomy to its seven municipal corporations, thus complying with both the letter and spirit of the 74th Amendment. These features are incorporated into Gujarat's law governing the municipal corporations:

- There are elected councillors with a term of five years. The councillors elect the mayor from amongst themselves for a term of 2.5 years.
- The state appoints the municipal commissioner as the chief executive. All other staff of the corporation are appointed by the commissioner, with the senior staff being selected by the councillors from amongst the short list submitted by the municipal commissioner. Most of the second layer of managers are appointed from amongst the ranks of state government officers.
- The 18 functions suggested in the 74th Amendment (including primary education and land use within the city boundaries) have all been fully transferred to the municipal corporations.
- The municipal corporations enjoy full autonomy for planning and implementation of their budgets without any reference to the state.
- The municipal corporations have introduced the concept of property taxes based on floor area, modified by factors related to location, type of construction, and quality and age of the building. The state specifies a broad range of tax rates (currently 20–80 rupees per square meter), within which the corporations can set their rate depending on their needs. The modification factors are determined by the corporation alone. The property tax records are publicly available on the municipal corporation website.
- The corporations can borrow within prescribed limits and are rated by recognized rating agencies.
- All municipal corporations have citizen service centres that provide one-stop service within prescribed standards for most public services, including the issuance of building permits.

Nonetheless, Gujarat's approach to municipal management has a few deficiencies:

- The mayors are not directly elected, and their terms are limited, which weakens the mayor and diffuses electoral accountability at the local level. Most citizens still view municipal management as a state responsibility.
- While the appointment of the commissioner from the state cadre is understandable, it is difficult to justify drawing the second rank officers from amongst the ranks of state officials. Over time, it would be useful to consider all municipal employees, irrespective of the level, being employed directly by the municipal corporation.
- Some municipal functions, such as water supply and garbage collection, are still carried out by departments within the municipal corporation. There is room for corporatization and commercialization of such services.

INDIA
2039

Part II

Chapter

7

Environmental
quality for
India's
citizens

Environmental quality for India's citizens: Meeting needs and expectations of a more affluent society

Harinder S. Kohli

One of the most visible improvements in the quality of life, as India moves from a poor society to an affluent society, must be in the quality of the environment in which its citizens live. Instead of the poor quality of air, water and sanitation and the general squalor amidst which the vast majority of Indians live today, citizens of an affluent India would expect and deserve high quality utility services (water and sanitation), clean air and clean (and safe) streets along the lines of Madrid, Singapore and Seoul today.

This transformation in the quality of life will not occur overnight. Its seeds must be planted now and nurtured carefully over the years. The process must start with a change in the basic focus and mindset of public officials and citizens alike.

Urgent need for a change in focus and mindset

In most countries the fundamental goal of national environmental policy and priorities is to improve the quality of life of its citizens. While global considerations are important and are taken into account to the extent feasible, the fundamental focus is on what is good for the citizens over the longer term and on how best to achieve this.

In India, the position appears to be the reverse. Instead of thinking of the environment from the perspective of its citizens, the current official Indian government thinking and statements on environment appear to be dominated by geopolitical considerations. As a result, the national debate seems to be dominated by the ongoing global negotiations related to climate change. Indeed, to a neutral observer it seems that the resolution of the issues of primary concern to Indian citizens is taking a backseat to the debate on how best to counter global efforts to have the major emerging economies fight climate change.

It ignores the fact that every sixth person on earth is an Indian and therefore any harm to the world as a whole would also harm India and make India a primary victim of any fallout from climate change over the longer term. Even more importantly, the time and energy devoted by the top policy makers to India's negotiating position in the international fora is crowding out the urgently needed focus on actions to improve the well being and health of over a billion Indians living today.

The position articulated on behalf of India at various international fora appears to be built around the following five propositions:

- On a per capita basis, emissions from India that harm world climate–CO_2 and the rest–are much, much less than those from the developed countries;
- India is affecting perceptible, indeed substantial improvements–in area covered by forests (that is, in sequestering carbon), and in energy efficiency (for instance, in energy-intensive industries like cement and steel);
- Several of the measures and protocols that are being suggested will curb India's growth rate, and, thereby, perpetuate India's poverty;
- Poverty is the greatest pollution, it is also the greatest polluter, and hence, India shall continue to strive to eliminate poverty and maximize growth; and
- As the developed countries are the principal doers of harm, they must do their bit first before compelling countries like India and China into curbing their growth.

India's self interest

Even though most of the above arguments are at least partly valid, the above position, if sustained, is not in

The author is grateful for valuable analysis and inputs provided by Arun Shourie (environment) and Richard Ackermann (water). The latter's paper "Creating Jobs in India: The Critical Role of Agriculture in Driving Labour-Intensive Manufacturing" is being issued separately and is also available on the website of the Centennial Group. However, the contents and conclusions of this chapter are solely the responsibility of the author.

India's own self interest; as it will inflict grave harm on India in the coming 30 years both in exacerbating problems—problems that it will be extremely expensive and difficult to remedy later—and in foreclosing the enormous opportunities that remedial measures taken now hold for India.

More fundamentally, the current policy is driven mainly by India's geopolitical negotiating stance rather than by a hard-headed and dispassionate analysis of what is good for the Indian citizens and what is in India's long term self interest.

This basic mindset must change to reflect the following considerations:

- The fact that some other countries have wrong policies and that others are exacerbating the problems is of little consolation to India's citizens. The deterioration in India's environment during the last 50 years is because of developments within India that inflict grave harm on Indians. Rivers like the Yamuna have become rivulets and, often, toxic drains. See box 1 on India's self-made looming problem on water management.

- The alarming increase in arsenic in North Bengal, the ailments that befall Indians because of polluted ponds or smoke within hutments of the poor as they cook over cow dung in closed areas, the woeful condition of sanitation, or the poor air quality in the cities—have nothing to do with what the developed countries are doing, and are not going to abate by anything that a global treaty on climate change may undertake to do.

- Neither India's formal policies on environment (or energy) nor the pattern of development that underlies it is sustainable:
  - o At even the optimistic forecasts for nuclear and hydro power projects, coal-fired power plants are expected to generate 60 percent of India's electricity in 2030;
  - o Only one in a 100 Indians owns a car today compared to 70 in the OECD countries.

What would happen to the air quality, traffic and availability of space in urban areas were India's over one billion middle-income citizens in 2039 to meet their transportation needs mainly through the private automobile? Should India not place much more emphasis on rail (rather than road) for long distance travel and on mass transit systems for intra-city transport?
  - o Underground fires in India's coal belt–in particular, in the Dhanbad-Jharia landmass, constitute the highest incidence of such fires in the world. Apart from the immediate danger such fires present to human life, they have severe long term consequences for the health of miners and their families and for all who live in the area.

- Were India and China to aim at attaining by 2039 the levels and pattern of consumption typical of the OECD countries today, what would be the impact on the world's resources? Would India be able to hold its own in the race that would ensue for resources?
  - o Look at the pressures that became evident in the energy and other commodity markets in 2007–08 when China and India were growing at a rapid pace in a global environment under which the world as a whole also enjoyed healthy growth. Can India continue on a growth strategy that depends on import of increasingly more expensive commodities?
  - o Would India be able to hold its own against China and other large economies to secure oil and other essential commodities?

- As Lester Brown has pointed out, the ecological footprint of the developed world is 32 times that of other countries. Were China and India to make the same draft on resources, it would be as if the population of the world had tripled;

> **Steps to preserve and restore the environment present an economic opportunity for India**

were all countries to do so, it will be as if the population of the world had increased to 72 billion. While the amounts of emissions and pollutants that India releases per capita are lower than those of the developed countries (and even China today), the totals in absolute terms are large. But, were China and India to persist in acquiring consumption levels and adopting production processes of the developed world today, they will become fatally large for the world as a whole as well as for their own citizens because of the size of their population.

- India must do its bit–both for itself, and also for the world. It is far more expensive to remedy the environment after damaging it than it is to take preventive action. The fate of the Aral Sea is a reminder that a society must change course early–the longer its gestation period, the earlier must the remedy be instituted.

- Steps to preserve and restore the environment present an economic opportunity for India. The trillion dollar market in carbon trade under the Clean Development Mechanism affords an immediate opportunity. Each solution that India develops for its own problems will be something that it can market to other countries that face the same problems: alternate fuels; microbes that break up pollutants; solar and wind energy; other clean energy technology; breakthroughs in energy efficiency technologies; an efficient and hygienic composting toilet; organic and bio-fertilizers, insecticides and pesticides; and technologies to recycle waste and water, etc.

- Successes in improving efficiency of resource use and reducing emissions have been registered everywhere–within India as much as in Europe and elsewhere. These have not curtailed growth; quite to the contrary, they have saved the countries the resources they would have had to expend to deal with the consequences of "growth".

- India aspires to being a responsible global citizen. Its aim should be to be, and to be seen as an example in this context. It will not be able to urge others to take steps that it is failing to take itself.

- Finally, what will happen if each country keeps putting off remedial action till the others begin to take it? To take just one instance, global warming will affect India in more ways than one. Forty six percent of the population of Bangladesh lives within 50 miles of the coast. If, following India's lead and that of China, each country keeps putting off remedial steps till the others have taken them, and global warming proceeds apace, how will India cope with the potential influx of scores of millions of refugees from the costal areas of Bangladesh?

Within India itself, there are many successful examples that can and should be emulated more broadly, starting now:

- The swiftness with which land has regenerated itself the moment elementary steps were taken to cordon it;

- The substantial increases that have ensued in the incomes and assets of the community once local water-bodies have been restored;

- Buildings–large office and research complexes—have been constructed, for instance, at the IIT, Kanpur, that consume 40 percent less power than conventional buildings of that size; and

- Considerable amelioration in pollutants discharged has been achieved even in traditionally notorious polluters like the leather and paper and pulp industries. Similarly, individual corporate firms have shown how they can benefit society as well as improve their bottom-lines simultaneously: for almost five years now, ITC has been storing and sequestering twice the amount of CO_2 than it emits; over the last seven years now, it has created rainwater harvesting

The management of surface and
groundwater presents an enormous challenge
that requires radical new thinking

Box 1 | **Water Management**

The management of surface and groundwater presents an enormous challenge that requires radical new thinking. Over 10% of India's GDP is linked to groundwater; with diminishing reliance on the traditional canal irrigation system which has been both unsuited for the rapidly-growing farming population (much of which is not located in command areas) and poorly managed. Over a decade of substantial investments in public irrigation systems has not resulted in any increase of net irrigated area! A large number of projects remain unfinished and/or poorly maintained.

By the mid-1980s already, India had became the largest groundwater user in the world–extracting 2½ times the amount extracted in the United States; and almost 3 times the amount in China. Small pump irrigation spread everywhere in India, including in canal commands, and it continues to grow today. Groundwater now accounts for well over 60% of net irrigated area.

In 20 years, up to 40% of India's aquifers could be exhausted in a business-as-usual scenario. Amarasinghe et al. (2007) calculate that while India's groundwater availability would be sufficient, on average, to meet most of the future food demand (not accounting for climate change), under the business-as-usual scenario, the country will suffer severe water crises at the regional level by 2050, with depleted aquifers and significantly reduced river flows in a large number of specific areas. In several river basins, essentially all available water would be consumed, leading to growing inter-state conflicts where these river basins cross state boundaries.

A worst-case groundwater scenario developed by the Planning Commission (2007) suggests that 60% of blocks will be overexploited by 2025.

To ensure the availability of uncontaminated drinking water, experts have urged starting with urban use, where it is easier to register and license tube wells and control industrial pollution, especially if water supply and wastewater management systems become more reliable (80% of domestic water depends on groundwater). Hard-rock areas and arid alluvial plain deserve special emphasis since that is where aquifers tend to be

unsustainably mined, For example, 82% of Punjab's tube-wells are running dry.

The focus of policy should therefore not be to try to hold on to the old paradigm of controlled water releases through public irrigation systems, managed by large but inept bureaucracies or unsustainable water users associations (farmers have anyway already moved beyond this in many areas), but to manage groundwater recharge so that groundwater abstraction throughout India again becomes sustainable.

Power Subsidies and Water Mining

More than 70% of the estimated Rs 250 billion farm power subsidies go to hard rock areas. The International Water Management Institute estimates that raising groundwater levels by 1 meter through recharge could save more than Rs 10 billion a year in power subsidy.

To achieve this, India needs to create incentives to wean affected states like Punjab away from heavy

Figure | **Growth of groundwater and surface water irrigation**

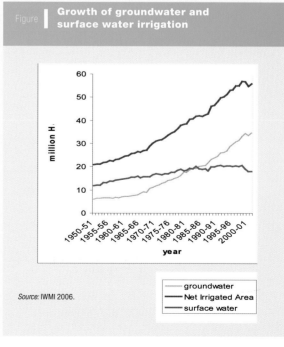

Source: IWMI 2006.

groundwater
Net Irrigated Area
surface water

> State Electricity Regulatory Commissions should increase pressure on State governments to charge farmers for electricity to create an incentive to get aquifers replenished and limit pumping depths

Water Management (contd.)

emphasis on water-intensive crops; the extensive canal water available in that state could be diverted first to manage aquifer recharge; and the State Electricity Regulatory Commissions should increase pressure on State governments to charge farmers for electricity to create an incentive to get aquifers replenished and limit pumping depths.

Arguably the most far-sighted experiment has been implemented with Gujarat's Jyotirgram Yojana scheme launched in 2003–06 at a cost of USD 260 million–one-third of the Gujarat Electricity Board's annual loss in 2001–02. The scheme goes "with the grain" of what farmers need but applies some simple yet effective ideas to slowly alleviate the fiscal burden of unsustainable subsidies: a "managed subsidy versus default subsidy" (Shah 2007). The scheme basically involves separating feeders/power lines to tube-wells from those to domestic and non-farm users. As implemented in Gujarat, tube-wells get eight hours of full-voltage electricity a day on a strict, pre-announced schedule and at a flat tariff, while non-farm connections receive 24/7 assured electricity. At the same time, new connections and pump sizes are being tightly controlled.

As a result of these changes, power supply to agriculture fell from 16 billion units in 2001 to 10 billion units in 2006, groundwater draft fell by 20–30%, and Gujarat government's electricity subsidies have come down from USD786 million in 2001–02 to USD388 million in 2006–07 (Shah and Verma 2008). The most satisfied group of stakeholders in this scheme are rural housewives, students, teachers, patients, doctors, and all non-farm trades, shops and cottage industries that get 24 hour uninterrupted electricity supply.

Figure | **Fraction of groundwater depleted in 2000, 2025 and 2050 business-as-usual scenario**

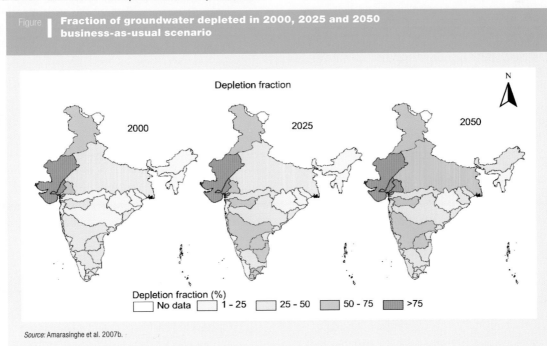

Source: Amarasinghe et al. 2007b.

> **The first and foremost imperative is much more rigorous and credible enforcement of the environmental laws and standards already on the books**

capacity that is thrice the amount of water it consumes; and by now it recycles all its waste. Such solutions can and must be widely publicized and massively scaled up.

Water is another international issue needing immediate attention that transcends environment and economics and affects the lives and livelihoods of India's 700 million people living in the rural areas. Box 1 discusses the dire plight of India's increasingly scarce and depleting water resources and the urgent measures needed to meet the needs of the country's agriculture, industry and households on a more sustainable and economic basis.

Things to be done

For all these reasons, and for sheer survival, India must take several steps to preserve and improve its environment—from the kitchen in the hut to its once-mighty rivers:

- The first and foremost imperative is much more rigorous and credible enforcement of the environmental laws and standards already on the books. On environment, as on so many other subjects, India has a plethora of laws and regulations. The basic problem is that they are not being enforced. As a start, as a matter of top priority, political and administrative leaders at the highest level in Delhi must demand and insist that all government organs implement all laws and regulations currently on the books without any exception.

- In addition to demonstrating its new resolve to make government organs more results-oriented and accountable, the central Cabinet must require all levels of government—at the center, state and local levels—to make every effort to deliver on the agreed programs and plans embedded in the official 11th Plan. As proposed in chapter 4 of part I, the government must monitor progress in these areas, report the results to the top national leadership and point out accountability for any shortfalls in

agreed programs. This should not only lead to a clear improvement in the quality of life of Indian citizens but also restore the government's credibility in their eyes.

- As part of efforts to dramatically improve the livability of India's 100 largest cities, as recommended in chapter 6, India should launch a crash program to radically improve the quality of air, supply of clean water, sewerage and solid waste collection services to every citizen within the next 5–7 years. Recent environmental measures and development of urban transports in Delhi clearly demonstrate that it is indeed possible to make dramatic improvements in the quality of city life under decisive leadership. Though the prodding to do so should come from within the government rather than from directives by the Supreme Court.

- While the above steps relate to implementation of existing policies, there is also a need for a few policy actions. Perhaps the most important policy actions that need to be taken are on the fiscal side. Ecologists estimate that the world spends $700 billion each year to damage the environment—in terms of harmful subsidies. India contributes its share—in terms of subsidies it gives to chemical fertilizers, petroleum products, coal, power and the like. These subsidies have already begun to impose a fiscal burden that cannot be sustained for long. They inflict even greater harm as they help conceal consumption and production patterns that injure the health of the people even as they make India more dependent on resources that will soon be exhausted. These subsidies should, therefore, be weeded out.

- India also has the opportunity to pioneer green taxation—to tax commodities and processes by their ecological footprint and the quantum of non-renewable resources used; it will do well not to defer action till it alights upon the ideal

Box 2	Looming threat from climate change

Climate change poses potentially devastating effects on India's agriculture.

While the overall parameters of climate change are increasingly accepted—a 1°C average temperature increase over the next 30 years, sea level rise of less than 10 cm in the same period, and regional monsoon variations and corresponding droughts—the impacts in India are likely to be quite site- and crop-specific. Some crops may respond favorably to the changing conditions, others may not. This emphasizes the need to promote agricultural research and create maximum flexibility in the system to permit adaptations.

The key ingredient for "drought-proofing" is the managed recharge of aquifers. To ensure continued yields of important staple crops (e.g., wheat), it may also be necessary to shift the locations where these crops are grown, in response to temperature changes as well as to water availability. The latter will be a key factor in making long-term investment decisions.

For example, water runoff from the Himalayas is predicted to increase over the next 30 years as glaciers melt, but then decline substantially thereafter. It will be critical to provide incentives to plan for these large-scale shifts in agro-ecological conditions.

In parallel, much more effort needs to go into disaster planning and management. Appropriate planning could yield enormous benefits. For example, relief and damage repairs from a single drought (2003) and flood (2005) in Maharashtra absorbed more of the State's budget (Rs 175 billion) than the entire planned expenditure (Rs 152 billion) on irrigation, agriculture and rural development from 2002–07. For instance:

• Denudation of eastern Tibet and intensified exploitation of mineral and other resources within Tibet will contribute to accelerating the pace at which Himalayan glaciers are already melting. As all the major rivers of north India except the Ganges originate in the Tibetan plateau, such acceleration will adversely affect all parts of the subcontinent.

• India—in particular, eastern India—is already suffering severely from the consequences of illegal migration from Bangladesh: about 20 million Bangladeshis are estimated to have crossed into India. If, to the factors that have been hitherto causing and facilitating this influx, is added the effect of climate change—the rise of the sea level and the consequential submergence of large swaths of Bangladesh, in particular of the densely populated coastal areas—the movement of Bangladeshis into India could assume the proportions of a social disaster.

• Overexploitation of the Indus in its upper reaches has begun to cause extensive salination of the soil in Sindh, just as its reduced flow is beginning to cause ingress of the sea. Slower development in Pakistan as well as uncertainties that bedevil the country have already begun to cause migrants to cross over the Indian border; the 2000 Census revealed that villages had sprung up on the Indian side, in Rajasthan, that did not exist even 10 years earlier.

• If on top of these factors, ecological deterioration continues, India will be faced with an influx from the west to compound the problems that arise today from influx of illegal migrants from Bangladesh.

rates of taxation of different commodities and processes. Levels that will make the commodities and processes expensive enough to make consumers and producers switch to alternatives is what should be mandated.

• In many spheres, technologies that can affect major savings are already at hand. The Integrated Energy Policy prepared by the Planning Commission and recently approved by

the full Cabinet estimates that India can save up to 15 percent of its electricity consumption just by better demand management. In the same way, to continue with the example cited earlier, major savings in energy consumption can be affected by more thoughtful design of buildings. Similarly, forestation still remains the least expensive way for mitigating carbon. It is necessary, therefore, that these better practices be

> *India's per capita income by 2039 could be the same as the average global income. This has a fundamental implication for India's negotiating stance*

pursued—through pricing, through enforcement, and through introducing them (to continue the buildings example) in more thoughtful curricula in schools of architecture.

- But in many areas new technologies have to be developed. With its large technological manpower, there is a great opportunity for India to develop these technologies by setting up national research missions to develop, for example: i) more efficient photovoltaic cell technology; ii) an efficient hydrogen fuel cell; iii) clean coal processes; iv) development of solar and wind energies that are available in virtually endless supply along India's long coastline; and v) fast breeder nuclear reactors as well as the thorium cycle for nuclear power. Government and industry must work together to harness India's technological and engineering talent for affecting breakthroughs in products and processes such as these. The pioneering work that Japan's MITI did in bringing industrial firms, government laboratories, and technological personnel together is the example that India should emulate.

India's stance on Kyoto protocol negotiations

Finally, ending with where this chapter started—India's stance on the Kyoto protocol negotiations. Part I of this book has suggested that India's per capita income by 2039 could be about the same as the average global income. This has a fundamental implication for India's negotiating stance.

Indian policy makers need to recognize that targets set on a per capita basis and on a GDP basis will not be very different for India in 25–30 years when the measures will start to become binding.

As India will anyway enjoy at least a 15 year grace period before being asked to take significant measures, it may be better for it to negotiate a slightly longer lead time, say 20 years, and then accept the use of GDP per capita targets because India will by then be at world average income levels anyway! And, as argued further in the section on energy, India should in return ask for significant financial assistance and preferential access to the latest technologies from the global community in return for its enthusiastic support of efforts to fight and reverse climate change. This point is taken up further in chapter 9 on Energy.

Such a strategy will be good for Indian citizens and the global community alike, and demonstrate India's desire to be a responsible global citizen.

INDIA 2039

Part

III

Moving to a globally competitive economy

INDIA 2039

Part III

Chapter 8

Infrastructure for a competitive edge

> **"** These massive requirements cannot be met without much greater involvement of the private sector than has been the case until recently

Table 2 | **Annual total cost by sector 2009–2039 (in million US$)**

Period	Airports	Rail	Ports	Roads	Power	Sanitation	Water	Phones	Mobiles	Total
2009	678	1,370	763	46,469	34,216	3,549	4,125	4,792	13,469	109,431
2010–14	726	1,592	1,236	54,281	43,018	4,015	4,385	7,598	30,902	147,753
2015–19	1,067	2,365	1,851	62,917	64,972	5,218	4,479	13,644	29,933	186,446
2020–24	1,615	2,724	2,982	71,485	99,351	6,626	4,763	25,864	19,788	235,199
2025–29	2,269	3,667	3,826	98,825	156,289	9,163	5,004	22,190	20,497	321,731
2030–34	3,283	4,412	5,281	132,993	242,137	12,128	5,325	17,933	21,328	444,820
2035–39	4,824	5,115	6,555	181,203	372,558	15,494	5,523	18,402	21,885	631,560

Source: Centennial Group 2009.

Table 3 | **Annual cost by sector 2009–2039 (as % of GDP)**

Period	Airports	Rail	Ports	Roads	Power	Sanitation	Water	Phones	Mobiles	Total
2009	0.06%	0.12%	0.07%	4.23%	3.11%	0.32%	0.38%	0.44%	1.23%	9.96%
2010–14	0.05%	0.11%	0.09%	3.79%	3.00%	0.28%	0.31%	0.53%	2.15%	10.30%
2015–19	0.05%	0.11%	0.08%	2.85%	2.94%	0.24%	0.20%	0.62%	1.36%	8.45%
2020–24	0.05%	0.08%	0.09%	2.11%	2.93%	0.20%	0.14%	0.76%	0.58%	6.93%
2025–29	0.04%	0.07%	0.07%	1.89%	2.99%	0.18%	0.10%	0.42%	0.39%	6.16%
2030–34	0.04%	0.05%	0.07%	1.65%	3.01%	0.15%	0.07%	0.22%	0.27%	5.53%
2035–39	0.04%	0.04%	0.05%	1.47%	3.01%	0.13%	0.04%	0.15%	0.18%	5.11%

Source: Centennial Group 2009.

Crucial importance of public-private partnerships

These massive requirements cannot be met without much greater involvement of the private sector than has been the case until recently. There are two main reasons for this. First, it is clear that the government budget does not have the capacity to finance on its own anywhere close to the level of investments required, or even at the levels assumed in the Plan. Second, the lack of management and technical skills in the public sector are an equally important, and perhaps the binding constraint. The capacity of the multitude of public sector bodies responsible for infrastructure (ministries, regulatory agencies, state owned enterprises) is simply not adequate for either carrying out the very large capacity increases necessary or for transforming the efficiency and quality of services.

India's Eleventh Five Year Plan mentioned earlier has assumed that the share of private financing would rise to about 30% of total investment during the next Plan period. This level of private investments would translate into a total of almost $400 billion during the next 10 years (based on our estimates of India's needs).

This will be a massive increase indeed over the current levels and can only be achieved through much more extensive public-private partnerships in all facets of

> **Actual achievement of these ambitious targets would make the country a leader amongst developing countries in public-private partnerships**

infrastructure development. Actual achievement of these ambitious targets would make the country a leader amongst developing countries in public-private partnerships in building and operating infrastructure.

Impact of past policy reforms

India started significant reforms in infrastructure policy some 15 years ago, as part of the overall economic reforms initiated in 1991. Within the infrastructure field, initial reforms focused on telecommunications and the power sector. These reforms included the break up of public sector monopolies, setting up of more transparent regulatory regimes and opening up to private sector entry. Over time, reforms were gradually extended to other sectors such as civil aviation, highways and ports.

Overall results from these reforms have been mixed. In some sectors such as civil aviation (passenger airlines, but not yet airports) the reforms have unleashed very significant changes for the better: long standing capacity bottlenecks have been overcome, consumers now have a choice between multiple service providers, service standards are much better and prices are lower. But in other important sectors such as power, water supply, sanitation and rural infrastructure, the results have fallen well short of what is needed and was expected.

The outcomes in various sectors are strongly co-related with their record in attracting private sector participation. In mobile telecoms and passenger airlines, private companies have become the dominant service providers and financiers of new capacity and services. But, overall private sector participation in infrastructure as a whole—of between 15–18% of total—has been well below the desired levels.

The contrast between telecommunications and power is particularly striking. The power sector was one of the two infrastructure sectors—the other being telecommunications—in which reforms were initiated in the early 1990s. When the reforms started, public sector entities had virtual monopolies in both telecom and power; and capacity shortages and poor service were the norm.

Some 18 years later, the results could not be more different. While the reforms have totally transformed telecommunications, the power sector persists as the most problematic part of India's infrastructure. In telecom, shortages have by now become a distant memory, the private sector has over 60% share of mobile phones, consumers have a choice of providers, service levels have improved dramatically, prices paid by consumers have dropped from being the highest in the world to becoming one of lowest, and consumer coverage is approaching 90% in some areas.

Electricity rates on the other hand remain high by international standards, shortages persist, quality of service remains poor, coverage of population is stagnant and power subsidies absorb an increasing share of budget deficits; over 85% of generation capacity, 100% of transmission and all distribution (except in one state and four large Indian cities) remain in public hands.

Role of the state

While a much enhanced role for the private sector in the development of India's infrastructure is both desirable and necessary, the state will continue to have a critical and large role.

In addition to the normal policy and regulatory role common to other sectors (e.g., banking and finance), the public sector will need to remain a major investor in infrastructure services not attractive to private entrepreneurs (e.g., rural roads, sanitation, parts of urban infrastructure etc.). For example, the Eleventh Plan document expects two thirds of total infrastructure investments to be financed through the public sector. And, if it takes longer to attract the remaining financing from the private sector, it may become necessary for the public sector to cover part of the gap in the interim.

In any case, over the next two decades the public sector would need to finance a significant share of total infrastructure needs. Thus, the public sector will still have a critical role in infrastructure development.

> **India's main focus should shift from policy formulation to policy implementation and on achieving visible results on the ground**

Is the main problem the policy framework or policy implementation?

An important development in the last five years is the major effort made by the last government to replace, or revise, some of the existing policies and rules relating to PPP in infrastructure. These revisions were designed to correct anomalies in the earlier policies and procedures identified as a result of the actual experience. Major efforts have been made to put in place new PPP related policies based on international best practice for airports, ports and highways.

As a result, India now has, albeit with a few understandable exceptions, a robust policy framework for improving infrastructure services and facilitating much greater private sector participation. The most robust framework is for the telecommunications sector and for passenger air services. The new policies for PPP in national highways and for privatization of four major airports are also sound and need no major revisions. In the power sector, the country has a progressive policy in the Electricity Act 2003.

Overall, India thus has a very progressive policy framework by now. This policy framework is capable of putting the country at the forefront of efforts within the developing countries to enhance the access to and quality of infrastructure services and to attract significant private sector participation.

However, policy implementation is the Achilles heel of India's infrastructure development plans. Implementation of the newly adopted policies in most sectors—other than telecommunications and civil aviation—leaves much to be desired. Fundamentally, almost all implementation problems are rooted in two main causes. First, is the implementation capacity constraints within the public sector as a whole to plan, build and operate in a timely and efficient manner the massive new generation, transmission and distribution capacity required by the economy. And second, even more critically, are one or more facets of governance that prevent implementation of the agreed policies at the necessary pace.

One way or the other, all seven facets of governance discussed at the end of part I (chapter 4), hamper resolution of infrastructure problems by stalling progress on policy implementation.

The way forward

Given the urgency to resolve the existing infrastructure bottlenecks but also the importance of making a start on developing infrastructure facilities that provide the foundations for meeting the needs of an affluent society and a globally competitive society, India needs to adopt a two pronged strategy. The first prong would focus on the immediate future, while the second prong would anticipate and start to address longer-term—inter generational—needs.

Immediate agenda

In the near term, India's main focus should shift from policy formulation to policy implementation and on achieving visible results on the ground. There should be a laser-like focus on overcoming the current infrastructure bottlenecks:

- Implementation of existing policies: The government must ensure that all ministries and government entities implement the agreed policies and guidelines within a set timeframe. They should be held accountable for doing so.
- Further increase of investments levels to overcome current bottlenecks: As mentioned, India needs to invest an average of between 9% and 11% of GDP (including about 2.5% of GDP on maintenance and rehabilitation) for the next 5 years in order to support economic growth of 9% per year. This suggests that, even if the Eleventh Plan expenditures levels were achieved in practice, infrastructure bottlenecks would most likely worsen should the economy resume rapid growth. Therefore, at the mid-term review of the Eleventh Plan, all efforts should be made to increase budget allocations to sectors and

> **By 2039 India would need infrastructure that matches that of Korea today, if not better**

states that implement agreed policies and have the capacity to use additional funds effectively.

- Strengthening of institutional capacity: Many government agencies responsible for planning, reviewing, awarding and overseeing PPP projects still have to acquire requisite skills and managerial systems. They must be augmented as soon as possible.
- Simplification and delegation of government decision-making: The present implementation constraints partly arise from the cumbersome processes and risk-averse decision-making culture at all levels of government. To remedy this the government leaders at the highest level must delegate authority to the most competent bodies at lower levels as well as support a major simplification of decision-making processes.
- Crash programmes to eliminate power shortages and accelerate completion of rural electrification and national highways programmes: It is also clear that the continuation of a "business-as-usual" approach, or tinkering at the margins, will not improve the situation in three critical areas: power generation and distribution; rural electrification; and the national highways programme. The only solution is the adoption of a "crash programme" in each of these areas with the full support and commitment from the highest levels of government.
- Monitoring of results and enforcement of accountability: In return for the above proposed simplification of decisionmaking and delegation of authority, government leaders should hold lower level decision-makers accountable for the results on the ground. The key to resolving the current worrisome situation and preventing further deterioration will be the willingness and ability of the top political leadership to force the "system" to move with a much greater sense of urgency and results orientation. Monitoring of progress under the three "crash programmes"

suggested earlier, delegation of authority and enforcing accountability could be part of the initial set of areas to be included in the writ of the new unit in the Prime Minister's Office recommended in part I, chapter 4.

Longer-term policy agenda

The basic goals of the longer-term agenda should be to ensure that India will indeed acquire truly world-class infrastructure—in terms of coverage, quality as well as efficiency—that meets the needs of both an affluent society and the businesses operating in a very large and globally competitive economy. By 2039 India would need infrastructure that matches that of Korea today, if not better.

Overall, the longer-term makeup should be driven by the following reforms advocated in part I, chapter 4:

- Decentralization of authority and accountability to states and cities: India is one of the two most populous countries in the world and rapidly becoming one of the largest and most complex economies. Some individual states are bigger than most countries in world: Uttar Pradesh, for example, has a larger population than Brazil. It is impossible for an economy of this size and complexity to meet its infrastructure needs through a process dominated by the central government. India must align the future roles, responsibilities and accountability in infrastructure sectors in line with our earlier proposal for a major decentralization of power to the state and local governments. For example, the primary responsibility for providing and financing municipal services like urban transport, water, sanitation and power distribution should be delegated to the municipal governments.
- Smaller, more focused and smarter government: With time, the primary role of not only the central government but increasingly also the state governments should be on long term planning, policy formulation and oversight for

" The single most important agenda item in this context is the need to make regulatory bodies stronger, more independent and credible

the markets. To the extent some of the services would continue to be provided by state-owned enterprises, they should be made fully autonomous and subject to financial discipline of the markets and regulation and supervision by the relevant regulatory authority. This will also facilitate trimming and streamlining of the ministerial structure.

- Greater role for the private sector: Using the U.S., Japanese and Korean models, most public services can and should be provided by private suppliers by 2039. In some sectors like telecom, this may be achieved quickly while in others (e.g., railways) the transition period would be longer. But, it is desirable that a longer-term vision is developed soon to allow all parties ample time to adjust and get ready for the changes.

- More competitive markets—stronger and more independent regulatory bodies: This is clearly a major pre-requisite for allowing the private sector a much greater role. The single most important agenda item in this context is the

need to make regulatory bodies stronger, more independent and credible, as is already the case with the Telecommunications Regulatory Authority of India (TRAI). The need is urgent in power, civil aviation, railways and ports. Over time, services like water and sanitation must also be covered.

- Focus on the longer term: Infrastructure is a primary example of areas that need a long-term and multi-generational perspective. It is imperative that governments at all three levels—centre, states and local—periodically formulate a long-term vision of infrastructure needs (quality as well as quantity) under their purview and make it publically available so that both consumers and producers take day to day decisions within this framework. Indeed, this will become a major role of the government as private provision of actual services expands. The plans should be formulated by the government (centre, state or local) closest to the markets and in consultations with both producers and users.

INDIA 2039

Part III

Chapter

9

Global competitiveness through technology

Global competitiveness through technology

Vinod K. Goel and R. A. Mashelkar

The Indian growth story has captured the imagination of the world. This growth has come mainly from productivity gains as workers move from farms to services. Sustaining a long-term growth trajectory can transform India into an affluent nation within a generation. India could become the second largest economy in the world (surpassing the United States) with a per capita income of 22,000 dollars. To realize this potential (and grow like South Korea and Japan, without falling into the "middle income trap" like Brazil), India must rapidly and continuously enhance global competitiveness and improve productivity of its economy. This needs a strong strategy, where perpetual gains from a workforce that creates, acquires, and uses knowledge aggressively, are harnessed, along with the imaginative use of existing technologies to raise productivity levels to best possible benchmarks—in both the formal and informal sectors. This will require bold and visionary leadership.

Today, India spends just 0.5–0.7 percent of GDP on tertiary education; the United States spends 2.6 percent; Europe 1.2 percent; and Japan 1.1 percent. India invests 0.9 percent of GDP on R&D; China spends 1.4 percent; Europe 2 percent; and the United States 2.6 percent. India invests only .025 percent of GDP on R&D devoted to civilian applications—75 percent of its total R&D spending is in the public sector. In India, the Gross Enrollment Ratio in higher education is 11.8 percent; it is 91 percent in South Korea, 82 percent in the United States, and 22 percent in China. India has two universities in the Shanghai Top 500 global ranking; China has 22. India ranks 48th (China 34th) on the Global Competitiveness Index and 119th among 149 countries in the science citations index. It produces twice as many engineers as the United States, but its pool of PhDs is less than one-tenth the size of the United States' pool. And only 2 percent of the workforce has skills training

against 96 percent in South Korea and 80 percent in Japan.

Total factor productivity growth in India is low compared with the rest of the world, particularly the United States. Moreover, there are large differences in productivity in India between formal enterprises in the same industry and between the formal sector and the massive informal sector, where most of India's entrepreneurial activity takes place. For example, the least productive domestic formal enterprises in auto components and textiles are hundreds of times less productive than the most productive domestic firms in those sectors. Productivity dispersion in formal manufacturing enterprises is wider in India than in all other major comparator countries (China, Mexico, and South Korea) except Brazil. Raising average productivity to the domestic adjusted maximum level would boost average productivity fivefold.

India is the second most entrepreneurial country in the world—18 percent of its workforce is engaged in entrepreneurial activities, compared with 2 percent in Japan, 10 percent in the United States, and 7 percent worldwide. However, less than 3 percent of India's workforce is in the modern private sector, while 94 percent is in the informal sector, mostly in low-productivity and low-skill activities. Because India is still so poor, it has considerable potential for total factor productivity growth and tremendous catch-up potential in technology.

With bold reforms, India's enormous population of young people can be prepared to create knowledge and innovative goods, concepts, processes, and methods on a large scale. As Nandan Nilekani, co-chairman of Infosys, said recently: "India has democracy, population, IT, globalization, English, and ideas—no country has all these six things together except India" (IANS 2008).

In the coming decades India's demographics will describe either its most significant comparative

> **With appropriate reforms, India can convert its young population into knowledge workers, build an environment conducive to innovation, and tap into this source of long-term growth**

Table 1 | Key education, technology and innovation indicators, selected countries

Indicator	Brazil	China	India	Japan	Mexico	South Korea	United States
Gross secondary enrolment ratio, 2006 (%)	105.5	75.5	54.0	101.4	87.2	93.9	93.9
Gross tertiary enrolment ratio, 2006 (%)	25.5	21.6	11.9	57.3	26.1	91.0	81.8
Science enrolment ratio, 2006 (%)	8.4	na	14.3	2.9	13.0	8.6	8.9
Science and engineering enrolment ratio, 2006 (%)	15.9	na	20.3	19.5	31.3	37.5	15.6
Researchers in R&D, 2006	84,979	926,252	117,528	677,206	33,484	179,812	1,334,628
Researchers in R&D, 2006 (per million people)	462	715	119	5,300	331	3,723	4,628
Total expenditure on R&D, 2006 (% of GDP)	1.0	1.4	0.8	3.2	0.4	3.20	2.7
University-industry R&D collaboration, 2007 (scale of 1, low, to 7, high)	3.4	4.1	3.5	4.9	3.2	5.1	5.6
Scientific and technical journal articles, 2005	9,889	41,596	14,608	55,471	3,902	16,396	205,320
Scientific and technical journal articles, 2005 (per million people)	52.9	31.9	13.4	434.1	37.9	339.5	692.5
Availability of venture capital, 2007 (scale of 1, low, to 7, high)	2.5	2.9	4.1	3.9	2.8	3.4	5.3
Patents granted by U.S. Patent and Trademark Office, 2002–06 average	135	448	316	35,469	96	4,233	94,217
Patents granted by U.S. Patent and Trademark Office, 2002–06 average (per million people)	0.8	0.4	0.3	278.0	1.0	88.4	324.1
Manufacturing trade, 2005 (% of GDP)	14.9	53.5	17.1	18.2	46.6	32.7	16.0
High-technology exports as share of manufacturing exports, 2005 (%)	12.8	30.6	4.9	22.5	19.6	32.0	31.8

Note: na is not available.
Source: World Bank 2008b.

advantage or its most disappointing failure of political will. In the new global economy a nation's wealth lies not in its land or capital but in its skilled people, who generate new knowledge and convert it into useful ideas, goods and services. With plenty of smart, young, and competent workers, the challenge for India is to deploy its resources to produce the highest possible return. For this, India needs a massive increase in the capacity and quality of higher education and in the amount and scope of investments in technology and innovation. Business as usual will not work. Currently, education quality and enrolment are low at all levels, India's R&D expenditures are inadequate, and the activities of its R&D system are

narrow and disconnected from market demands (table 1). A radical change is needed in the political commitment, mindset, and approach—including a redefinition of the roles of the government and the private sector. With appropriate reforms, India can convert its young population into knowledge workers, build an environment conducive to innovation, and tap into this source of long-term growth.

Transformation agenda and milestones

In an advanced economy, many sectors require workers with specialized knowledge, who can create knowledge and use it as a productive tool. An educated workforce

> **An educated workforce is a prerequisite for a vibrant technology and innovation system that serves as a major source of growth**

| Table 2 | Key milestones in higher education, technology, and innovation for 2039—difficult but possible with the right leadership and timely and bold policy actions |

Milestones	2007	2039
Gross enrolment ratio in tertiary education (%)	11.8	50
Total enrolment in tertiary education (millions)	11	80
Stock of college graduates (millions)	51	300
Certified and skilled technicians (millions)	—	500
Annual output of PhDs	18,000	400,000
Number of universities	378	1,500
Number of world-class universities	—	100
Number of community colleges	260	100,000
Public funding for education (% of GDP)	4	8
R&D expenditures (% of GDP)	0.9	3
Share of private sector in R&D expenditures (%)	20	70
Resident Indians Nobel Prize winners	—	10
Centres of excellence in research & innovation	—	25

Note: — is not available.

Source: Data for 2007 are from India Planning Commission (2008); and MHRD (2007) Goals for 2039 are authors' estimates.

| Table 3 | India needs a paradigm shift in higher education, technology, and innovation |

Current approach	Achievable aspirations
Skills deficit nation	Skills capital of the world
Occasional world-class university builder	Builder of a 100 world-class universities
Copier of best practices in education and research	Creator of centres of excellence in education and research
Weak and hesitant private sector partner	Strong practitioner of privately managed nonprofit institutions of higher education
Tentative destination for occasional foreign students	Preferred global destination for foreign students
Suspicious viewer of foreign institutions	Aggressive partner and competitor of foreign institutions
Minor follower and player in R&D and innovation	Global leader and a giant in R&D and innovation
Uninspired incremental innovator	Aggressive disruptive innovator
Exclusive top of the pyramid innovator	Frontier and inclusive innovator catering to the entire society
Protective and restrictive intellectual property practitioner	Confident and competitive intellectual property promoter

is a prerequisite for a vibrant technology and innovation system that serves as a major source of growth. Rising labour productivity accounted for at least half of per capita GDP growth in high income countries during 1990–2000. Better educated workers are generally more productive and help to boost the productivity of co-workers. Larger stocks of human capital facilitate investment in physical capital and enhance the development

> **India needs a radical shift in political commitment, mindset, approach, and investment in higher education, technology, and innovation**

Box 1 | Agenda for transforming higher education, technology, and innovation

Several bold steps are needed to transform higher education, technology, and innovation in India:

1. Massively expand and improve the higher education system.
   - Double investment in education.
   - Increase tertiary enrolment eightfold.
   - Pursue a multi-tier system and create 100 world-class universities, 1,000 universities, 20,000 colleges, and 100,000 community colleges.
   - Increase the supply of qualified and trained faculty.

2. Greatly increase technology development and use, and innovation.
   - Increase R&D expenditures and outputs, by both the public and private sectors.
   - Create an innovation ecosystem and right-size (and refocus) major public R&D networks.

- Pursue frontier as well as inclusive innovation.
- Create centers of excellence in key research, such as clean energy technologies and public health.
- Enhance commercializable R&D and technology diffusion and absorption.

3. Radically shift the roles of the government and the private sector, including foreign direct investment.
   - Overhaul the regulatory and governance framework, with government playing a facilitating role with smart regulations, light oversight, and financing.
   - Enhance private sector participation (and foreign direct investment) with proper policies, including tax and other incentives.
   - Leverage international knowledge and financial resources, and capitalize on the demographic dividend by exporting skilled labor and higher education.

---

and diffusion of new technologies, raising output per worker.[1]

India must dramatically increase its supply of trained and highly educated workers to sustain its high growth trajectory over the next 30 years, create more and better quality jobs, and enable all of its people to realize the aspirations created by the country's recent economic success. To do that, India needs to transform its education system (table 2). India's education system suffers from serious problems of low capacity, poor governance and over-regulation, low quality and inadequate outputs, funding and skills deficits, and faculty shortages (table 3). In addition to spreading knowledge, a quality education system provides the foundation for future learning, creative thinking, and innovative energy.

In order to continue its climb up the global technology ladder, India needs to develop an integrated higher education, technology, and innovation system that is driven by the private sector. It should be a highly productive and globally competitive system (see table 3 and box 1) similar to ones developed by Japan and South Korea

in the past 50 years and as China is working on now. India must leverage its technology strength and establish an R&D and innovation ecosystem that conducts cutting-edge and globally competitive research and innovation, meets the demands of a modernizing economy, boosts productivity in the informal sector (which employs almost 94 percent of India's workforce), and contributes to the global good. The R&D sector must also address key strategic issues such as low-cost universal health care, clean water supply, low cost housing, efficient energy use, clean environment, management of urban congestion, agricultural and rural development, and others. India's technology and innovation system should also enable the efficient diffusion and absorption of knowledge, whether newly created or already existing.

To achieve these goals, India needs a radical shift in political commitment, mindset, approach, and investment in higher education, technology, and innovation. A business-as-usual approach will not work. India has much to learn from its "islands of excellence", such as the Indian Institutes of Technology and the Indian

> **❝❝ India must increase its output of skilled graduates tenfold over the next 30 years**

| Box 2 | **New thrust in Indian education** |

To succeed in a knowledge-based economy, a country needs the capacity to generate knowledge and the skilled human capital to convert knowledge into value-added goods and services. For this, it needs a well-developed education system at all levels, a system that creates knowledge workers. Basic education needs to be of highest quality, to establish a flow of solid students for higher education and research.

The recently passed "Rights to Education" bill is a step in the right direction, but a lot more needs to be done to improve the quality of basic education.

India must improve the quality of its basic education system while investing in higher education. In addition to the technical subjects, students need to learn soft skills—creativity, innovation, intellectual curiosity, communication, and team work. Schools need to move away from rote learning to the acquisition of learning skills to prepare students for the global challenges ahead. Teaching institutions need to do their job efficiently and effectively. Schools need to encourage research, strengthen the analytical abilities of students, and create leaders in business, academia and public service, as well as technology. And special attention needs to be paid to improving and expanding liberal arts institutions, as well as science and technology institutions.

Institutes of Management, and its space and nuclear research initiatives. These successes demonstrate that a primarily public sector effort will not work. A large private sector presence and foreign direct investment are needed to ensure rapid expansion, high quality output, and relevance where public sector initiatives and overregulation have been inefficient, insufficient, and unreliable. Ongoing, highly successful initiatives must be encouraged, supported, and scaled up across the country. India must ultimately learn from the U.S. model—with its creative, productive, and market-relevant higher education and research system that excels globally.

Expand and improve massively the higher education system

Despite many islands of excellence—including the institutes of technology, management, and science—India's education system is dysfunctional, with low capacity, poor governance and overregulation, with low quality and grossly inadequate outputs, with funding and skill deficits, and with faculty shortages.

The Indian education system must undergo a major transformation in order to meet the growing demand of its modernizing economy, fulfil the aspirations of its people, and contribute to the global good (box 2).

Demand for higher education and vocational training
India must increase its output of skilled graduates tenfold over the next 30 years. Several factors go into estimating the demand for higher education. They range from the projected demand of various sectors of India's fast-growing economy to the rising aspirations of the country's youth and society at large. Demographic trends in India and patterns of higher education in western nations and other emerging economies could also help to estimate demand. Although some data are available on demand from a few sectors over the next 10 years (information technology and electronics, textiles, and automobile), reliable long-term demand projections for the next 30 years are unavailable. Therefore, projections must be based on demographic trends, the aspirations of the Indian people, and education patterns in other economies. On this basis, the number of India's higher education graduates needs to increase some eight- to tenfold in the next 30 years.

Demographic projections of demand for higher education and vocational training. In the coming decades, India's demographic change will reflect either its greatest comparative advantage or its most disappointing failure of political will. In a world where

Box 3 | The Skills Development Mission and employment potential in selected sectors

To create a pool of skilled personnel in appropriate numbers with adequate skills in line with the employment requirements across the entire economy, with particular emphasis on the 20 high-growth, high-employment sectors, the government has set up a Skills Development Mission aimed at enhancing training opportunities of new entrants to the labour force from the existing 2.5 million in the non-agricultural sector to 10 million per year.

Dialogue with the private sector is focusing on developing skills for workers in 10 high-growth sectors in manufacturing (automobile and auto components, electronics hardware, textiles and garments, leather and leather goods, chemicals and pharmaceuticals, gem and jewelry, building and construction, food processing, handlooms and handicrafts, and building hardware and home furnishings), and 10 in services (information technology and software services; information technology-enabled services and business process services; tourism hospitality and travel; transportation, logistics, warehousing and packaging; organized retail; real estate services; media, entertainment, broadcasting, content creation, and animation; healthcare services; banking, insurance, and finance; and education and skills-development services).

A Confederation of Indian Industry employment potential study of 36 sectors found that the financial sector could employ 1.1 million people. The construction industry could employ 9.9 million more people, whereas the defence equipment sector sees the possibility of generating only 160,000 jobs. Other important sectors where high employment is possible are tourism (19.6

million), retail (9 million), tobacco and tobacco products (6.4 million), gems and jewellery (3.16 million), horticulture (2.6 million), oil and gas (2.3 million), state transport (2.3 million), food (2.1 million), khadi (1.9 million), railways (1.9 million), healthcare (6.1 million), and media and entertainment (1.0 million).

In the auto sector (with turnover of $28 billion), an employment increase from 10.5 million to 25.0 million is targeted by 2016. A skill-intensive industry (90 percent skilled workers), it will require 6.25 million technical and managerial personnel. The Auto Components Manufacturers' Association envisions $20 billion in domestic sales, $20 billion in exports, and 1 million new jobs.

The electronics hardware industry is growing at an average annual rate of 25 percent and expects to scale up by 2016 from a current turnover of $30 billion to $320 billion, with employment rising from 1.5 million direct and 3 million indirect to 7 million direct and 14 million indirect. The industry requires 5 percent graduate engineers, 15 percent diploma-holders, 50 percent skilled workers and 30 percent semi-skilled workers.

The textile and garments industry expects to scale up by 2016 from current turnover of $47 billion to $115 billion, raising employment from 35 million to 41.5 million. Of the 6.5 million new workers, only 20 percent will be unskilled—50 percent will be semi-skilled, 20 percent will have Industrial Training Institutes certificates, and 10 percent will be management and technical graduates.

Source: Indian Planning Commission 2008, India Department of Heavy Industries, Government of India 2006.

information technology, and even education itself. Some sectors are losing their competitive advantage because of the tightness of the labour market. Moreover, because the current higher education system is able to meet only a fraction of potential demand, many qualified and talented young Indians are forced to attend substandard institutions or to go abroad. Education abroad comes at a high cost to the country since many students do not return. (Box 3 describes the Skills Development Mission and employment potential in selected industries.)

Many of India's graduates lack critical skills for the new economy. A recent McKinsey study estimates that only 10 percent of Indian arts and humanities graduates and only 25 percent of engineering graduates are globally competitive[4]—symptoms of a quality deficit in both public and private institutions. These conditions have already resulted in shortages of skilled workers in industry and academia, creating faculty shortages, throttling advances in science and technology, and constraining competitiveness. With a few exceptions, India's higher

> **" With a few exceptions, India's higher education system does not have the high-quality institutions, public or private, that can produce the creative, intellectual leaders that India requires for sustainable growth**

education system does not have the high-quality institutions, public or private, that can produce the creative, intellectual leaders that India requires for sustainable growth.

Higher education outputs and standing

India has the third-largest higher education system in the world, behind China and the United States. It has 369 universities—222 state universities, 20 central universities, 109 deemed universities, 5 institutions established under states legislation, and 13 institutes of national importance established by central legislation[5] (figure 5). It also has 18,064 colleges, including some 1,902 women's colleges, according to the *2006/2007 Annual Report of the Ministry of Human Resource Development* (figure 6). Enrolment in 2006/07 was 11.028 million—1.427 million (12.9 percent) in university departments and 9.6 million (87.1 percent) in affiliated colleges (that is, colleges associated with a university for awarding degrees but not a part of the university

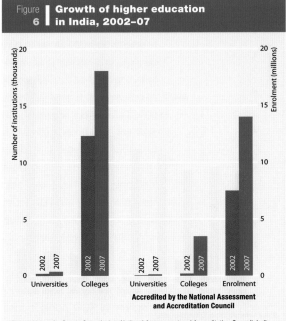

Figure 6 | Growth of higher education in India, 2002–07

Source: University Grants Commission, National Assessment and Accreditation Council; India Planning Commission 2008.

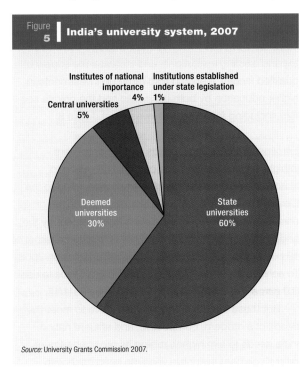

Figure 5 | India's university system, 2007

Source: University Grants Commission 2007.

itself). The 2,240 engineering colleges admit about 700,000 students annually. Two-thirds of the engineering institutions are located in four southern states, plus Maharashtra, even though these states account for less than one-third of the population (India National Knowledge Commission 2008). Only 15 percent of seats are open to students from outside the state, so students in under-provided states have considerably less access than in-state students. The intake in most premier institutions is quite low—just 3,500 undergraduates for all seven Indian Institutes of Technology, for example (The Georgia Institute of Technology in the United States alone has 20,000 students). Most private professional education is controlled by politicians for profit and self-promotion, with the heavy influence of black money.

universities, with enrolments of 20,000–30,000 students to benefit from economies of scale (not the 12,000 limit set by the University Grants Commission).[8]

The central government's current plans for the higher education sector are not adequate. The government plans to establish 30 new central universities, including 16 in each of the 16 uncovered states. The other 14 new central universities, to be called national universities, are expected to achieve world-class standards. In addition, the government plans to open a number of institutions of national importance including eight new technology institutes, six management institutes, and five institutes of science education and research.[9] Added to that are plans to open 20 other institutes of technology; 1,617

engineering and technology colleges; 1,292 polytechnic schools; 91 schools for hotel management; and 4 architecture institutions. The government has also identified five universities with potential for excellence (Jadavpur University, Jawaharlal Nehru University, University of Hyderabad, University of Madras and University of Pune). The plan falls short of the 100 world-class universities required to meet India's needs, and it fails to call for all central universities (new and existing ones) to be brought up to world-class level (see box 4 on creating world-class universities).

To compete successfully in the knowledge-based economy, India needs enough universities that not only produce world-class graduates but also support

---

Box 4 | Creating a world-class university—India's universities of tomorrow

India's universities of tomorrow should embody innovation, acting as a laboratory for experimentation, adventure and curiosity, where education takes the form of learning to learn and where information is converted into new insights about the world. They would be open-source, holistic, multidisciplinary institutions, continuously adapting and offering courses to enhance the creative, analytical and entrepreneurial skills of students and their ability to learn, unlearn and relearn. While India needs to produce more science and engineering graduates, it also needs to improve and expand liberal arts colleges and universities across the country. Most top institutions offer education across a range of disciplines from natural sciences, social sciences and humanities to engineering, technology and medicine. The Massachusetts Institute of Technology in the United States offers science, technology, economics, business, media and social sciences, while Stanford University also offers medicine and law.

Universities should have the authority to determine the locations of new campuses, admission policies and faculty hiring and salary policies, hiring the best available faculty including from abroad. They should do teaching and research, be free of any external affiliation, welcome private sector funding and set fees to generate adequate income while supplementing that funding with contract

research and donations. They should have performance-based rewards for the faculty and should be able to decide with whom to collaborate (both in India and abroad). They should also introduce flexible programmes such as a four-year BS (with broad based education) leading directly to admission to a PhD programme, offer integrated five-year BS/MS degree programmes with research, and provide mobility of course credits. They should offer special honours courses for exceptional students, so that they can learn in an environment of intense competition, and continuing education courses to enable the workforce to keep pace with changing skills demand in the marketplace.

The location of new public universities should be determined competitively, through evaluation of alternative offers of land by the state. The state could allocate land for private universities through a transparent auction process. New universities should be located where there are opportunities for synergies arising from co-location with existing renowned institutions and laboratories to attract the best faculty and high-quality students, rather than simply to ensure better geographic coverage. Proximity to bigger cities and towns will also help faculty spouses and graduate students find employment, important for attracting quality faculty and students and reducing the burden of providing faculty and student housing.

Source: Authors' formulation.

❝ **With more than 75 percent of students finding employment, the community colleges that have been developed in the past decade primarily through nongovernmental initiatives are a resounding success deserving of replication and support**

Figure 9 | **Education and research are interdependent, selected countries, 2007**

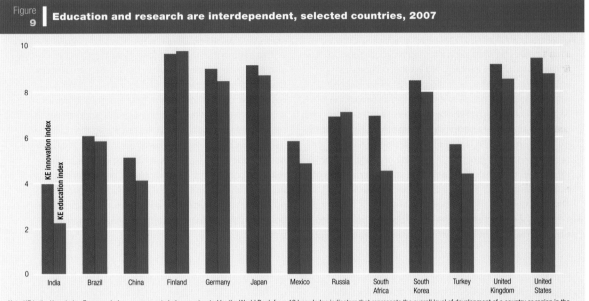

Note: KE is the Knowledge Economy index, an aggregate index constructed by the World Bank from 12 knowledge indicators that represents the overall level of development of a country or region in the knowledge economy.
Source: World Bank 2008a.

sophisticated research that contributes to the knowledge and technology needed for an expanding economy. That means not only working at the frontiers of research but also creating new frontiers. India needs to empower universities to use R&D labs to teach. Teaching without research is sterile. Research enriches the quality of teaching—and teaching enriches research (figure 9). Many universities around the world conduct research free of government interference. Success in research requires collaboration with the best universities in the world, along with exchange programmes for faculty and students. Universities such as the Massachusetts Institute of Technology, Stanford and others offer outstanding education and research opportunities and create billions of dollars in wealth through broad support for university-based start-ups. These include financing, intellectual property management, training, and incubation facilities.

India needs to establish 100,000 community colleges. An interesting model is emerging in the

community colleges that have been developed in the past decade primarily through nongovernmental initiatives, including some 260 concentrated mainly in southern India. These colleges have flexible entry norms that do not require prior formal academic qualification. Curricula include 21 weeks each of life skills and work skills, with eight weeks of internship and hands-on training and two weeks of preparation for employment and evaluation. With more than 75 percent of students finding employment, these community colleges are a resounding success deserving of replication and support. In appropriate cases, course credits from community colleges should be transferable to universities.

Increasing the capacity of existing institutions. India needs to substantially increase the quality, efficiency, and intake levels of existing institutions (see box 5 on balancing expansion, inclusion, and excellence). Most higher education institutions have some slack, and capacity can be expanded with additional

> ❝ **India's challenge while expanding higher education is to find ways to include the excluded without compromising efficiency and excellence**

Box 5 | **Balance between expansion and efficiency, inclusion and excellence**

India's challenge while expanding higher education is to find ways to include the excluded without compromising efficiency and excellence. In the long run, expansion will naturally solve the inclusiveness problem as capacity in higher education grows and as the increase in the supply and quality of education and training reduces inequities in society.

In the meantime, solutions require an honest recognition of the fact that the quality of students follows the normal distribution. There are a small percentage of outstanding students, a majority that are average and a small percentage that are below average.

Thus a small percentage of the population tends to account for most of a country's intellectual energy. Much

of this segment of the population has been lost to Europe and the United States by brain drain. India must learn to court these intellectuals and to devise systems that recognize, encourage, retain, and promote them. While it is important that all children have the opportunity to realize their potential, this does not mean that standards need to be based on the lowest performers. The country needs special provisions (such as incentives and reservations) for the disadvantaged groups in society, but this can be done without compromising on quality by providing such students with opportunities for catching up—such as special courses and programmes and scholarships.

investments and flexibility. This can include providing evening classes, making greater use of information and communication technology, and establishing distance learning. One size fits all is not the model to follow. The Indian Institutes of Technology and the Indian Institutes of Management should differentiate themselves through course offerings, outputs, and international benchmarking, including the possibility of converting themselves into full-fledged universities (like the Georgia Institute of Technolgy in the United States).

Investment requirements. The share of spending on higher (and technical) education in India is meagre, at just 0.5–0.7 percent of GDP, compared with 2.6 percent in the United States, 1.2 percent in Europe, and 1.1 percent in Japan. Successive governments have promised to increase investment in education to 6 percent of GDP but have never achieved more than 4.3 percent (in 2000; other highs have been 2.98 percent in 1980 and 3.49 percent in 1997). Recognizing the importance of education, the government has again pledged to increase public spending on education to 6 percent of GDP (from 3.46 percent in 2005). The 2004 central budget earmarked 2 percent of major

central taxes and duties for elementary education, and the 2007 budget earmarked 1 percent for secondary and higher education. Further, the Eleventh Five-Year Plan (Indian Planning Commission 2008) allocates 19.3 percent of total plan outlays for education—a

Figure 10 | **Education allocation in Indian Tenth and Eleventh Plans**

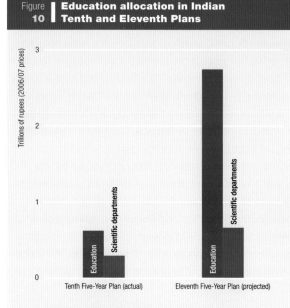

Source: India Planning Commission 2002, 2008.

> **India needs a technology and innovation system that is highly productive, globally competitive, and capable of meeting the needs of its globalizing economy and lifting the productivity of its informal sector**

fourfold increase over the Tenth Five Year Plan (Indian Planning Commission 2002)—seeing education as a central instrument for achieving rapid and inclusive growth (figure 10).[10] But even with these increases, the proposed investment is still too low.

India will need a much larger increase in investments in education by both the public and the private sectors. In the new knowledge economy, investment in education is an investment in the nation's future, not just social expenditures. National returns are high from increases in technology and productivity. India should increase public investment in education from the current 4.2 percent of GDP to around 8 percent to fund the massive expansion of the education system needed to compete in a knowledge economy. The cost of a new university could vary from 15 billion rupees ($300 million) to 50 billion rupees ($1 billion), depending on size, location, type of programmes, quality and other variables. Faculty salaries at a world-class university would alone cost more than 3–4 billion rupees ($75–$100 million) a year. Investments of $600–$1,000 billion will be required over the next two decades or so just to establish 1,000 new universities; additional investments will also be needed to establish new colleges and vocational institutions and expanding existing institutions.

Increase greatly technology development and use, and innovation

With a comprehensive network of research institutions, India has the world's third largest scientific establishment. It has done well in strategic research on space, defence, atomic energy, and supercomputers. It is also becoming a top global player in biotechnology, pharmaceuticals, information technology, and automotive parts and assembly. The recent crowning glory of India's space research—the first moon orbiter project, Chandrayan-1—has placed India among a handful of nations that have a credible capability in space science and technology.

But India's expenditures on research and development, at 0.9 percent of GDP (70–80 percent public),

are lower than the 1.4 percent in China, 2 percent in Europe and 2.6 percent in the United States—and only 0.25 percent of GDP is focused on civilian applications. Moreover, the research and development system is narrow in scope, has low outputs and is disconnected from the market.

India needs a technology and innovation system that is highly productive, globally competitive, and capable of meeting the needs of its globalizing economy and lifting the productivity of its informal sector. This requires an increase in research and development investments from 0.8 percent of GDP to 3 percent—driven largely by the private sector—pursuing frontier, strategic, and inclusive innovation; enhancing commercializable research and development; and creating a foundation to diffuse and encourage the absorption of new technologies.

Need for reform

Limited level and scope of research. India has a well developed science and technology infrastructure, but R&D expenditures are concentrated in only a few areas. India's major public R&D networks include the Council of Scientific and Industrial Research, the Indian Council of Agricultural Research, the Indian Council of Medical Research, the Indian Space Research Organization, the Defence Research and Development Organizations, the Atomic Energy Research Establishments, the Indian Institutes of Technology, the Indian Institutes of Management, and the Indian Institutes of Science. The public sector accounts for 70–80 percent of total R&D investment (0.9 percent of GDP), with the bulk of it concentrated in mission-oriented R&D in defence by the Department of Defence (25 percent), in space research by the Department of Space Research (17 percent), and in energy by the Department of Atomic Energy (9 percent). Less than 20 percent of public support for R&D is for civilian applications, and within industrial R&D expenditure, nearly 40 percent is for drugs and pharmaceuticals.[11]

III/9

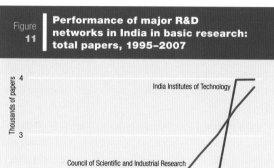

Figure 11 | **Performance of major R&D networks in India in basic research: total papers, 1995–2007**

Source: Indian Council of Scientific and Industrial Research data New Delhi, India.

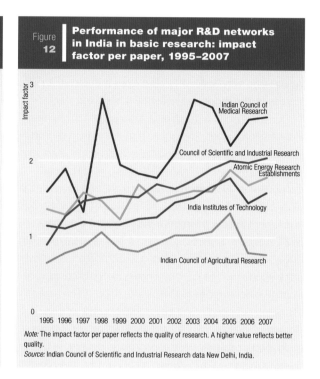

Figure 12 | **Performance of major R&D networks in India in basic research: impact factor per paper, 1995–2007**

Note: The impact factor per paper reflects the quality of research. A higher value reflects better quality.
Source: Indian Council of Scientific and Industrial Research data New Delhi, India.

Limited output of the R&D system. Research of world-class calibre is limited to a few top-level institutions in India (figures 11 and 12). Few universities conduct research, primarily because they lack adequate research infrastructure, an academic environment with free debate and discussion, and a drive for creating new knowledge, and research groups of critical size. India produces only 6,000 PhDs a year in science and fewer than 1,000 in engineering and technology because of very low enrolment and inadequate facilities and incentives for individual research. India ranked 119 of 149 countries in the 2004 Science Citations Index.[12] India compares poorly in its share of world research publications, remaining almost static at about 2 percent during 1993–2003. In the same period, China increased its share from about 1.3 percent to about 4.5 percent, South Korea from 0.4 percent to about 2 percent, and Brazil from 0.6 percent to 1.5 percent.

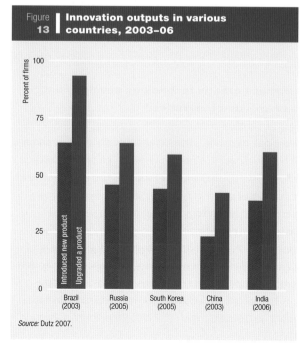

Figure 13 | **Innovation outputs in various countries, 2003–06**

Source: Dutz 2007.

" The performance of the Indian Council of Agriculture Research network is well below desired levels—India has not produced any major breakthroughs in agriculture since the Green Revolution in the late 1960s

Even when the comparisons are made with India's best institutions, the outcomes are poor. A McKinsey study found that a typical Indian Institute of Technology was granted 3–6 patents a year compared with 64 for the Stanford University engineering faculty and 102 for the Massachusetts Institute of Technology engineering faculty.[13] The number of citations in scientific publications per faculty member over a five-year period was 2–3 for a typical Indian Institute of Technology, compared with 52 for the Stanford University engineering faculty and 45 for the Massachusetts Institute of Technology engineering faculty. India filed 363 patents in 2004, compared with 84,271 by the United States and 35,350 by Japan.

The absence of excellence in research has seriously constricted India's scientific and technological output (figure 13). India's Council of Scientific and Industrial Research, established in 1942, is the largest public R&D network in the world, with some 18,000 staff, 5,400 researchers, and 37 national R&D labs representing all major industrial sectors. It receives 8 percent of total public spending on R&D and holds more than 1,000 U.S. patents. However, it lacks a culture of commercialization and spin-offs and income from patents remains minimal. Some of its labs are well advanced in public-private collaboration and applied research (National Chemical Laboratory, Indian Institute of Chemical Technology), but many are still lagging (National Aerospace Laboratory). The performance of the Indian Council of Agricultural Research network is well below desired levels—India has not produced any major breakthroughs in agriculture since the Green Revolution in the late 1960s. While India has more than 60 facilities approved by the U.S. Food and Drug Administration, regulations and red tape (plus lack of experience and a risk-averse culture) are hampering the development of India's pharmaceuticals industry through slow reviews and approvals of clinical trials and drugs. As a result, some companies seek external assistance to avoid costly delays in a global industry where timing is critical.

Low R&D commercialization. Commercializable research and technology absorption are low in India, except in a few institutions (such as the Council of Scientific and Industrial Research, the Indian Institutes of Science, the University Institute of Chemical Technology in Mumbai, and the Indian Institute of Technology in Mumbai). With few exceptions (such as Tata Motors and some firms in pharmaceuticals, biotechnology, and auto components), the private sector has not invested adequately in R&D.[14] For example, Reliance Industries, India's largest conglomerate, has minimal R&D facilities (except for its Life Sciences Division, which has 130 scientists, 80 PhDs and 300 patents, 30 percent from the United States). Reliance did not invest substantially in R&D until 2007, when it set up a high-level Innovation Leadership Council (chaired by Dr. R. A. Mashelkar and including Dr. Lawrence H. Summers and Noble laureates). While R&D investments remain low, there has been a significant increase in private sectors investments since India began to liberalize its economy in the early 1990s. In 2004, enterprise R&D was more than seven times higher than in 1991. This trend needs to continue.

Limited diffusion and absorption of existing knowledge. India also needs to increase its technology absorption. Despite some centres of excellence, total factor productivity growth is low in India compared with the rest of the world, especially the United States, and productivity dispersion is high. There are large differences in productivity between formal enterprises in the same industry and between the formal sector and the much larger informal sector. A key reason for these disparities is the limited absorption and diffusion of existing knowledge. India ranked 48 (China was 34) on the 2007 Global Competitiveness Index (table 4) and 26 on the Global Innovation Index (China was 50).[15] Given the comparatively low cost of diffusion compared with the production of new knowledge, these disparities evidence a lack of basic technological infrastructure, insufficiently developed human capital, and limited investment in R&D.

> **While having an economy-wide scope, R&D must also address key national policy issues such as public health and cheaper drugs, low cost housing, clean water supply, efficient and clean energy use, the environment, urban congestion, agriculture, and rural development**

Table 4 | Global competitiveness: Innovation Capacity Components Index

Country	Innovation Capacity Index		Quality of scientific research institutions		University-industry research collaboration		Availability of scientists & engineers		Utility patents (per million of people)		Public procurement of advanced technology	
	Rank	Score	Rank	Score	Rank	Score	Rank	Score	Rank	Score	Rank	Score
Brazil	27	4.0	43	5.13	50	3.6	57	4.4	58	0.5	84	3.4
China	25	4.2	37	5.12	23	4.5	52	4.5	54	0.6	20	4.2
India	35	3.8	27	5.1	45	3.6	3	5.7	57	0.5	88	3.4
Japan	2	5.9	15	5.4	21	4.6	2	5.9	3	260	42	3.9
South Korea	9	5.3	14	5.5	12	5.1	19	5.1	7	131	2	5.1
United Kingdom	14	14.0	7	5.7	9	5.1	32	4.8	18	55	32	4.0
United States	6	5.5	1	6.3	1	5.8	6	5.5	1	262	4	4.9

Note: Rank refers to the economy's global rank on each indicator among 134 economies. Scores range from 1 low to 7 highest, except for utility patents, where the score shows the number of patents per million people.

Source: WEF 2008.

Details on the index of various components of innovation capacity are given in table 4.

Vision for technology and innovation in India
For India's size, capability and needs, its current R&D performance is grossly inadequate. To attain global leadership in the knowledge economy, India needs a vibrant, comprehensive R&D system that generates state-of-the-art knowledge (both basic and applied). It must be focused on commercialization and should assist workers in both formal and informal enterprises in using and adapting knowledge to improve their productivity and competitiveness. While having an economy-wide scope, R&D must also address key national policy issues such as public health and cheaper drugs, low cost housing, clean water supply, efficient and clean energy use, the environment, urban congestion, agriculture, and rural development.

To accomplish these ends, India needs an integrated science, technology, and innovation policy that encourages competition among enterprises, greater diffusion of knowledge, and increased support for early-stage technology development and grassroots innovators. It should foster increased collaboration among R&D institutes, universities, and the business sector and leverage their cumulative strengths in designing and implementing research and innovation programmes. The government and the corporate sector should introduce vigorous and attractive recruitment policies for science and technology personnel, with flexible salary support and start-up grants to attract world-class scientists to work in India.

Building on India's innovation successes. India has done well in strategic research in aerospace, defence, atomic energy, and supercomputers and is becoming a global innovator in biotechnology, pharmaceuticals, automotive parts and assembly, and information technology (software and information technology-enabled services). It has created a global R&D platform for multinational corporations, with more than 300 R&D and technical centres. India has developed missiles, rocket systems, sophisticated sonar systems, satellites, helicopters, combat, and small civilian aircraft, a light-combat aircraft, and remotely piloted vehicles. India's first moon orbiter

> **❝ To become globally competitive, India needs to increase R&D investment from 0.9 percent GDP to 3 percent over the longer run**

project, Chandrayan-1, placed a spacecraft in polar orbit. India is now ranked among a handful of countries that have a credible capability in space science and technology. India's space programme has led to the creation of the largest domestic communication system in the Asia–Pacific region. India developed the entire range of nuclear technologies, from prospecting for raw materials to designing and building large nuclear reactors, on a self-reliant basis. Other breakthroughs include low-cost generic drug production and a role as an emerging hub for clinical research and drug discovery (asthma, tuberculosis, vaccines); almost 20 percent of drugs entering Europe and the United States come from India. India has more than 60 facilities approved by the U.S. Food and Drug Administration. All this has been possible because of the availability of the high-quality science and engineering workforce produced by the Indian higher education system. However, with increasing demand by the Indian private sector and the multinational R&D centres, these systems will be under increasing pressure to attract and retain talent.

Meeting investment targets. To become globally competitive, India needs to increase R&D investment from 0.9 percent of GDP to 3 percent over the longer run. Gross expenditures on R&D have lagged far behind comparator countries (figure 14). R&D investment by multinational corporations and the domestic private sector—concentrated in pharmaceuticals, information and communication technology, electronics, and auto parts—has raised total R&D spending from a 20-year average of 0.88 percent of GDP to 1.1 percent in 2005. But domestic gross expenditures on R&D never exceeded 1 percent of GDP, although outlays (753 billion rupees or about $16.5 billion) in the Eleventh Plan are triple those in the Tenth Plan.[16] Moreover, these numbers, already low, mask the full extent of the problem. The share of the private sector is quite low, with the public sector accounting for 70–80 percent of R&D investment, the bulk of it in mission-oriented R&D, and only 20 percent is spent on civilian applications.

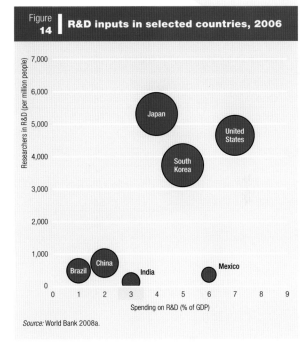

Figure 14 | R&D inputs in selected countries, 2006

Source: World Bank 2008a.

Making the most of existing knowledge. Creating new knowledge, while necessary, is costly and risky and requires scientific talent and other infrastructure. Economies that are still behind the technological frontier get larger gains in productivity and improvements in welfare from adopting existing knowledge than from doing R&D to push back the technological frontier. The main means of tapping into rapidly expanding global knowledge are trade, foreign direct investment, technology licencing, copying and reverse engineering, foreign education and training, and foreign technical information in print and on the Internet.

India has made little use of global knowledge, except to a small degree in education and, more recently, in foreign direct investment and trade (table 5). Thus there is a tremendous potential to increase productivity by diffusing global knowledge throughout the economy. This requires appropriate technological commercialization infrastructure, including intellectual property protection, technology transfer units at universities and R&D

Table 5 | **Global knowledge acquisition indicators, selected countries**

Indicator	Brazil	China	India	South Korea
Trade (% of GDP)				
1990	16	44	23	59
2006	26.5	73.9	47.6	85.3
Merchandise exports (% of GDP)				
1995	6.1	20.4	8.6	24.2
2006	12.9	36.6	13.2	36.7
Manufactured exports (% of merchandise exports)				
1995	54	84	74	93
2006	51	92	70	89
High-technology exports (% of manufactured exports)				
1998	9	15	5	27
2006	12	30	5	32
Commercial service exports (% of GDP)				
1995	0.8	2.5	1.9	4.3
2006	1.7	3.5	8.2	5.7
Computer. information, communication, and other business services (% of service exports)				
1995	23.6	24.4	31.4	34.5
2006	50.9	39.1	73.7	32.3
Tariff and nontariff barriers[a] (%)				
1995	56	20	0	69
2006	71	70	51	66
Average tariffs, 2006 (%)				
Average simple tariffs (%)	12.1	8.9	16.8	9.1
Average weighted tariff (%)	6.7	4.3	14.5	7.4
Foreign direct investment (FDI)	Much FDI is for production for protected domestic market rather than for export	One of main means of rapidly modernizing China	Much less FDI overall; only recently liberalized FDI regime	Very little FDI until after the 1997 Asian financial crisis
Average gross FDI (% of GDP)				
2000–05	3.4	3.2	0.90	0.90
Average gross FDI (% of GDP)				
2000–05	3.4	3.2	0.90	0.90
Royalty and licence fee payments, 2006 ($ millions)	1,404	5,321	421	4,487
Royalty and licence fee payments, 2006 (per million people)	7.5	4.1	0.4	92.7

Note: a. Normalized so that 0 is very high protection and 100 is very low protection.

Source: Dahlman 2008; World Bank 2008a.

> **Innovation and R&D can mitigate increases in social inequiality and relieve the pressures created by rapid urbanization**

institutes, science and technology parks, incubators, early stage finance, and venture capital. Further, human capital is critical for tapping into knowledge. India's low average education level combined with little access to global knowledge (because of inward-oriented public policies) has constrained the assimilation of foreign knowledge. Increasing enrolment of the rural and urban poor should advance the spread of new ideas, best practices, newer technologies, and the application of knowledge to low-productivity agriculture and industries.

Providing public support for public benefits. An innovative India will be inclusive as well as technologically advanced, improving the lives of all Indians. Innovation and R&D can mitigate increases in social inequality and relieve the pressures created by rapid urbanization. The growing divergence in productivity between agriculture and knowledge-intensive manufacturing and services threatens to increase income inequality. By encouraging India's R&D labs and universities to focus on the needs of poor people and by improving the ability of informal firms to absorb knowledge, an innovation and research agenda can counter this effect. Inclusive innovation can lower the costs of goods and services and create income-earning opportunities for poor people.

The Indian Council of Agricultural Research and the Council of Scientific and Industrial Research have demonstrated the potential for inclusive innovation to improve lives of rural residents. For example, as a result of technology developed by the Council of Scientific and Industrial Research's Central Institute of Medicinal and Aromatic Plants in Lucknow, India now exports almost 80 percent of the world's menthol mint essential oil. University and formal private initiatives, such as eChoupal and Amida's simple computer—the Simputer—have provided essential and timely information to farmers and improved rural literacy. Further, the National Innovation Foundation has a repository of 70,000 grassroots innovations and traditional knowledge practices—most of them developed in Indian towns and villages—that could provide significant benefits for both

innovators and consumers. A higher quality of life in rural India together with productivity gains in informal enterprises and agriculture might counterbalance some of the forces driving rapid urbanization. They could also ease the development challenges resulting from urbanization, including land use and infrastructure problems, environmental problems, and endemic poverty.

An innovative India will increase research and the dissemination of knowledge in the agriculture sector, which contributes more than 20 percent of GDP and provides livelihoods for more than half the population. While Indian agriculture has changed considerably—even achieving national food self-sufficiency—growth in agriculture remains low, with total factor productivity on the decline during the 1980s and 1990s.[17] The Indian Council of Agricultural Research has 47 R&D labs, complemented by one central and 39 state agricultural universities. Nonetheless, since the Green Revolution of the 1960s, India's agricultural research system has not produced any major breakthroughs. Private players account for only 12 percent of investments in agricultural research. To improve productivity, Indian agriculture needs to shift from resource- and input-based growth to knowledge- and science-based growth. It also needs to shed labour and move people from agriculture into agro-processing and other services. This will require the elimination of subsidies (power, water, fertilizer, food and others), consolidation of farms and substantial investments in training, education, irrigation, and rural infrastructure.

Global warming and climate change threaten India's ability to fully realize its development potential. An innovative India will harness its R&D capacity to improve energy efficiency, develop alternative and renewable energy and reduce carbon emissions, and meet India's vast and rising demand for energy. The National Action Plan on Climate Change, released in June 2008, outlines government policies for addressing climate mitigation and adaptation (India, Prime Minister's Council on Climate Change 2008). The plan proposes establishing eight core "national missions" on important areas,

Policies needs not rely on vague theories about the strengths and weaknesses of the government and the private sector—India need only look at its own experience to make the argument for a shift in the role of government

including solar energy, energy efficiency, and strategic knowledge for climate change. India needs to do more, however, including providing incentives (such as tax credits, matching grants, and results-based technology rewards) for innovation to promote behavioural change for improving efficiency and developing new technologies and processes. India should set up a centre of excellence—an advanced energy research centre to meet domestic needs. It should also lead global efforts in developing clean energy technologies by deploying its best scientific and engineering minds to this challenge.

Shift radically the roles of the government and the private sector

India needs a major paradigm shift in thinking among all groups—politicians, academicians, researchers, industry, students, parents, and civil society—with a new role for the government and the private sector.

The reform agenda to improve higher education, technology, and innovation needs a commensurately bold strategy to leverage the strengths of the public and private sectors. Incrementalism and band-aid solutions will not deliver the desired results. The government should become a catalyst for the provision of high-quality higher education and for cutting-edge R&D, rather than a proprietor and operator. It should primarily facilitate, support, and empower the private sector to undertake investments with public financial support and should focus on setting policy and implementing smart regulations and light oversight. It should link financial support to performance and outcomes and supply funds to the private and public sectors on a competitive basis. It should provide incentives such as tax credits (for students, education providers, and enterprises for R&D and skills upgrading) and financial incentives to expand capacity, improve quality and performance, and promote inclusivity. It should allow any remaining public institutions to function as business corporations and to make their own decisions in a market environment with suitable regulatory and accountability mechanisms. It should collaborate with international partners and encourage

an influx of new ideas and financial resources. Changing the stock of the educated workforce takes a long time. Action needs to start now.

Policies need not rely on vague theories about the strengths and weaknesses of the government and the private sector—India need only look at its own experience to make the argument for a shift in the role of government. First and foremost, given the scale of the required expansion, the Indian government simply cannot carry the full burden of necessary investments. Second, a crisis of governance is the largest barrier to the provision of high-quality higher education and R&D outputs in India, created largely by an imbalance of public and private sector roles. Last, against a backdrop of seemingly intractable challenges, India's successes— as well as those of the United States—suggest that a major shift in the role of government together with a large private sector presence will create a higher education, technology, and innovation system marked by high output, quality, efficiency, and relevance.

Scale of required expansion

As already mentioned, massive investment is needed in both higher education and technology development and use. In a country where total government expenditure hovers around 20 percent of GDP, doubling national commitments in higher education to 8 percent of GDP and more than tripling R&D investments to 3 percent of GDP would pose insurmountable fiscal challenges to a primarily public sector effort. Private sector investments and foreign direct investment—enabled by public investment and incentive regimes—must do the heavy lifting.

Moreover, India's political system has proven itself to be unreliable as a driving force of large-scale expansion in higher education and R&D. Over the past 30 years, the government's proposed expansions have been too timid, and many promises were never kept—the result of well-meaning but illusory political will that has yet to produce necessary action. Several successive governments, recognizing the importance of education and research, have announced the intention of reforming the

> The most critical weakness plaguing the Indian higher education and R&D system is a crisis of governance—a lack of political will at the highest level and a lack of execution at lower levels

| Box 6 | Factors that have made the Indian Institutes of Technology a global brand |

Five Indian Institutes of Technology were set up in the 1950s and 1960s, each with a foreign partner (France, Germany, Russia, United Kingdom and United States) and following international best practices. They shared certain successful characteristics:

- Autonomous, with independent professional governing boards.
- Generous public financial support and light oversight.
- Highly qualified and dedicated faculty, with conducive environment and remuneration.

- Merit-based student intake—5,000 (1.7 percent) selected annually out of 300,000 taking the entrance test.
- International brand name, with creative, open and supportive environment.
- Combined research and teaching, with strong partnership with industry.
- International collaboration and partnership, in both education and research.

sector and increasing funding, but actions have fallen far short of pledges.[18] India has also seen political concerns compromise opportunities to expand higher education through foreign direct investment and the export of education. Partnerships with foreign universities, including the establishment of satellite campuses in India, could expand domestic enrolment capacity and faculty supply without using scarce public resources. Allowing higher intakes of foreign students could expand opportunities for domestic students by tapping foreign financial inflows for tuition and living expenses. These modes of expansion, however, have been expressly excluded from reform agendas because of political arguments founded on false premises. Market rather than political forces must lead implementation of the reform agenda.

Crisis of governance and weak institutional capacity
The most critical weakness plaguing the Indian higher education and R&D system is a crisis of governance—a lack of political will at the highest level and a lack of execution at lower levels. Excessive centralization of higher education has resulted from overregulation and lack of autonomy in decision-making, pressures on admission, demand for quota-based reservations, political interference, and poor leadership. Also contributing to the poor health of the Indian higher education system are weak curricula, inappropriate teaching–learning methodologies, inadequate monitoring and quality assurance

mechanisms, uncommitted teachers who fail to keep current in their area of expertise, archaic evaluation procedures, and lack of accountability. Further, heavy reliance on public sector R&D structures, opaque governance, and regulatory red tape has contributed to the suboptimal performance of India's scientific establishment. The system lacks competition, a focus on excellence, and open debate as well as a supportive environment to pursue bold and risky ideas. A corps of dedicated and able teachers work at the management and technology institutes, but the lure of jobs abroad and in the private sector makes it increasingly difficult to attract the best and brightest to academia. Political pressures are adversely affecting even the small top-tier institutions, jeopardizing the generally effective meritocracy that has characterized them. The so-called independent governing boards have not functioned with independence and have routinely undermined education and R&D quality.

India's areas of excellence and the U.S. model
India must convert its "islands" of excellence into "rivers and mountains" of excellence by following the example of its premier institutions and encouraging, supporting, and scaling up its highly successful initiatives. India has not only the ingredients for success, including creative and entrepreneurial human capital and a comprehensive science and technology infrastructure but also several areas

> **India must replicate and scale up islands of excellence as the Indian Institutes of Technology and Indian Institutes of Management and space and nuclear research**

Box 7 | Examples of bold, highly successful initiatives that need to be scaled up throughout India

The University of Pune system has some 15,000 foreign students (up from 10,000 in the past two years), representing more than 40 percent of the national total. Almost 3,000 of 7,500 are at the university campus, paying five times more in tuition than Indian students do.

Central Leather Research Institute, the largest such institute in the world, has the goal of spreading and sustaining a technology culture in India's leather sector (the Leather Mission). The institute trains workers in all areas, from collecting raw materials to designing products. The global leather industry sources personnel from workers trained in India.

Several Council of Scientific and Industrial Research labs are implementing bold initiatives in partnership with the private sector. The Institute of Genomics and Integrative Biology has set up a state-of-the-art public–private R&D centre in New Delhi. The National Chemical Laboratory in Pune operates GE's plastics market intelligence service. The Central Institute of Medicinal and Aromatic Plants has developed a technology of menthol mint essential oil plant cultivation and processing in the Lucknow region.

India School of Business, a fully private initiative (except for the land, which was provided by the Andhra Pradesh government), offers world-class management education. It employs Indian and foreign faculty and conducts research. Its graduates are in high demand globally.

The University Institute of Chemical Technology, a premier state institution in Mumbai with a faculty of 80, produces 80 PhDs annually (10 percent of India's engineering PhDs) and plans to expand its capacity by 150 percent in the next two years with little public funding. It pioneered the practice of topping off its director's salary with private funds.

Reliance Industries established an Innovation Leadership Council (with Nobel laureates and other highly regarded international and national members) to lead its R&D and innovation agenda.

Piramal Health is developing several new drug molecules for the global market, using state-of-the-art R&D and clinical trial technologies.

The Indian Institute of Technology in Mumbai operates a business incubator providing faculty and students with a favourable environment for startups and commercialization of R&D.

The Department of Biotech of the Ministry of Science and Technology introduced an R&D support programme for the Indian pharmaceuticals industry, following international best practices including the model of the U.S. Small Business Innovation Research programme.

The Indian Institute of Science Education and Research in Pune attracts a large portion of its faculty from among nonresident Indians and began an integrated five-year MS/PhD programme for science graduates and several joint appointments with the National Chemical Laboratory.

The Technical Education Quality Improvement Program, launched in 1999 with World Bank help, supported scale-up efforts to improve the quality of technical education in India. The programme targets include graduating 10,000 students and training 1,000 teachers annually. Participating in the programme are 40 lead institutions (including 18 centrally funded National Institutes of Technology) and 88 state engineering/network institutions (including 20 polytechnics) in 13 states. Phase II is expected to be substantially enlarged to cover 200 more state engineering institutions.

where success has been demonstrated—such islands of excellence as the Indian Institutes of Technology and Indian Institutes of Management and space and nuclear research. India must replicate and scale up such successes, rather than allow these institutions to become mediocre by failing to cultivate the conditions that made

them a success (box 6). It should also support and scale-up highly successful initiatives that are being implemented throughout Indian institutions (box 7).

In higher education, technology, and innovation, India should move closer to the U.S. system, not the European or Japanese models. The United States has

> **❝ The government must collaborate globally to expand the exchange of knowledge, enable foreign direct investment and other financial inflows to fund expansion, and encourage commercialization of R&D**

| Box 8 | **U.S. system of higher education and research** |

- One of the best performing higher education and research systems in the world, with 7 of the 10 top universities—has 68 percent (34) of the world's top 50 universities with only 5 percent of world population (Zakaria 2008).
- With 30 percent of total foreign students globally, it is the preferred destination for foreign students.
- Multitier and flexible, with a mix of public and private not-for-profit and for-profit institutions.
- Universities as places for learning, experimentation, debate, and exchange of ideas.
- Autonomous, free of government interference and political pressures.
- Competitive and merit-based recruitment of students and faculty nationally and worldwide.
- Mobility of students, faculty, and administrators between academia, business, and government.

- Combined research and teaching, with competitive funding for basic and applied research.
- Limited government financial support, with major funding coming from the private sector and philanthropy.
- Strong international collaboration and partnership in both education and research.
- Comprehensive student financing programs, with a mix of loans, grants, scholarships, and part-time jobs.
- Strong collaboration between business and education institutions.
- Many centers of excellence, but only a few public research institutions in strategic areas such as National Institutes of Health, nuclear research labs (managed by a university).
- Major portion of research funded and conducted by private sector, with limited public support for risky and early-stage technology development.

a highly creative, productive, and market-linked higher education and research system that is the finest in the world (box 8). It attracts the best and the brightest from all over the world to study in its universities and research institutions. Dr. Lawrence H. Summers, former president of Harvard University, identifies five key lessons for India from the U.S. experience in higher education: the importance of competition, flexibility, the authority of ideas, generous philanthropy, and the combination of research and undergraduate study—"Universities must be places based on the authority of ideas, rather than the idea of authority" (Summers 2006).

In defining the new role for the government, India has much to learn from the key success factors of its "islands of excellence" and the U.S. system (see boxes 7 and 8). These include a major role for the private sector; real institutional autonomy with no government interference; strong focus on efficiency and excellence with merit-based selection of students and faculty; and vibrant competition, with strong links to the domestic and global markets.

Vision for government's role and proposed reforms
The government must enable the rapid expansion of higher education and India's technology development by establishing the requisite technological, institutional, and human infrastructure. It must respond to the crisis of governance by implementing smart regulations and limited oversight while granting institutions genuine autonomy to make independent decisions. To realize the full extent of the proposed expansion quickly, reliably, and efficiently, the government must embrace public-private financing schemes that permit direct links between institutions and market forces. At the same time, it must maintain public sector commitments to meet desired social ends, including the production of public goods and increased social equity. The government must also collaborate globally to expand the exchange of knowledge, enable foreign direct investment and other financial inflows to fund expansion, and encourage commercialization of R&D (box 9). In keeping with this vision of public, private, and international roles, India should enact the following reforms to seize its transformation opportunity.

> **❝ An independent Regulatory Authority for Higher Education should be created, drawing on the lessons of agencies such as the Telecommunications Regulatory Authority of India and the Securities and Exchange Board of India**

A modern intellectual property regime is critical for promoting innovation and facilitating technology commercialization. At the same time, India must protect its knowledge dissemination interests at the lowest possible costs, especially in areas of public concern such as health. It also must defend its interests in new technologies not yet fully regulated by international agreements. The government, recipients of funds, the inventor, and the public benefit from the protection and commercialization of intellectual property in the legislative framework introduced recently (similar to the U.S. Bayh-Dole Act of 1980) for incentivizing innovators and commercializing public funded R&D. While India has a fairly well developed metrology, standards, testing, and quality system, it is dominated by the public sector, and coverage, quality, and use of services are low.

Smart regulations and light oversight. The current regulatory and accreditation model for higher education institutions and programmes needs major overhauling. The University Grants Commission, the All India Council of Technical Education, and most other regulatory bodies are incapable of meeting today's challenges. In their place a new mixed public–private sector model should be installed, with strong links to market participants. An independent Regulatory Authority for Higher Education should be created, drawing on the lessons of agencies such as the Telecommunications Regulatory Authority of India and the Securities and Exchange Board of India—India's modern, booming telecommunications industry was created through intelligent regulation and re-regulation. The new universities should be set up under national umbrella legislation, with the state providing free land and signing a memorandum of understanding for a minimum set of education reforms that would enable the new institutions to serve as benchmarks of excellence. Similar umbrella legislation is needed for private and foreign participation in Indian higher education, such as the Not-for-Profit Education Corporation Law.

The new Regulatory Authority for Higher Education must be independent and have the authority to reward and impose sanctions. All institutions—public and private—should be required to fully disclose details on student intake, faculty, laboratory and other facilities, output standards, and other relevant information. There should be no licencing requirements, and accreditation should be optional for institutions that do not require public support. The private sector (and trade associations) should develop and manage accreditation bodies with transparent international standards. These bodies could be accredited by an independent professional public body, following practices in line with those practiced by the Quality Council of India.

Colleges should be free to award their own degrees and diplomas, and the unwieldy affiliation system should be gradually dismantled. Major R&D labs (such as the Council of Scientific and Industrial Research, the Indian Council of Agricultural Research, the Indian Council of Medical Research, and some of their more selective labs such as the Centre for Cellular and Molecular Biology, the Indian Institute of Science, the National Chemical Laboratory, and the University Institute of Chemical Technology in Mumbai) and large colleges should receive university status, giving them autonomy and reducing the burden on the universities.[20] For assessing the quality of outputs from different institutions, national standards could be developed for entry to graduate and postgraduate programmes, similar to the Graduate Record Exam, Graduate Management Admissions Test, Law School Admissions Test, and Medical College Admissions Test in the United States. For vocational and professional trades, certification programs could be set up by industry and trade associations. In the longer run, the market (employers, parents, and students) will recognize and reward quality and penalize poor performing higher education institutions.

Governance and autonomy. Academic and research institutions need full autonomy—institutional, financial, academic, and pedagogic—which demands a radical

> **India should enable its private sector to play a major role in financing and managing the institutions of higher education**

shift to liberate these institutions from political and bureaucratic control. Indian academic and research institutions lack true autonomy today. Continuous erosion of autonomy is evident even in institutions such as the Indian Institutes of Technology and the Indian Institutes of Management, which have experienced pressures in recent years from the sudden increase in students due to quota-based reservations, application of reservations to faculty, and centralization of the selection of directors. While a vigilant academic community can defend the institutions against government incursions, sound governance systems should be able to avoid the need to do so.[21]

Full autonomy would require fiscal and managerial autonomy; high-quality leadership; greater private sector participation in management and funding; professional accreditation of colleges and universities; merit-based selection of students, faculty and institutional managers, subject to constitutional provisions and guarantees; high opportunity of mobility for researchers; and active collaboration with R&D laboratories and industry. There is no justification for reservations in faculty recruitment, particularly when Indian institutions are facing a severe shortage of faculty at all levels. Institutes of higher education and research should function like modern business corporations in their management, administration, and financial processes. The University Acts, as well as the enabling legislations for the Council of Scientific and Industrial Research, the Indian Council of Agricultural Research, and the Indian Council of Medical Research networks, need to be rewritten to reflect a new culture of innovative, effective and accountable governance, and efficient management. The location of new universities should be based on potential synergies (not just on achieving a more uniform geographic coverage) arising from co-location with existing highly regarded institutions and laboratories.

India needs to improve the performance of public R&D investments by reforming and examining the relevance of national R&D laboratories. As the private sector engages increasingly in its own research and development, international review boards should examine the performance and even the relevance of the vast chains of public institutions, such as the Council of Scientific and Industrial Research (CSIR), the Indian Council of Agricultural Research (ICAR), and the Indian Council of Medical Research (ICMR). These reviews should guide government actions, including a public sector retreat from certain R&D labs, by privatizing some public institutions, transferring some to universities, converting some into research universities, and closing some. Those that remain in the public sector should be operated as commercial corporations, generating revenues and subject to transparent management with full accountability and a performance-based rewards system. Steps should also be taken to increase cross-institutional synergies and focus on market needs and commercialization of the R&D outputs of the CSIR, the ICAR, and the ICMR networks.

After restructuring, these national R&D networks should focus on two key areas of national importance—inclusive innovation and development of cutting-edge technologies, such as those related to climate change and public health. The public R&D networks must play a strong role in these areas as the private sector is not likely to invest in such technologies, at least not within the next decade. To improve the relevance and quality of research at the public R&D labs, a major part of their research funding should be allocated on a transparent and competitive basis (instead of as an automatic annual budget allocation) involving other labs, universities, and the corporate sector—along the lines of how the U.S. National Science Foundation allocates research funding, with most universities competing fiercely for research funding among themselves and with industry. The regulatory regime for technology development and innovation also needs a major overhaul, with smart regulations and oversight, to make it market driven and to enable Indian industry to compete globally.

Public–private financing. India should enable its private sector (as well as foreign direct investment)

> **Under new public-private partnerships, most institutions, programmes, and initiatives would be publicly funded but privately managed, bringing the professionalism, efficiency, and growth characteristics of the private sector into the education system**

to play a major role in financing and managing the institutions of higher education. Under new public-private partnerships, most institutions, programmes, and initiatives would be publicly funded but privately managed, bringing the professionalism, efficiency, and growth characteristics of the private sector into the education system. Government should focus its energy and resources on public goods—such as primary and secondary education, where social returns are highest—to provide a solid foundation and adequate inflow of students for higher education and research. At the higher education level, a substantial portion of services provided are private goods, related to employment and earning potential. Vocational education and training is completely employment-related and thus should be left entirely to the corporate sector. Many prestigious U.S. institutions, such as the Massachusetts Institute of Technology and Stanford University, are funded almost entirely by private money.

India needs to set up comprehensive student loan programmes. Through a public-private partnership, the government should establish a Student Loan Finance Corporation (like Sallie Mae in the United States) to provide student loans and loan guarantees directly and through commercial banks. Further, tuition expenses on higher education should be tax deductible. As in China and the United States, establishing financing mechanisms for scholarships and soft loans through special instruments funded by the government and private sector would establish a balance among accessibility, social equity, and competitive quality. It would meet the country's responsibility towards the public goods component of education and provide returns to investors in for-profit institutions.

Tuition fees should be increased gradually in existing institutions, but the new norms could be implemented from the start in new institutions. Students should also be encouraged to "earn while they learn". Tuition levels, which have been kept very low, mostly for political reasons, need to be raised across the board to provide necessary financial resources for academic institutions.

This would enable them to compete for high-quality faculty and students, provide competitive compensation to faculty, create modern infrastructure, and invest in global programmes. In many cases, fees do not cover even 5 percent of operating costs. Since most university students come from the wealthiest 10 percent of the population, they should be able to pay fees amounting to 20–30 percent of the operating costs of a general university education. The fees for professional courses could be much higher—close to full costs—and even more for foreign students. Most parents and students, rich or poor, are already paying high fees to get into most private (and some public) professional institutions. Disadvantaged students can be supported through means-based public scholarships. A competitive environment in fees will eventually reduce the cost of education for all.

India needs a huge expansion in vocational education, training, and skills-development capacity, but this should be done by the private sector. Certificate-level training in India is provided by 5,114 industrial training bodies—1,896 are state government–run industrial training institutes and 3,218 are private industrial training centres. Their total intake capacity is 773,000 students (415,000 seats in government-run industrial training institutes and 358,000 in private industrial training centres). In addition, there are 1,292 polytechnic institutes with an intake capacity of 265,000. More than half of these vocational training institutes are in southern India. Although certificate holders have relatively better labour market outcomes than students with only a grade 10 or 12 education, more than 60 percent remain unemployed three years after earning their certificates. The central government provides vocational training to about 20 percent of the annual additions to the labour force; thus 80 percent of new entrants have no opportunity for skills training.[22]

Since vocational education and training are entirely employment related, they should be left to the private sector. The government should withdraw from all vocational institutions, turning them over to the private sector or closing them. Industry should take full responsibility

> **" More favourable matching grant support for inclusive early-stage technology development could significantly increase collaboration among public R&D entities, universities, nongovernmental organizations, industry, and global networks**

for the provision and financing of vocational education and training. This would result in better linkages with markets, higher quality, more efficient service delivery at a lower cost, and financing entirely from user fees, freeing scarce public resources for investment in primary and secondary education. The government should provide matching grants to small and informal businesses and grants or loans to students who cannot afford the fees. (The informal sector in India contributes 59 percent of GDP, and employs 94 percent of the total workforce.)

Financing technology development. The government should finance basic research and support applied research and technology dispersion, since R&D has both public and private good elements. Such support should be result-based and provided competitively. The government should provide incentives (such as R&D tax credits, matching grants, loan guarantees, technology rewards, and training support) to the private sector for applied research, technology development, use and dispersion. For example, the United States government provides 20–25 percent of funds for early-stage technology development through programmes such as the Small Business Innovation Research Programme and the Advanced Technology Programme (a stage in the innovation cycle that private investors often find too risky).[23] Such programmes help to develop synergies among universities, R&D labs, and industry. The flagship New Millennium India Technology Leadership Initiative (and other public R&D support programmes) should be scaled up and transformed, following international best practices, to enhance commercialization, accountability, business participation, and global collaboration.

India's innovation infrastructure should aim to reconcile internal asymmetries and serve the dual purposes of global competitiveness and inclusive growth. India should pursue frontier as well as inclusive innovation to benefit all its people. The National Innovation Foundation has a depositary of almost 70,000 grassroots innovations. The government, in collaboration with technical schools and the private sector, should implement

appropriate schemes to convert many of these innovations into viable products and business. Further, more favourable matching grant support for inclusive early-stage technology development could significantly increase collaboration among public R&D entities, universities, nongovernmental organizations, industry, and global networks. India's successes with inclusive innovation can be of interest to other developing and emerging market economies.

International collaboration and global citizenship. India should welcome foreign investment in higher education and R&D. Even though many of India's premier institutions (such as the first five Indian Institutes of Technology and the India School of Business in Hyderabad) were set up with strong foreign collaboration, India has not taken adequate advantage of the resources available at foreign academic and research institutions. India should invite reputed foreign universities to establish campuses or full universities in India (and allow Indian institutions to open campuses abroad). This will help to expand capacity without using scarce public resources, will increase the supply of faculty, and will bring diversity and competition that will improve the quality of domestic institutions. Partnerships between Indian and foreign universities will help to attract and retain high-quality staff and will provide opportunities for students to receive internationally-recognized credentials. It could also save a part of the $4 billion spent annually by some 100,000 Indians who study abroad.[24] Such changes will require a forward-looking policy and legal framework that welcomes foreign direct investment in higher education rather than shuns it.

India should capitalize on its low-cost advantage and English-speaking traditions for exporting higher education. Some two million higher education students are currently studying outside their home country, according to United Nations Educational Scientific and Cultural Organization (UNESCO) estimates.[25] A U.K. study based on UNESCO data estimated "that the total global

> **If India gets its skills-development policies right, it could have a skilled workforce surplus of about 47 million**

demand for international student places will increase from about 2.1 million in 2003 to approximately 5.8 million by 2020, with demand in the Main English Speaking Destination Countries forecast to increase from about 1 million places to about 2.6 million places."[26] India currently has 35,000 foreign students in its higher education system but has the potential to increase this to as much as 1 million in the next decade. By tapping the financial inflows of foreign students for tuition, Indian institutions can develop a new and reliable revenue stream that will allow them to expand domestically and reach even more foreign students. The indirect benefits of exporting education are also important. For example, no small part of the influence and strength of the United States in its global policies over the last few years have been derived from the way foreign students who studied in the United States view that country.[27] A rising superpower such as India should consider this as an explicit strategy and should devise open and progressive policies for bringing higher education into the world market, including proper visa and travel norms, infrastructure, and other facilities.

India has the potential to become a global skills centre by seizing high value-added global employment opportunities (including in R&D). The unprecedented opportunity for skills development arises from a unique 25-year window of opportunity—India's demographic dividend. According to the Indian Planning Commission, India has the youngest population in the world; its median age in 2000 was less than 24 compared with 41 for Japan, 38 for Europe, and 30 for China, giving India a comparative cost advantage over others for the next quarter century. The ageing of those other economies is expected to create a skilled personnel shortage of 56.5 million by 2020. If India gets its skills-development policies right, it could have a skilled workforce surplus of about 47 million. Already, India accounts for 28 percent of the graduate talent pool among 28 of the world's lowest cost economies. In the 1990s, the Indian diaspora made a large contribution to the Silicon Valley information technology revolution in the United States, creating almost 25 percent of the start-up companies. Further,

Indians represent more than 20 percent of staffing at major information technology corporations in the United States—including Cisco, Intel, and Microsoft.[28]

India needs to improve the capacity of the private sector (including the informal sector) to harness domestic and global knowledge. This would include making appropriate changes in foreign direct investment, trade, technology licencing, and royalty payment regulations as well as leveraging Indian diaspora talent (and that of a higher skilled workforce). Some 2 percent of India's population—20 million people—lives abroad, with earnings almost equal to two-thirds of India's GDP.[29] India cannot remain solely a supply system of talents. Re-inventing and reverse engineering models of growth are also not sustainable for a modern, growth-oriented economy. India needs to transform this "brain drain" to a "brain gain" and eventually to "brain circulation". It will take unusual measures—such as those that Singapore and South Korea implemented and that China is implementing now—to attract the best talent from other parts of the world, particularly people of Indian origin living abroad and excelling in their areas of science and technology, and management. India also needs to leverage such technology-led diplomacy.

India should create centres of excellence in key education and strategic research areas. That effort should include increased efforts in producing more economically relevant public goods such as pre-competitive research, and socially relevant innovations, such as access to clean water, low cost housing, urban congestion, urban transport, clean energy technologies, renewable energy, Ayurveda and traditional medicine, public health, and technologies for sustainable livelihoods. These centres should be established and operated with strong public-private partnership and international collaboration. India should set up a clean coal technology research centre to develop state-of-the-art technologies for national and global use and become a global leader in this critical technology. Because of the global public goods nature, such a centre might be organized under a new consultative group for energy research,

" **India should create centres of excellence in key education and strategic research areas**

with support from the international community. It could follow the example of the best-known international public goods R&D effort, the Consultative Group for International Agricultural Research, which led the Green Revolution. This is also a practical way of tapping into international resources (financial and technological) that are becoming more available in the context of international agreements on climate change. This initiative will not only help India meet its energy needs, but will also add to its global citizenship credentials.

INDIA
2039

Part III

Chapter

10

Energy and
sustainability
in affluent
India

Energy and sustainability in affluent India: Unleashing an energy revolution

Hossein Razavi

The International Energy Agency (IEA) refers to India as a slumbering giant who will soon awaken with a ravenous thirst for energy. In 2005, India's total primary energy demand was 537 million tons (Mtoe) of oil equivalent, roughly equal to that of Japan. While India's current energy consumption rate is considered inefficient, the most serious concern, in lieu of its rapid economic growth, is its future energy demand. Because of its sheer size, India's future energy needs will have a substantial impact on world energy markets, while also increasing India's exposure to the market's instability.

India is facing unprecedented challenges in the energy sector, which include:

- Sustained surge in economic growth, resulting in a rapid growth in energy demand.
- Noticeable increase in dependence on energy imports as demand outstrips domestic supply.
- Substantial increase in the level and fluctuations of international energy prices, translating into costly and uncertain sources of energy imports.
- A growing political pressure by the international community that it reduce carbon emissions. This is a result of increasing recognition by the international community of the potential impact of energy use on climate change.

Adding to the complexity of India's energy challenge are such contentious issues as the lack of access to electricity services by some 400 million people, widespread environmental damages of energy use, slow progress in the sector reform process, and the social and political constraints in dealing with energy subsidies.

This chapter examines India's energy sector in the context of emerging international trends and identifies the challenges and opportunities that India faces over the next three decades. It compares the implications of a "business-as-usual" scenario of energy growth on energy supply, security, and climate change. Using various measures of energy efficiency and fuel diversification options, it aims to arrive at policies that would enable the country to move toward a more sustainable scenario. The chapter also proposes a benchmark for energy efficiency that gives India the flexibility to meet the energy requirements for economic growth while also enabling it to pursue the efficiency standards that industrial economies plan to achieve. Associated with this benchmark is a package for cooperation between India and the international community that would allow India to access—and afford—the most advanced energy technologies as they become available.

The international context

While some forecasts of world energy consumption predict enormous growth over the next several decades, the two most highly regarded forecasts—by the International Energy Agency[1] and the U.S. Energy Information Administration[2]—assume that continuous improvements in energy efficiency will keep global energy consumption growth rates at 1.5–2.0 percent a year over 2005–30. Under these business-as-usual scenarios, world energy consumption would expand 55 percent during the next 25 years, with developing countries accounting for some 80 percent of the overall growth. Developing countries today account for 52 percent of energy consumption; that share would rise to 62 percent by 2030 under this scenario (figure 1).

Two consequences of this growth path make it unacceptable. First, the oil component of the projected increase in energy consumption (figure 2) would require a 27 million barrels a day (mbd) expansion in global capacity, resulting in increases of oil imports from about 40 mbd in 2005 to 65 mbd in 2030 (figure 3). Much of these imports are expected to come from a few Middle Eastern countries (figures 4 and 5), which raises concern about the reliability of oil supply.

Second, a much more serious concern is that the increase in carbon dioxide emissions associated with rising energy consumption would cause an irresistible

> **Global carbon dioxide emissions associated with rising energy consumption would soar from 28 gigatonnes in 2005 to 42 gigatonnes by 2030 and 62 gigatonnes by 2050**

Figure 1
Developing countries are expected to increase their share of world energy consumption relative to industrial countries through 2030

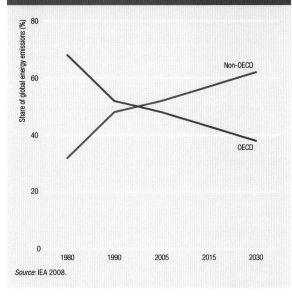

Source: IEA 2008.

damage to the global environment. World-wide, the energy-related carbon dioxide emissions were about 28 gigatons (GT) in 2005. Under this business-as-usual growth scenario, emissions would soar to 42 GT by 2030 and 62 GT by 2050 (figure 6). This level of emissions would lead to a concentration of greenhouse gases in the atmosphere of 650 parts per million (ppm), which could raise global temperatures by around 6° C above pre-industrial levels, causing irreversible changes in the global climate. To limit the average increase in global temperatures to a maximum of 2.4° C, which is considered necessary to ensure stability of the global climate, the concentration of greenhouse gases in the atmosphere would have to be stabilized at around 450 ppm. This so-called 450 stabilization case would require that energy-related carbon dioxide emissions peak at around 30 GT by 2015 and decline thereafter to 23 GT by 2030 and 14 GT by 2050. This ambitious target was translated by the IEA (2008) into a new scenario that advocates a global revolution in energy supply and

Figure 2
The mix of energy sources will change, but oil will still be the most important in 2030

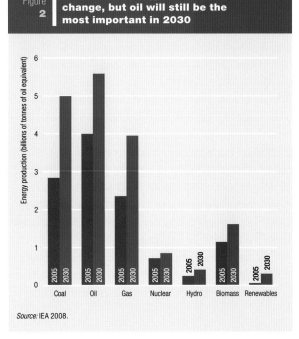

Source: IEA 2008.

Figure 3
OPEC producers are expected to account for most of the increase in oil production through 2030

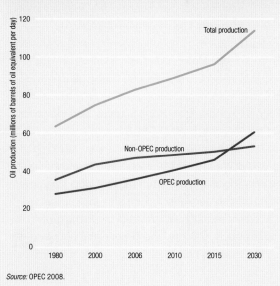

Source: OPEC 2008.

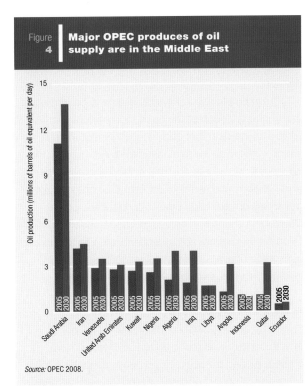

Figure 4 | Major OPEC produces of oil supply are in the Middle East

Source: OPEC 2008.

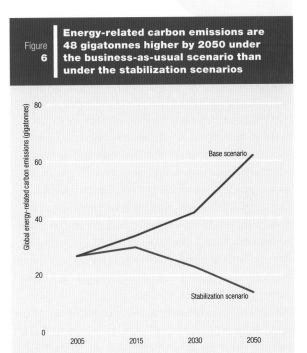

Figure 6 | Energy-related carbon emissions are 48 gigatonnes higher by 2050 under the business-as-usual scenario than under the stabilization scenarios

Source: Author's estimates based on IEA (2008).

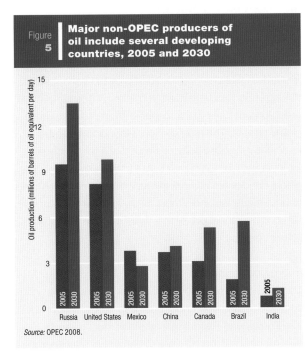

Figure 5 | Major non-OPEC producers of oil include several developing countries, 2005 and 2030

Source: OPEC 2008.

use. It would require far greater energy efficiency, large-scale use of renewable and nuclear energy, and deployment of carbon capture and storage technologies.

Reduction of carbon dioxide to 14 GT by 2050 is not a forecast but a target path. While current technologies and trends do not foresee a feasible way of moving onto this target path, the international community has decided that it has no choice but to push towards it. The shift from the business-as-usual scenario to the stabilization scenario will cost an estimated $40 trillion in additional investments in research, technology development, and improved energy supply infrastructure.

Reversal of world carbon emissions to this extent requires a fundamental change in the carbon intensity of economic growth. The long debate about the tradeoffs between economic growth and lower carbon emissions has generally reached the conclusion that a programme of action on climate change has to both stabilize carbon emissions and maintain growth. That leaves just one

> **India needs to decouple energy consumption from economic growth to avoid jeopardizing its potential for economic growth**

choice: to dramatically increase carbon productivity. This "carbon revolution" has been compared to the industrial and technology revolutions of the 20th century (figure 7).[3]

The histories of the industrial and information technology revolutions show that, with the right incentives and institutional structures, dramatic change and innovation are possible. These experiences have led to increased productivity and have created opportunities for growth and prosperity. The carbon revolution could do the same, although the speed of increase in productivity would have to be much faster than in those previous revolutions (see figure 7). There are also some other major differences. The eventual benefit of a carbon revolution—management of climate change—is a global public good rather than a private good. The industrial and technology revolutions were driven by the opportunity to make exceptional profits; the carbon revolution is driven by the imperatives of world survival. While the rise

in labour productivity resulted in cost savings and higher standards of living, the increase in carbon productivity will require substantial spending and some reduction in comfort.

The international community seems to be arriving at a willingness to accept the need for collective sacrifice while also insisting that each country contribute a fair share. In the medium term, sacrifice by some countries will create opportunity for others. Most industrial countries provide substantial funds to finance greenhouse gas emission reduction projects and technologies. Developing countries can use this unprecedented opportunity to adapt advanced technologies and to take advantage of available financial resources, while also fulfilling their role as good international citizens.

India's energy picture

Under the above global conditions, India will not be able to consume as much energy as it would have otherwise used to support its process of economic expansion. Energy supplies, moving forward, will likely become more scarce, less reliable, and increasingly expensive. Energy consumption will be under more strict international scrutiny. India thus needs to decouple energy consumption from economic growth to avoid jeopardizing its potential for such growth. It should also decouple carbon emissions from energy consumption in order to contribute to international efforts to protect the global climate. The next section will outline a number of forecasts regarding business-as usual energy scenarios for India. All will be unsustainable under expected future global conditions. Later sections will deal with a sustainable scenario that India must follow in order to be a responsible global player that wishes to join the ranks of affluent nations.

Energy consumption

There is a wide range of forecasts for India's future energy consumption under business-as-usual scenarios. The Energy and Resource Institute of India predicts an expansion of more than 400 percent in total energy

Figure 7

Carbon productivity growth needs to be three times faster than the rise in labour productivity during the industrial revolution

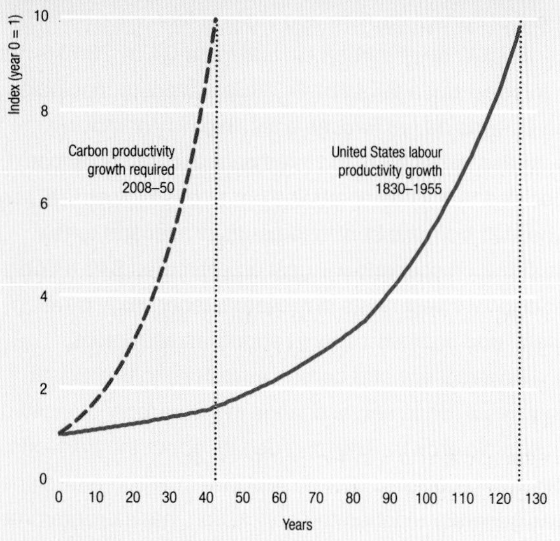

Carbon productivity growth required 2008–50

United States labour productivity growth 1830–1955

Source: McKinsey and Co. 2008.

❝ The carbon emission of electricity generation in India is about 50 percent higher than the international average, even compared with countries that rely heavily on coal

use over the next 25 years.[4] The baseline projection of the Indian Planning Commission's integrated energy policy for the country, developed by a team of experts in 2005, also foresees a 400 percent expansion in energy demand over the next 25 years.[5] In contrast, the IEA forecasts a total growth of 140 percent during the same period.[6]

This chapter suggests a slightly different business-as-usual scenario. It assumes an average annual economic growth of 9 percent, which is higher than the growth rates used by the IEA. It further assumes that India will continue on its path of improving energy efficiency. The forecast period that it uses is extended to 2050 since the global debate on energy consumption is focused on a timeline that extends until 2050. The results can thus be compared with the parameters of the international context. Based on the assumptions mentioned earlier, total energy consumption can be expected to grow at an average annual rate of 4.91 percent, for a total expansion of 230 percent over 2005–30.

This business-as-usual forecast is based as well on various assumptions about growth specific to the different sectors. First, it assumes that energy demand in the residential and services sectors, the largest components of energy demand, will be met largely by oil, electricity, and biomass. It further assumes that the share of total energy consumption used by those sectors can be expected to decline from 51 percent in 2005 to 28 percent in 2050. Second, it assumes that the industrial sector's energy use will be met largely by coal, oil, and electricity. It further assumes that industry's share in total energy consumption can be expected to rise from 28 percent to 33 percent. Finally, regarding the transport sector, it assumes that it is the major consumer of oil and will account for 28 percent of energy demand in 2050, up from 10 percent in 2005.

This energy consumption scenario translates into substantial growth for all primary energy sources. The largest increase is expected to be in coal, whose share is predicted to increase from 39 percent in 2005 to 48 percent in 2050. The share of natural gas is predicted to

increase from 5 percent to 7.5 percent, while the share of oil is predicted to remain stable at 24–25 percent. Biomass will account for a declining share, from 29 percent in 2005 to 9.5 percent in 2050, with its use growing from 158 Mtoe to 402 Mtoe. Nuclear energy's share will be less than 4 percent, although its use is expected to increase from 5 Mtoe to 169 Mtoe. The share of solar and wind energy will be less than 2 percent of total energy supply, though its use will grow from 1 Mtoe to 63 Mtoe.

While some of these primary energy sources are used directly by final consumers, a substantial part is often converted to electricity. In fact, electricity demand is the fastest growing component of final energy consumption. It is expected to grow at an average annual rate of 5.5 percent, which would require an expansion of about 1,500 gigawatts (GW) in generating-capacity over 2005–50.

Carbon emissions

India was the fifth-largest emitter of energy-related carbon dioxide in 2005. Two-thirds of emissions came from burning coal, mainly in the power sector. The efficiency of coal-based power plants remains low by international standards. As a result, the carbon dioxide emission of electricity generation in India is about 50 percent higher than the international average, even compared with countries that rely heavily on coal, such as Australia, Indonesia, South Africa, and the United States. The transport sector accounted for 8 percent of India's carbon dioxide emissions in 2005 and its share is expected to grow to 15 percent by 2050. In comparison, the transport sector's share of carbon dioxide was 31 percent in the United States and 24 percent in the European Union in 2005.

Implications for energy security

The key factors that go into assessing energy security are the diversity of a country's fuel mix, its dependence on imports, the concentration of sources of imports, and political stability in the exporting countries.[7] India

> **India has a reasonably diverse energy resource base, including coal, oil, gas, hydro, biomass, and wind and solar, but the most serious security concern relates to the increasing dependence on imported oil**

has a reasonably diverse energy resource base, which includes coal, oil, gas, hydro, biomass, and wind and solar. The development of some of these resources, however, has remained below potential, particularly with regards to coal, gas, and solar. Furthermore, a most serious security concern relates to the increasing dependence on imported oil.

Oil—reducing the heavy reliance on imports

India has limited oil reserves (5.6 billion barrels) and a small and declining oil production capacity. Total oil production was about 800,000 barrels a day in 2006, which is expected to expand slightly in the next two years before declining gradually to 500,000 barrels a day by 2030. Under the business-as-usual scenario, India would need to increase its oil imports from about 2 mbd in 2006 to 3 mbd in 2015, 6 mbd in 2030, and 15 mbd in 2050. India's major oil suppliers are Saudi Arabia (25 percent), Nigeria (16 percent), Kuwait (12 percent), Iran (10 percent), Iraq (8 percent), United Arab Emirates (7 percent), Malaysia (4 percent), and Yemen (4 percent). Smaller amounts are also imported from Angola, Egypt, Libya, and other countries. Long before 2050, India's sources of oil imports will be concentrated in just a few countries, as many of its current foreign sources lose their export potential because of declining production and increasing domestic consumption.

Total oil export capacity in the Middle East will be around 19 mbd in 2030, mainly from Saudi Arabia, Iraq, Kuwait, and the United Arab Emirates (table 1). Considering that competing demand for their oil exports will be high, India's first concern would be how much of these exports it would be able to access.

A second concern relates to the security of oil supplies from such concentrated—and sometimes vulnerable—sources of supply. Iraq's security situation is an obvious difficulty. Kuwait's reliability as a source of long-term supply became more questionable after the 1991 invasion. And the picture is changing in Saudi Arabia, once seen as a secure source of supply because of its substantial excess capacity and political stability.

With the emerging demand–supply situation, Saudi Arabia's ability to maintain any excess capacity is more uncertain, while the planned terrorist attacks against its major oil installations (though uncovered in advance) create further uncertainty. The shipping route for these oil imports, through the Straits of Hormuz at the mouth of the Persian Gulf, gives rise to other misgivings. Although the Straits of Hormuz have never been closed for military or political reasons, the growing tensions over Iran's nuclear programme force consideration of the risks of disruptions to shipping in the event of a serious conflict in the region.

To mitigate the risks of short-term supply disruptions, the government decided in 2004 to build a strategic stockpile of crude oil. The stockpile will eventually reach about 110 million barrels, to be accumulated in three phases between now and 2016. The first phase of about 35 million barrels is to be completed by 2012 at an estimated cost of $2.7 billion.

Natural gas—uncertainty of supply

India has proven natural gas reserves of 1,100 billion cubic metres (bcm), with good prospects for additional discoveries. Domestic production totalled 29 bcm in 2005 and is expected to increase to 45 bcm by 2015 and peak at 60 bcm by 2025 before declining to 50 bcm in 2030 and 42 bcm in 2040. To meet its surging natural gas demand, India would need to increase its imports from 6 bcm to 12 bcm by 2010. After that, the growth in domestic gas production could meet the increase in demand until 2020. Then, between 2020 and 2030, gas imports would need to expand rapidly, and to reach about 60 bcm by 2030. Liquefied natural gas (LNG) would be the most effective way to import gas. Several pipeline projects have been proposed, including ones from Burma, Iran,[8] Oman, and Turkmenistan, but they all face significant technical (gas availability) and geopolitical challenges. They are thus not likely to be completed in the foreseeable future.

Until a few years ago, dependence on imported natural gas was considered less risky than dependence

> **❝ The perception that dependence on imported natural gas is considered less risky than dependence on imported oil is quickly changing as sources of natural gas are dwindling**

Table 1 | **Oil production and consumption by major OPEC producers, 2007 and 2030**

Country	Reserves (billion barrels)	Production (million barrels a day)		Consumption (million barrels a day)		Exports available (million barrels a day)	
		2005	2030	2005	2030	2005	2030
Indonesia	9	1.1	1.0	1.1	1.6	0.0	0.0
Iran	138	4.2	4.5	1.6	3.8	2.6	0.7
Iraq	115	1.9	4.0	0.4	1.2	1.5	2.8
Kuwait	96	2.7	3.3	0.3	0.6	2.4	2.7
Qatar	12	1.1	3.2	0.1	0.1	1.0	3.1
Saudi Arabia	264	11.1	13.7	2.0	4.2	9.1	9.5
United Arab Emirates	97	2.8	3.1	0.4	1.2	2.4	1.9
Total Middle East	756	23.8	31.8	5.9	12.7	17.9	19.1
Algeria	12	2.1	4.0	0.3	0.5	1.8	3.5
Libya	41	1.7	1.7	0.4	0.8	1.3	0.9
Angola	9	1.4	3.1	0.3	0.6	1.1	2.5
Nigeria	36	2.5	3.5	0.6	1.2	1.9	1.3
Ecuador	6	0.5	0.6	0.2	0.3	0.3	0.3
Venezuela	87	2.9	3.5	0.6	1.2	2.3	2.3
Total OPEC	935	36.1	49.3	8.2	17.3	27.9	32.0

Source: OPEC 2008.

on imported oil. This perception is quickly changing as sources of gas imports are dwindling. From at least 10 nearby countries that were previously considered potential exporters of substantial volumes of natural gas, the list is now down to one or two countries.

The most likely scenario involves gas imports in the form of LNG from Qatar. Although Qatar has declared a moratorium on commitments of future gas exports, it is likely to expand export volumes once its ongoing reserve study is completed. Iran might be a future source of LNG, but it cannot be relied on right now. Its gas production capacity is insufficient to meet its own requirements, which include vast and growing domestic consumption and the rapidly increasing volumes for re-injection into oil wells. It is conceivable that under exceptionally improved circumstances, Iran could develop enough production capacity to meet its own needs, plus some limited exports. However, the internal

debate over the gas export policy is far from concluded, and the lack of a resolution prevents the country from making any major export commitments. While Iran's gas production is managed by its national oil company, there is also a gas-exporting company that continues to negotiate purchases that are not forthcoming in the foreseeable future. While India may want to continue to pursue such negotiations, it should not count on such gas volumes until contracts are completely finalized. Whether LNG imports are sourced from Qatar or from both Qatar and Iran, the fact remains that these supplies have to be shipped through the Straits of Hormuz, and that itself would carry a potential risk of interruption, as explained earlier.

> **For India, improved energy security depends mainly on reducing energy requirements, increasing domestic production of gas and coal, and diversifying on a large scale towards solar and nuclear energy**

Coal—abundant, but low quality and costly to transport

India has the world's fifth largest coal reserves (after the United States, Russia, China, and Australia) and is the third largest consumer of coal (after China and the United States). Its recoverable coal reserves are estimated at 36 billion tons, for a reserve-production ratio of 80 years at current rates of production. Indian coal is typically of poor quality (low heat and high ash content), however, making it inefficient to use and costly to transport. Total coal production was 252 metric tons carbon equivalent (Mtce) in 2005 and it is expected to increase to 354 Mtce in 2015, 637 Mtce in 2030, and 725 Mtce in 2040. Coal deposits are located mainly in the east, while consumption is concentrated mostly in the north, south and west. Therefore, transport costs play an important role in the economics of coal use.

Domestic coal is normally competitive in mine-mouth types of use, while imported coal is advantageous for users adjacent to a port. The recent increase in international coal prices has made domestic coal more attractive to many users, except those whose quality requirements cannot be met by local coal. A shift to imported coal is taking place in the steel industry, where the quality of domestic coking coal does not meet the industry's requirements, and also in power generation, where production of local steam coal is not keeping pace with demand with respect to quality and quantity. Coking coal is imported mostly from Australia. Steam coal is imported from Indonesia, with smaller quantities from China and Australia. Total coal imports were 36 Mtce in 2005, accounting for 12 percent of consumption. The share of imports is expected to rise to 28 percent by 2030. Coal India has invested in coal mining in Australia and Indonesia.

Implications

Although energy trade is a proven instrument for improving the economic efficiency of energy supply, it introduces considerable uncertainty to the energy security equation. For India, improved energy security depends mainly on reducing energy requirements, increasing domestic production of gas and coal, and diversifying on a large scale towards solar and nuclear energy. To a limited extent, India could also improve energy security by making more strategic use of natural gas, particularly where it can be substituted for oil rather than coal. This policy would translate into larger coal imports, which creates its own tradeoffs between energy security and environmental impacts.

Prospects for improving energy efficiency

There are prospects to improve energy efficiency in all uses , particularly the power sector. India had 146 GW of power-generating capacity in 2005, with coal accounting for more than 70 percent. India's coal power plants are among the least efficient in the world, with an average conversion efficiency of 27–30 percent, compared with 37 percent in industrial countries (table 2). Over the next three decades, the overall efficiency of coal plants will increase, as new larger plants that rely on more efficient technology are introduced. The efficiency of coal plants could be increased by at least 6 percent, bringing them up to the current industrial country average, and eventually up to the 42–45 percent that industrial countries are expected to achieve based on existing technologies. Other phases of efficiency improvement can also be attained if India uses the best available technologies as they become available.

China's experience is relevant in this regard. The Chinese government decided in 2004 to increase the efficiency of coal use in power generation by closing small plants, installing large ones, and switching to supercritical and ultra-supercritical technologies. The plan called for the closing of 50,000 MW of small plants during 2006–10, and efforts are currently on track. The shift to advanced technologies has been similarly successful. Before 2004, China had 20 plants with supercritical technology, at a capacity of 12,600 MW and accounting for 4 percent of thermal power-generating capacity. By the end of 2007, more than 140 plants with a capacity of 89,000 MW of supercritical and

> **A major part of industrial output in India is produced by small-scale, often village-based plants, which use inefficient motors and equipment. There is thus considerable room for efficiency improvements**

ultra-supercritical technologies had been commissioned and another 100,000 MW were under construction. According to government plans, more than 70 percent of new coal plants will be based on these advanced technologies.

India could gain significant efficiencies by pursuing an aggressive strategy such as the one that China has adopted. The potential for efficiency gains goes beyond generation and into transmission and distribution. India has total transmission and distribution losses of 25 percent, compared with 6.7 percent in China and 4.6 percent in Japan (see table 2). Losses could be reduced by at least 2–3 percent a year during a well designed five-year plan.[9]

Growth in industrial energy demand is projected to accelerate in the medium term. A major part of industrial output is produced by small-scale, often village-based plants, which use inefficient motors and equipment. There is thus considerable room for efficiency improvements. The iron and steel sectors are expected to continue their rapid expansion to meet the surging demand for steel-based goods for the domestic market. The cement industry is also expected to grow in response to the extraordinary expansion in infrastructure and building construction. These sectors will be the major users of coking coal. The energy intensity of these industries is high by international standards because of the poor quality of local coking coal and outdated technologies. As mentioned, a major part of domestic coal is not suitable for steel production, and the industry is shifting to imported coal. Demand for energy is also expected to grow in chemical and petrochemical production, although most of the demand increase will be in the form of oil and electricity—and natural gas, if available. Coal will account for 42 percent of industrial energy demand in 2050, compared with 30 percent in 2005; electricity's share will rise from 18 percent to 31 percent.

The transport sector will account for a major part of growth in oil demand in the coming years as more people can afford private vehicles. The number of vehicles in India soared from 19 million in 1990 to 75 million in 2005 and it is expected to grow almost sixfold over the next three decades. Oil demand in the transport sector will rise to meet the fuel requirements of this surge in vehicle ownership and the shift from two-wheel to four-wheel vehicles. Two-wheelers now account for 80 percent of the vehicle stock. This ratio is expected to be cut in half by 2040, to 40 percent. However, vehicle fuel efficiency is expected to improve with the new vehicle fleets, particularly considering the large number of partnerships between local and foreign vehicle manufactures, which are likely to introduce more efficient technologies.

Prospects for improving the energy mix

India needs to change the energy mix in order to deal with issues of energy security, and local and global environmental impacts. The most promising options include the expansion of gas use, nuclear power, and solar energy.

Gas-fired plants have problems with supply

Gas-fired generation accounted for 9 percent of power generation in 2005. The power sector faces gas supply shortages because adequate supplies are not always available at agreed prices and because government supply allocations favour the fertilizer industry. Many gas-fired power plants have had to substitute naphtha for natural gas, and some remain idle because naphtha is too expensive. Future growth in gas-based generation, both utilities and auto producers, depends critically on the availability of gas: how fast domestic gas can expand, and how much imported gas will be available and at what price. As discussed earlier, gas is becoming too valuable to be used in substantial volumes in electricity generation. Its use could be limited to peaking units that supplement coal-based and nuclear plants.

Nuclear energy has several obstacles

Nuclear energy offers a significant potential for changing the energy mix. India now has 3,000 MW of nuclear capacity, accounting for 2.5 percent of electricity generation. The government aims to raise that capacity to 20,000 MW by 2020 and 40,000 MW by 2030.

> **A recent agreement with the United States is expected to improve India's access to nuclear fuel and technology**

Table 2 | **Potential for improving the efficiency of power supply, India and selected countries**

Country	Power generation		Power transmission and distribution		
	Average efficiency of coal plants (%)	Grams of coal equivalent per kWh	Direct use in plant (%)	Transmission and distribution losses (%)	Total (%)
India	27–30	488	6.9	25.0	31.9
China	29–33	457	8.0	6.7	14.7
United States	37–42	352	4.8	6.2	11.0
Japan	42–45	305	3.7	4.6	8.3
World	32–35	400	5.3	8.8	14.1

Source: Mao 2008; NETL 2007; ESMAP 2008.

Earlier targets have not been achieved, partly because of India's exclusion from international trade in nuclear plants and materials. A recent agreement with the United States is expected to improve access to nuclear fuel and technology. India plans to build light water reactors if it can access international markets. In the second stage, India would develop fast breeder reactors, coupled with reprocessing and fuel fabrication plants using plutonium. This stage has begun, with the construction of a 500 MW plant at Kalpackam with a fast breeder reactor based on Indian technology. During the subsequent phase, India will develop plants that use a thorium-uranium-233 cycle. Construction of a 300 MW demonstration project is under way.

Worldwide, nuclear energy accounts for 15 percent of electricity generation. Almost 60 percent of global nuclear capacity is in the United States, France, and Japan. The United States has the largest number (104) of reactors, while France has the highest share (78 percent) of nuclear power in total power generation. Although nuclear power has the capacity to provide large-scale and carbon dioxide-free electricity, its development has remained limited for reasons of cost and safety. However, the development of nuclear power is receiving growing attention in response to the recent spike in international oil prices and concerns about global carbon emissions.

Using nuclear energy to generate electricity depends on the availability of uranium. Uranium demand is currently about 70,000 tons a year. Conventional uranium resources are estimated at about 5 million tons, providing 85 years of supply at current levels of demand. Geological evidence indicates that potential uranium resources may be three times as large. In addition, spent-fuel reprocessing and use of fast-breeder reactor technology would enable uranium supplies to last much longer. There is therefore less concern about the availability and the cost of fuel. However, the cost of nuclear energy can vary significantly, based on capital costs and construction time. Reliable estimates of capital costs are difficult to obtain because of a sparse track record in recent years. Vendors' estimates are often self-serving and subject to change. Similarly, construction time depends heavily on location.

Two other obstacles to nuclear energy are concerns about safety and proliferation. The main safety issues are the risks of a meltdown and the safe disposal of nuclear waste.[10] Some of the by-products of nuclear power include highly radioactive actinides, which remain toxic for thousands of years. They have to be housed in waste dumps isolated from all possible contact with the environment for up to 10,000 years. Part of this waste can also be reprocessed into weapons-grade plutonium, increasing the risk of nuclear proliferation.

> **Renewable energy—hydropower, wind power, and solar power—represents another option for the change in energy mix**

Despite uncertainties about construction costs and public concerns over the risk of meltdown, disposal of radioactive waste, and proliferation of weapons-grade by-products, the momentum for building new plants is growing. The largest additions are expected in China, which plans to build 40,000 MW of nuclear capacity by 2020. In the United States, there are plans to build 22,000 MW of capacity, although the implementation period is unclear. The U.S. Nuclear Regulatory Commission has established a new process for licensing advanced reactors. The process is intended to eliminate the long delays experienced during the 1980s when the last plants were licensed. However, utilities, financiers, and the public at large have not yet reached consensus on support for a big push into additional nuclear capacity.

Renewable energy still a small share of overall power generation

Renewable energy represents another option for the change in energy mix. In 2005, renewable energy, mainly hydropower, accounted for 15 percent of India's electricity generation.

Hydropower. Installed hydropower capacity reached 34 GW in 2005. The share of hydropower in total electricity generation has steadily declined, from 40 percent in 1971 to 25 percent in 1990 and 14 percent in 2005. The development of hydropower faces strong environmental opposition (particularly because of the flooding caused by dams and the need for resettlement) and financing difficulties. Government policy has consistently emphasized hydropower, although more recently the government has also signalled a significant shift to other renewable energy sources, particularly wind and solar power.

Wind power. India's wind power capacity has grown fast, reaching 8 GW (fourth largest in the world) in 2007 and is expected to rise to 27 GW by 2030 and to account for 2.5 percent of electricity generation.

Worldwide, wind power capacity in 2007 was 94 GW. The largest capacities were installed in Germany (22 GW), the United States (17 GW), Spain (15 GW), India (8 GW), and China (6 GW). Under the IEA's business-as-usual scenario for world energy supply, wind power capacity is expected to grow fourfold (reaching 400 GW) by 2050, accounting for 2 percent of world electricity generation. However, under the carbon reduction scenario, wind power capacity would grow 20-fold (reaching 2,000 GW) by 2050 and account for 12 percent of world electricity generation, reducing global carbon dioxide emissions by 2.1 GT a year.[11]

Wind power technology is an example of renewable energy R&D successfully improving technology, lowering cost, and rapidly dispersing around the world. The cost of wind power depends on site characteristics, but the average cost has declined from more than 20 cents a kilowatt hour in the early 1990s to 6–7 cents a kilowatt hour today. Advances in wind power technology were initiated in Denmark in most of the early stages but are now emerging from Germany, Spain, the United States, and other countries.

There are clear prospects for further cost reductions with larger-scale wind turbine production and advances in technology. R&D efforts are focussing on building large (10 MW) wind turbines, reducing the material weight of turbine blades, and designing more intelligent rotors to improve reliability. There are also initiatives to improve the availability of wind power through storage facilities or through combinations with other energy resources, such as hybrid systems that use wind and gas, or wind and solar.

Solar power. India receives abundant solar radiation, which is its largest source of untapped energy. Its theoretical solar potential is about 5,000 terawatt hours (TWh) a year, far above the country's total electricity consumption of 700 TWh in 2005. Actual solar energy use is negligible, however. Some photovoltaic systems are being promoted primarily in rural and remote applications, but their use is limited. These decentralized

> **❝ To implement large-scale nuclear capacity, India and the international community would need to end the embargo and allow India access to nuclear equipment, fuel, and technology**

Table 4 | Energy mix under sustainable scenario

Energy source	Business-as-usual scenario			Sustainable scenario		
	2005	2030	2050	2005	2030	2050
Total energy (millions of tons of oil equivalent)	537	1,793	4,241	537	1,431	2,792
Energy mix (%)						
Coal	39	48	48	39	40	38
Oil	24	27	28	24	23	20
Gas	5	7	7.5	5	9	8
Hydro	2	2	2	2	3	3
Nuclear	1	3	4	1	5	9
Renewables	0	1	2	0	3	10
Biomass	29	12	10	29	17	12
Emissions (gigatonnes)						
Carbon emissions	1.1	3.9	8.3	1.1	3.2	3.9
Carbon capture and storage	0	0	0	0	0	1.0
Net emissions	1.1	3.9	8.3	1.1	3.2	2.9

Source: Author's analysis based on data from IEA 2008.

Table 5 | Estimated market value of carbon dioxide savings from India's pursuit of a sustainable energy scenario, 2010–50

Calculation	2010–19	2020–29	2030–39	2040–50	Total
Carbon dioxide savings (gigatonnes)	2.4	6.2	18.6	36.8	63.6
Discounted value at fixed price ($ billions)[a]	16.8	38.3	63.8	92.6	211.5
Discounted value at variable price ($ billions)[b]	19.3	49.8	108.6	203.7	381.4

Note: a. Using a 5 percent discount rate at a price of $10 a ton of carbon dioxide in 2008 dollars.

b. Using a 5 percent discount rate at a price of $10 a ton of carbon dioxide in 2010, increasing to $25 a ton by 2050, in 2008 dollars.

Source: Author's analysis based on data from IEA 2008.

technologies. Each of these technologies has to be developed aggressively, shared generously, and commercialized as quickly as possible.

Nuclear. To implement the large-scale nuclear capacity put forward in the proposed scenario, India and the international community would need to end the embargo and allow the country access to nuclear equipment, fuel, and technology.[17] India would need to allow large-scale

imports rather than limit itself to domestic manufacturing capacity. Industrial countries are undertaking numerous R&D activities to improve the safety and cost effectiveness of nuclear power. A promising area is the development of small- and medium-scale nuclear plants, with some 60 designs in preparation. These are expected to become commercial after 2010. Most current reactors have capacities of 1,000–1,700 MW and may not be suitable for the power networks of some developing

> **" To implement large-scale solar enegry capacity, India would need access to new technologies as they become available**

countries. The reduced size and complexity of the new designs could mean shorter construction time and enhanced safety and reliability. India has developed some of its own small plants, with a domestic production of 200 MW and 490 MW pressurized heavy water reactors.

Another area receiving international attention is thorium-based nuclear energy. This is attractive for India, which has an abundance of thorium, and for the international community because of the potential safety benefits. Thorium, a lighter element than uranium, is fertile but does not produce as many heavy and highly radioactive by-products. Whereas a uranium-fuelled reactor might generate a ton of high-level waste, a thorium-fuelled reactor might generate a fraction of that. However, thorium is not fissile, so it cannot undergo nuclear fission by itself or sustain a nuclear chain. The challenge is therefore to provide thorium with enough neutrons to initiate and sustain a reaction in an efficient and economic way. Current research is concentrating on combinations of enriched uranium, plutonium, and thorium.[18]

Solar. To implement the large-scale solar energy capacity of the proposed scenario, India would need access to new technologies as they become available. Solar technology is in transition, with several new technologies under development. Most solar energy produced today is based on photovoltaic technology, and more than 90 percent of photovoltaic modules use wafer-base crystalline silicon. This is a well established and reliable technology, but it uses large amounts of silicon as primary feedstock material. Numerous efforts are under way to improve the resource effectiveness and cost efficiency of this technology. Nonetheless, it is expected that by 2020, most photovoltaic applications would shift to thin-film technology, which is based on a different manufacturing approach. The main advantages of thin films are the relatively low cost of raw materials, the high degree of automation, the resource effectiveness of the production process, the suitability for integration with buildings, and their better

appearance. Photovoltaic technology is expected to go through another transition after 2020, when a third generation of photovoltaic systems is expected to further reduce cost and to increase efficiency. As a result of these developments, the electricity generation cost of solar photovoltaic systems is expected to decline to around 5–7 cents a kilowatt hour by 2050.

Another emerging technology is concentrated solar power, which uses direct sunlight, concentrating it several times to reach higher energy densities and thus higher temperatures. The heat is then used to operate a conventional power cycle through a steam turbine that drives a generator. This technology is at the early stages of large-scale production. Four demonstration plants are under construction in developing countries (Egypt, India, Mexico, and Morocco), all supported by the Global Environment Facility. All are facing implementation problems at this stage because of a recent surge in equipment cost. The U.S. Department of Energy has targeted 2020 as the date for concentrated solar power to become competitive with conventional electricity generation. Several projections by the Department of Energy and others indicate that the cost of concentrated solar power electricity generation would decline to less than 10 cents a kilowatt hour by 2020. Such cost reductions would require a scale-up in the volume of manufacturing, which is not yet scheduled.

Carbon capture and storage. Carbon capture and storage are integrated into the proposed scenario for the period after 2030, though India is considered a promising candidate for carbon capture and storage at its earliest stage. The government has shown an interest and has joined international efforts to speed up the development and dissemination of carbon capture and storage technologies. Estimates of the geological storage potential of India are large, in the range of 500–1,000 GT of carbon dioxide, including onshore and offshore deep saline aquifers, basalt formation traps, unmineable coal seams, and depleted oil and gas reservoirs. Analysis of early opportunities for carbon capture and storage in

> **A prerequisite for implementing the energy agenda is a total reshaping of the relative roles of government, private sector, and civic society**

India, matching sources and sinks, indicates a potential for disposal of 5 MT a year within 20 km of large carbon dioxide sources, storing carbon dioxide in depleted oil and gas fields or using it for enhanced oil recovery. Saline aquifers could absorb a further 40 MT a year.

With strict limits on global carbon emissions a near-term prospect, the application of carbon capture and storage is considered essential. Most carbon dioxide emissions come from power generation and large-scale industrial processes. The cost of capturing carbon dioxide from these large-scale sources is much less than from distributed sources such as transport. Carbon capture and storage involve capture, transport, and underground injection. The bulk of the costs are associated with capture. The cost of carbon capture from a coal-based power plant is estimated at $25–$50 per ton of carbon dioxide (Kemp and Kasim 2008). Transport and storage would add another $10 per ton. On average, carbon capture and storage is expected to add 3–4 cents a kilowatt hour to the cost of electricity generation in a new coal plant. The incremental cost of adding carbon capture and storage to an existing plant could be much higher and may not be feasible if there is no suitable space for additional capture equipment or suitable storage reservoir in the vicinity. Most carbon capture and storage capabilities worldwide are expected to emerge after 2030 and to reach a total capacity of 5 GT a year by 2050.

Today, there are only a few carbon capture and storage projects under way (two in Norway, one in Algeria, and one in the United States). The objectives of all four projects are commercial rather than global carbon emission reductions. For example, the U.S. Weyburn project in North Dakota captures more than 1.7 MT a year of carbon emissions from a coal gasification plant, compresses the carbon dioxide, and transports it through a 330 km pipeline to the Weyburn oilfield in Canada to enhance oil production. There are also some 20 projects in the pipeline, 70 percent of them based on the integrated coal gasification combined cycle technology.

Coal gasification. Integrated coal gasification combined cycle is an important new technology that is likely to take a prominent position among clean coal technologies. Its thermal efficiency matches that of ultra-supercritical technology. However, it has further advantages when used in combination with carbon capture and storage processes. It provides a more effective way of dealing with local and global environmental impacts of coal use in power generation. There are currently only five coal gasification plants operating in the world, so the track record on construction and operation costs and risks is thin. The capital cost is 15–25 percent more than for conventional coal plants. However, the average cost of manufacturing is expected to decline at larger scales. Thus, there is support from the international donor community and some potential suppliers for the construction of new plants.

Current projections indicate that some 27,000 MW of integrated coal gasification combined-cycle units are under preparation, 70 percent of them in the United States, 14 percent in Europe (Germany, Netherlands and United Kingdom) and the rest in Australia, China, Japan, and a small one in India. All of these projects receive grants and other financial support. The future of integrated coal gasification combined cycle depends on the prospects for carbon capture and storage. A strong push towards carbon capture and storage, as currently appears to be the case in international discussions, would provide an attractive opportunity for the rapid expansion of coal gasification capacity.

Refocusing the roles of government, private sector, and civil society

A prerequisite for implementing the energy agenda is a total reshaping of the relative roles of government (at all levels), private sector, and civic society. India needs to develop a consensus on the desirable roles of government, the private sector, and citizens in 2039, and start immediately to move in that direction.

Well before India becomes an affluent society and possibly one of the three largest economies, it will need

> **The government's chief role is to create the incentive system, to lead the strategy, and to manage interactions with the international community**

a much smarter, much more focused, and more effective government. Public sector enterprises would ultimately need to be privatized; in the meantime, they should be required to compete on equal footing with the private sector and be subject to the same financial discipline and accountability for promised results. The private sector should have the primary responsibility for implementing the agreed energy policy and strategy. All energy enterprises should be subject either to adequate market competition or to oversight by strong and independent regulators. And civic society and the media must make sure that government, the private sector, and regulators are performing their jobs well:

- *Government.* Establish a single central entity responsible for all energy policy. The fundamental role of the government should be to create the incentive system and to lead a consolidated energy strategy. Instead of having many separate ministries with overlapping responsibilities for individual aspects of the energy sector, the responsibilities for setting policy, formulating strategy, monitoring results and establishing the appropriate legal and autonomous regulatory bodies should be given to a single entity at the centre. The government must establish an enabling business environment to attract the private sector to meet the huge energy investment needs efficiently. The most important part of this business environment is an energy pricing policy that provides financial incentives for timely investments and for the transfer and adoption of new technologies by the private sector.
- *Private sector.* Businesses should have the primary role in producing and distributing energy and in conducting most research and development. In addition, they should lead efforts to adopt and implement energy-efficiency standards and practices, reduce carbon emissions, create new businesses to promote a worldwide

energy revolution, develop clean energy technologies and eliminate energy wastage.
- *Regulatory bodies.* Establish independent and specialized regulators that can encourage competitive market behaviour. Give regulators financial autonomy and clear authority for setting tariffs. Limit price regulation to the segments of the energy industry characterized by significant economies of scale (natural monopolies).
- *Civil society and media.* Encourage civic society and the media to play their proper role in the energy sector by promoting transparency and enforcing accountability.

Institutional aspects of the energy sector

The institutional and policy aspects of India's energy sector, though complex, have been well debated and well articulated.[19] Described here are a few aspects that are crucial to the proposed strategy.

Implementing a sustainable energy development strategy requires carefully-designed and well-coordinated institutional and policy environments that provide clear incentives for unprecedented energy efficiency improvements, private investments, and adoption of advanced technologies. The government's chief role is to create the incentive system, to lead the strategy, and to manage interactions with the international community. The current structure of the energy sector disperses policy responsibilities over several ministries (power, petroleum, coal, and others). A consolidated and coherent energy strategy requires that responsibilities for formulating energy policy, monitoring results, and setting up appropriate legal and regulatory structures be given to a single entity.

The Energy Conservation Act of 2001 and the Planning Commission's energy policy of 2006 both incorporate energy efficiency as a policy objective. The act requires energy consumers to follow relevant codes and standards (for example, energy performance codes for new appliances and energy conservation codes for new buildings). There is, however, a worldwide push

> **Following the practices of industrial countries, India needs to establish and enforce aggressive standards for energy-intensive industries, major energy consumers and the manufacture of energy-consuming equipment**

towards much stricter standards of energy efficiency and more holistic codes that enforce energy conservation while encouraging the adoption of new technologies.

Following the practices of industrial countries, India needs to establish and enforce aggressive standards for energy-intensive industries, major energy consumers, and for the manufacture of energy-consuming equipment. Particularly important is an emphasis on transparent monitoring and reporting of efficiency gains (or losses). Energy efficiency improvements in the transport sector are potentially especially rewarding, reducing the need for oil imports while offering environmental, congestion, and economic efficiency benefits. Achieving them will require a well-coordinated strategy for strengthening mass transport and encouraging the use of fuel-efficient vehicles. More powerful than technical and regulatory measures for energy efficiency is energy pricing policy. Subsidies should be aggressively removed or redesigned and relegated to some limited and targeted schemes. Time-of-day tariffs should be introduced to shift part of the load from peak to off-peak periods.

The policy environment for encouraging renewable energy development has its own characteristics. Industrial countries have realized the need for varying levels of subsidies to encourage development of renewable energy technologies. Most countries try to keep these subsidies transparent, well targeted and within a confined time frame. Subsidies include R&D support, feed-in tariffs, tax incentives, and access to soft sources of finance. However, the predominant instrument is the feed-in tariff—that is, the price at which the utilities are obligated to buy the electricity—found to be most conducive to the private sector supply of renewable energy technologies and services.

The electricity sector is the major vehicle for improving energy efficiency and altering the fuel mix. The institutions and policies for this sector can make or break India's energy strategy. The Electricity Act of 2003 restructured the electricity industry, unbundling the vertically integrated electric supply utilities of each state into a transmission utility and several generating and distribution utilities. Each state's electricity regulatory commission sets tariffs for electricity sales. The restructuring has introduced a framework for the proper functioning of the sector, but the details remain to be worked out.

The poor performance of the sector is evidenced in persistent power shortages and the failure to expand electricity supply capacity. Investment requirements are estimated at $1.6 trillion over the next three decades. The sheer size of these investment needs, together with the poor track record of past investments, raises serious concerns about the sector's future. Investments at this level are possible only with considerable participation by the private sector. Yet private investment in the power sector has been limited and unstable. After an enthusiastic start in the early 1990s, private investment remained low and unstable until 2002. In 2003, a new enthusiasm emerged, with investments peaking at $4 billion in 2004. Still, it is too early to tell whether private investors are ready to make substantial commitments, particularly considering that their investments in 2005 and 2006 have been lower than in 2004.

Most important for attracting new private investments is the sector's financial performance. High operating costs, inadequate tariffs, and failure to collect payments have resulted in deterioration of the financial health of most of India's state electricity boards. The boards receive large subsidies—estimated at 30–40 percent of total revenue—but still cannot cover the full cost of electricity supply. The weak financial state of the state electricity boards discourages the private sector. A few state electricity boards (Chhattisgarh, Goa, and Orissa) have had positive financial results and are considered benchmarks for rating the performance of the other boards. The Ministry of Power has introduced a rating system that measures the performance of all 28 state electricity boards based on technical and operational performance of power facilities, tariff policy, cost recovery, and commercial viability.

In addition to financial performance, private sector investors are concerned with fuel availability, already a strain for investors in the power sector. Most private

> **India needs to strengthen two major aspects of R&D: be much more open to drawing on international experience and advances and ensure much greater reliance on the private sector for technology imports and adaptation**

power producers favour gas-based power generation plants, but they cannot be assured of a reliable supply of gas. And although coal is plentiful domestically, the industry structure does not lead to reliable supplies of coal at competitive prices. The coal sector needs substantial investments in mining and transport. Attracting such investment will be a challenge because the sector lacks commercial discipline. The sector is isolated from competitive forces, and its poor financial performance is unacceptable in an environment of high international coal prices. The government needs to organize the industry, ensuring that Coal India does not have monopoly power over activities best left to commercial entities. Reform of the coal sector is needed not only for its own viability but also for the good of the power sector, which requires assurance that reliable and suitable quality coal will be available to meet technology needs and manage the risks of fuel supply.

Finally, regulatory bodies, civil society, and the media have important roles in the proper functioning of the energy sector. Independent and specialized regulators are needed, to encourage competitive market behaviour. Regulators need financial autonomy and clear authority for setting tariffs. At the same time, regulation has limits and should be confined to segments of the energy industry with significant economies of scale (natural monopolies). Finally, the impact of regulation on technological innovation and adoption needs to be taken into account. India should consider the ongoing revisions of the EU energy regulations as a possible model.

Civil society and the media play an important role in exposing governance issues in the energy sector. Worldwide, the energy sector is considered a potential source of institutional and technical inefficiencies, environmental damage, political abuse, rent seeking, and financial misconduct. Having a transparent role for government and a credible regulator is essential for avoiding such pitfalls. So is having a strong civil society and media to insist on accountability.

Global leadership—Establishing a Centre of Advanced Energy Technologies

Worldwide, the energy industry has always depended very heavily on research and development. But the role of research and development has never been as great as it will be in the next three decades. India should aspire, as part of its energy revolution, to global leadership in advanced energy technologies, establishing a global centre focused on such technologies as a first step.

An important aspect of a sustainable energy development strategy is the adoption of new technologies. The energy industry worldwide has always depended heavily on R&D. But its role has never been as vital as it will be in the next three decades, when the industry needs to undergo a revolution. India must consider this global trend as well as its own technology challenges in redesigning its energy R&D strategy. Historically, India has systematically promoted indigenous R&D. Its progress in nuclear energy and manufacturing power system facilities attests to the success of domestic R&D.

Going forward, however, India needs to strengthen two major aspects of R&D. First, India must be much more open to drawing on international experience and advances. Second, it should ensure much greater reliance on the private sector for technology imports and adaptation. The government's role remains critical, however. The government should direct the overall R&D strategy and oversee implementation of a well-prepared approach to the international community. But it should structure the incentive system to catalyze private sector resources, innovation, and entrepreneurship.

The government should consider establishing a Centre of Advanced Energy Technologies as a public-private partnership. The centre would have the agility and business orientation of a private enterprise, while pursuing the strategic directions set by the government. It should be opportunistic in accessing the rapidly increasing facilities that the international community is offering in support of advanced energy technologies. For example, the World Bank is launching an initiative to help remove the barriers

> **To meet its growing energy demand while managing energy security and mitigating local and global environmental impacts, India needs to achieve an unprecedented level of energy efficiency and diversification**

to private sector commercialization of climate technologies by supporting accelerated climate technology innovation. It envisages establishing three innovation centres as regional hubs for climate technologies. India should attempt to qualify as a candidate for one of these centres.

Almost all the climate change funds (as discussed earlier) would look positively on the establishment of the proposed Centre of Advanced Energy Technologies. The Centre's functions—demonstration, adaptation, and dissemination of advanced technologies—reflect the key elements in the support menu of these climate change funds. Mobilizing support from such funds would need to take place in two phases. In the first phase, these funds should be approached to finance the establishment of the Centre. In the second phase, the Centre would approach climate change funds and other sources of resources to mobilize large amounts of financing for its projects, with the Centre as a channel for transferring technology and finance to relevant energy projects.

In addition to creating the global centre, India needs to strengthen two other major aspects of research and development. There should be a much greater degree of openness to drawing on international experience and advances. And the modes of research and development support should ensure much more reliance on the private sector for technology imports and adaptation.

Conclusions

India needs to meet its growing energy demand while managing energy security and mitigating local and global environmental impacts. To this end, India needs to achieve an unprecedented level of energy efficiency and diversification. Though a formidable challenge, India will not face it alone. During the next three decades, the world will experience an energy or carbon revolution that will create opportunities as well as challenges for India. India will have access to extensive technological and financial support if it joins the revolution, but it will be subject to severe international scrutiny if it decides to continue on a business-as-usual path. The international community recognizes that India cannot be expected to curb its economic growth, but it also recognizes that the global carbon emission target cannot be achieved without India's cooperation.

By joining this worldwide movement, India gains more than the appreciation of the international community. It reduces the vulnerability of its economy to costly and unreliable energy imports. It diminishes damage to its local environment. And it places India in the forefront of some very advanced technologies. These benefits can occur only if India shifts from a business-as-usual scenario to a sustainable scenario. Though many have advocated this move, they have not clearly articulated what a sustainable scenario would look like. This chapter proposes a framework for defining a sustainable scenario based on a set of assumptions regarding progress in energy efficiency and use of renewable and nuclear technologies. These assumptions are in line with the emerging policies of the government.[20]

INDIA 2039

Part IV

Improving governance

INDIA
2039

Part IV

Chapter

11

Role of the
State and
governance

Role of the State and governance

Bimal Jalan

Cutting across all aspects of the Indian economy and society, there are two issues which deserve major attention. These are: the role of the State and governance. Admittedly, both of these issues are highly intertwined and difficult to tackle. But, without doing so India cannot hope to become an affluent and cohesive society and a leading economic power in the world.

It is a striking fact that economic renewal and positive growth impulses are now occurring largely outside the public sector—at the level of private corporations (e.g. software companies), autonomous institutions (e.g. IIMs or IITs), or individuals at the top of their professions in India and abroad. In the governmental or public sector, on the other hand, there has been a marked deterioration at all levels—not only in terms of productivity and fiscal disempowerment but also in the provision of vital public services in the fields of education, health, water and transport.

Recent developments and trends

Excessive scope and power of government

A refocused government will be crucial for bringing about the anticipated dramatic transformation in the Indian economy. There is a need to rethink not only what the government does but also how. For example, while the current dominant role of the state in both policy making and delivery of many public services was a major strength immediately after independence, the system has become outdated by now, if not suffocating. Similarly, the central government is still performing a large number of functions which are better left to local or state authorities. We discuss below some areas relating to the role of the State, which require correction in order to deliver high growth with better distribution and less poverty.

In India, despite liberalization of the economy and openness of the economy at the macro-level, the power available to multiple ministries to control and allocate economic activity is truly enormous. This ranges from the ability to impose price controls on specific items (say, steel or coal), to allot land for specific purposes (such as Special Economic Zones), control of imports/exports, and allocation of raw materials (such as minerals). Similarly, foreign investment in individual sectors, external commercial borrowings, and mergers and acquisitions (at home and abroad) require government approvals.

Unlike other democracies, another area which confers substantial powers on governmental authorities in India is control over public sector enterprises. In addition to major industries, like oil and steel, public sector enterprises are dominant in the financial field (particularly banking and insurance) and transport (particularly railways, ports and airports). Award of contracts as well as operational priorities, in addition to appointments, are decided by multiple government ministries.

Trend toward short life expectancy of governments

In addition to the above-mentioned two factors, i.e., the enormous power available to ministries to allocate resources and their control over public enterprises, an over-riding factor which would have a crucial bearing on the role of the State in shaping India's economic future is the emergence of coalitions as a "regular" form of government, particularly since 1989. This has led to what may be best described as a short life expectancy of governments at birth. Some governments may last their full term, as is the case with the present government. However, the crucial point is that at the time of their formation or birth, the general expectation is that they will not survive for long. Short life expectancy has important behavioral implication for ministers who take office, as well as for members of Parliament. If ministers expect to be in office only for a short period, the tendency to maximize gains of office and minimize accountability for performance becomes paramount. Almost anything

IV/11

goes, including switching sides, in the event of loss of majority by a particular coalition of parties.

Under the present Constitutional provisions, as a consequence of amendments carried out in 1985 and again in 2003 to prevent defections, there is now a built-in incentive for fragmentation of political parties at the time of election. This is because the smaller a party, the greater the power of an individual legislator to defect to another party in search of political power. Thus, e.g., a member elected from a large national party has very little discretion to defect without the support of a substantial number of other members, who also wish to defect. However, if the same person is a member of a small party of 5 or 10 members, a consensus to defect among all of them or only 3 or 4 of them, and switch from one coalition to another, is easier to achieve. The same is true of so-called "independent" members. In a situation where multi-party coalitions are the norm, all regional or caste leaders naturally have a much greater incentive to form their own separate parties.

Weakened parliament and non-democratic leadership of parties

In addition to a fragmentation of parties and a short life expectancy of coalition governments at birth, in recent years, there has also been a subtle change in the role of Parliament, and the accountability of the executive to Parliament. Parliament now has multiple centers of power (in addition to the party leading the government, and the party leading the opposition). An important consequence of the emergence of multiple centres of power is that what the Parliament does or does not do depends on 'behind the scene' agreements among different sets of party leaders within and outside government. As long as the government has the backing of a sufficient number of leaders, it is supreme and it can get Parliament to do what it wishes. As Eric Hobsbawn, the noted historian and political analyst, has pointed out in another context, when important national decisions are taken among small groups of people in private in a democracy (as was the case, e.g., with respect to the

U.S. decision to invade Iraq), the situation is not very different from the way they would have been taken in non-democratic countries.

Politicization of the bureaucracy

A related development is the politicization of India's bureaucracy, which has gathered further momentum in recent years. India, at the time of independence, inherited a civil service structure which was generally referred to as the "steel frame" and was supposed to be the envy of the post-colonial world. What made India's civil service an extremely effective instrument of governance was the independence that civil servants enjoyed in effectively implementing policy decisions, which were taken by the political leadership. There was a clear separation of executive powers between ministers and civil servants within the executive. Gradually, all this seems to have undergone a change, particularly after the emergence of coalition governments at the centre and states with short life expectancy.

In theory, under the Indian system of executive responsibility, there is supposed to be a clear division of roles between the permanent civil service and the political leadership. Government's policy priorities and its work programme are set by politicians. However, the bureaucracy is supposed to ensure that implementation of the approved programme is done according to the laws and procedures in force, without fear or favour, for the benefit of all the people regardless of their political affiliations.

Over the years, slowly but surely, the role of the bureaucracy has been seriously compromised. Any party which comes to power and joins a multi-party coalition, is inclined to appoint favoured bureaucrats in sensitive positions who, in turn, are expected to carry out the wishes of its party leaders, irrespective of their merits or legality. According to one study, in one year alone, in the state of Uttar Pradesh (when there was a six-monthly rotation of the government headed by leaders of two parties in coalition) there were 1,000 transfers

> **" There is no item of government business for which a single ministry can be held responsible**

among members of the elite Indian Administrative Service (IAS) and Indian Police Service (IPS).

The deleterious effects of frequent transfers on the morale and effectiveness of top civil servants have been substantial. Lack of motivation at the top has led to acts of passive resistance and delays by subordinates. Corruption has become widespread, both to prevent transfers as well as in efforts by corrupt officials to get remunerative postings.

Deterioration in governance of public services

As universally recognized, periodic elections to seek the people's mandate for the government to continue in office (or otherwise) are truly the hour of triumph for India's democratic traditions. In the last national elections, held in June 2009, as many as 714 million people were entitled to vote. More than 417 million persons exercised their franchise. This was the largest democratic election ever held in the history of the world. What is also remarkable about Indian elections is that a pre-ponderant proportion of the voters is from poor rural areas. In urban areas also, there is evidence that the poor tend to vote much more than the middle and upper classes.

Yet the fact remains that along with the largest electorate in the world, India also has the largest number of persons living below the poverty line. Even the most conservative estimates released by government agencies show that as many as 300 million Indians are below the poverty line, and do not earn enough to provide even the minimum intake of food and nutrition. The conditions prevailing in India's urban slums and rural areas are among the worst in the world.

India perhaps also has the largest number of programmes, launched by the government, to provide subsidized food, primary education, housing and improved rural infrastructure for the benefit of the poor. Yet, the absolute number of persons below the poverty line has been rising rather than declining. Assuming that as many as 200 or 250 million people are currently benefiting from the high rates of growth in manufacturing and services in

the private sector, more than 800 million persons in India would still continue to be at the periphery of the circles of prosperity for quite some time. This paradox can only be explained by the poor state of governance and rising incidence of corruption in the public delivery system.

Proliferation of ministries and government offices

There are multiple reasons for the failure of the administration to deliver services to the poor, or for that matter, improve public infrastructure. The most important reason, in addition to some of the political factors mentioned above, for this state of affairs is the proliferation of ministries and offices of government over time. There is no item of government business for which a single ministry can be held responsible, except perhaps taxation or budget-making. The number of ministries has shot up from 18 in 1947 to 65 or more now, and there has been a sharp increase in the number of cabinet ministers, independent ministers of state in charge of separate ministries, and large number of ministers of state who report to cabinet ministers. Many of these ministries have very little to do. All ministries also have more than one department and several subordinate agencies. The rigid hierarchy in the delivery and decision-making process further ensures that horizontally as well as vertically, a dozen or more offices are likely to be involved from different ministries, including the Planning Commission even when there is no policy to be decided, such as, say, provision of drinking water or electricity to rural areas.

In addition to the centre, there is a similar proliferation of governmental organizations at the state and district level. It has become a routine matter for policy to be announced by the central government, but implementation to be in the hands of state government and their subsidiary organizations. The central government blames state governments, and the latter blame the central government for rigidity in the provisions of the scheme or inadequate allocation of funds. Within the central government, it is now common for one department or ministry to blame another department

> **Corruption is now a major hurdle in growth, development and poverty alleviation in India, as indeed in several other countries**

Box 1 | Evidence of failure of governance of public services

A good example of substantial diversion of subsidies and budgetary resources to unintended beneficiaries under an important poverty alleviation programme is that of the Targeted Public Distribution System (TPDS). Under this programme, in order to provide food security, a certain quantity of food grains is provided under the public distribution system (PDS) at highly subsidized prices to households with incomes below the poverty line (BPL) families. The objectives of this programme are indeed laudable and are supported by all sections across the political spectrum. However, an evaluation study covering 60 districts and 3600 households, undertaken by the Planning Commission in 2005, has found widespread diversion of grain from genuinely poor families to other households. Among its findings, the following are particularly disturbing:

- During 2003–04, 16 large states covered under the study were issued 14 million tonnes of food from the central pool for distribution to BPL families. Of this, less than 6 million tons (or only about 40 percent) were delivered to the BPL families, and the rest never reached them;
- Thus, for every 1 kg of food grain delivered to the poor, the Government of India had to issue 2.4 kg of subsidized grain;
- Out of an estimated budgetary consumer subsidy of Rs. 72 billion for sixteen states in 2003–04, as much as 60% did not reach BPL households;
- The government spent Rs. 3.65 through budgetary food subsidies to transfer Re. 1 to the poor. There could not be a more serious indictment of the governance system in India than the above findings.

for any drawback in either policy formulation or policy implementation.

Increased "demand and supply" of corruption

The proliferation of multiple government agencies involved in the decision-making process combined with the complexity of administrative rules and regulations has had the inevitable result of increasing both the demand and supply of corruption in India. Thus, according to the widely quoted Transparency International's corruption index (EPI), India was ranked as having one of the highest levels of corruption in the world. India's rank was higher than non-democratic countries like China. It was also substantially higher than other East Asian countries like Japan, Malaysia and South Korea.

In addition to the wide acceptance of corruption as a necessary evil, another area of grave concern is the interlocking or "vertical integration" of corruption at various levels of the government hierarchy—elected politicians, higher bureaucracy and lower bureaucracy. Along with vertical integration, there is also horizontal spread of corruption to other public institutions, including legislatures, parts of judiciary, media as well as independent professions. This has made the prevention and control of corruption even more difficult. As if all this were not enough, another unfortunate development has been the politicization of corruption. Increasingly, cases of corruption are being given a political colour without any serious intent to tackle the problem. This has facilitated the entry into politics of persons with a track record of corruption. The public no longer knows whom to trust—the accuser or the accused.

Corruption is now a major hurdle in growth, development and poverty alleviation in India, as indeed in several other countries. Research has established that in the long run corruption reduces productivity, lowers investment, causes fiscal drain and has a debilitating effect on efficiency. Unfortunately, these adverse effects of corruption are not generally appreciated either by India's political and legal institutions, or its public.

> **The most important priority for the future in the area of governance is to redefine the primary role of the government in the economy**

It is abundantly clear that unless the Indian authorities take some measures to improve governance and reduce the "demand and supply" of corruption in the economy, there is simply no way in which India can fully achieve its growth potential over the long run or reduce the rising disparity (and perhaps despair) among the bulk of its people. Given the current political scenario of multiple-party coalitions with no shared economic agenda, dramatic reforms or "hard" measures to improve administrative efficiency may not be feasible in the near future. However, over a period of four to five years (particularly in light of the results of the general elections in 2009), it should be possible to evolve a consensus on introducing a package of reforms which are relatively benign and are likely to be in the overall interest of the country as a whole. Some suggestions to this effect are given below.

An agenda of essential reform measures

Corruption is now a major hurdle in growth, development and poverty alleviation in India, as indeed in several other countries. Fortunately, India's democratic system of government is still robust. Elections supervised by an autonomous agency outside the government (i.e. the Election Commission), are free and fair. All citizens enjoy multiple freedoms, including the right to free speech, the right to choose their own professions or jobs, and the right to property. There is a vibrant civil society and free media, which keep a watch on the activities and programmes of multiple parties in power as well as in opposition. India also has an independent judiciary, which is the final arbiter of deciding what is legal under the Constitution and what is not.

Ultimately, it is likely that a favourable change in India's politics in the years to come can only be brought about by the civil society and media. This will happen only if they are vigilant and generate sufficient pressure on leaders of parties to undertake urgently required political reforms. Views on what needs to be done by way of political reforms, and what can actually be done in the near future, are likely to vary among experts as well as observers. Based on a review of developments in the past two decades, it appears that the following reforms are essential to enable India to improve governance, reduce the "demand and supply" of corruption and seize the global economic opportunities that lie ahead:

- Within the framework of the parliamentary form of government, the most important priority for the future in the area of governance is to redefine the primary role of government in the economy. At the macro-economic level, the political (i.e. ministerial) role of the government should be to ensure a stable and competitive environment with a strong external sector and a transparent domestic financial system. While the macro-economic priorities (e.g. the trade-off between growth and inflation) may be decided by the government, the instrumentalities for achieving these objectives must be left to autonomous regulatory and promotional agencies. Similarly, the government's direct role in economic areas should be re-set in favour of ensuring the availability of public goods (such as roads and water) and essential services (such as health and education) to the people. In these areas, the government's role must expand substantially.

- At the same time, an important priority is to further reduce the political role of the government in the economy, particularly the power of multiple ministries and short-lived governments over public sector enterprises. This objective should be achieved without in any way affecting the financial and other benefits of those who are presently employed. Privatization is not the only answer. The real question is whether India can create an "arm's-length" relationship between the government and these enterprises. One option is for the Board of Directors of public enterprises to be appointed by an autonomous agency, such as Public Sector Enterprises Board (PSEB). The Board should have exclusive power of supervision over the management of public enterprises. As a shareholder, the

INDIA
2039

Part IV

Chapter

12

Governance
for a modern
society

> **Government functions that can be done over the telephone, online or by mail in many countries can take days or weeks in India and require considerable time and money**

IV/12

Yet, paradoxically, India stands out amongst developing countries as having well established institutions of governance. It has long had a Constitution and a strong system of checks and balances amongst the legislature, the executive and the judiciary. The legislatures, both at the national and the state levels, are duly elected with a long record of fair multiparty voting. Keen electoral competition yields regular changes in the governing party. The executive branch, modelled after the British government, comprises competent civil servants at the professional levels. The judiciary has a proven record as the protector of individual rights. Overall, the country has the right institutions for good governance. So why does India continue to have relatively poor governance? Why do the checks and balances fail to ensure that public institutions serve the people? Some bold changes in the relationships amongst India's politicians, bureaucrats and citizens are now essential to make the existing institutions function more effectively. Incremental changes simply will not solve India's governance problems.

India's governance problems

Two related symptoms of India's governance problems are the highly complex, time-consuming and unpredictable procedures that underlie the infamous Indian red tape and the widespread corruption facilitated by the red tape.

Red tape

Government functions that can be done over the telephone, online or by mail in many countries can take days or weeks in India and considerable time and money. The simplest government services can require multiple steps, numerous follow-ups, applications in triplicate and unnecessary expense. A number of factors contribute to this situation:

- Most procedures are not adequately defined or disclosed, leaving the citizen to rely on personal visits to government offices, professional intermediaries to complete the paperwork or

most often multiple efforts to rectify rejected applications.
- Even when the prescribed procedure is ostensibly straightforward, there are often hidden requirements that are revealed only after the process is started. (Annex 1 illustrates a case involving a visa extension.)
- The front line of the bureaucracy is staffed by low-level functionaries with little professional training—known as "*babus*" in the Indian civil service terminology. These *babus* are responsible for making "notations" on the "file" that moves from desk to desk until reaching the "higher-level officers" for decision. These officers have little direct contact with the citizen and in most cases do nothing more than endorse the notations made by the *babus*. As one state ombudsman ("*lokayukta*") pointed out: the higher-level officers routinely sign the file as prepared by the lower levels and exercise independent judgement only when the matter involves a personal interest or pressure from politicians or other influential people.
- The movement of the file can be stopped at any of the desks through which it passes for no ostensible reason or for the slightest actual or concocted deficiency. There are no consequences for inaction. People have to resort to bribes and personal influence to get the file to move.
- There is an unwritten understanding that one role of the government is to provide direct employment. Thus, a large hierarchy of file handlers persists, despite sporadic efforts at downsizing, partly because politicians tend to perceive the unionized clerical cadres as potential votes.
- A lack of transparency in the rules and procedures allows politicians and bureaucrats at all levels to exercise considerable arbitrary power

216

❝ **Transparency International's surveys of corruption in the judicial system place India eighth from the bottom of 60 countries. Over 75 percent of the citizens in the Centre for Media Studies survey indicated that corruption is getting worse**

to deny or delay a legitimate request or to approve an illegitimate one.

- Government officials are well aware of the many unnecessary steps built into most government procedures, and many individual officers have made isolated efforts to simplify them. Nonetheless, few bureaucrats think of streamlining processes and improving service to citizens as a normal part of their job. Some officers claim lower-level bureaucrats resist simplification because it reduces their opportunities for bribes; others choose not be proactive out of apathy, careerism or unwillingness to disturb the status quo.

To be sure, the business environment has significantly improved for the large corporations that have gained power and influence as the economy has opened up. The small and medium-size businesses have benefited much less, and the average citizen has hardly experienced any change. Successful development requires a coevolution of better governance for the society as a whole.

Corruption

Surveys by the Centre for Media Studies and Transparency International confirm the widely held view that corruption is widespread and permeates all branches and levels of government. Transparency International's surveys of corruption in the judicial system place India eighth from the bottom of 60 countries. Over 75 percent of the citizens in the Centre for Media Studies survey indicated that corruption is getting worse. Indian citizens can provide egregious examples of corruption from their personal experiences; the following are a small sample:

- Without notifying the aggrieved party, a chief justice unilaterally moves a major land use dispute to his jurisdiction and advances the date of the hearing two days before his mandatory retirement. The aggrieved party discovers the change from the daily docket posting and is

able to get the action reversed only upon vigorous protest.

- In a notorious criminal trial before the Delhi high court, the prosecutor and the defence lawyer are caught on tape planning to tamper with witness testimony.
- An engineer in the Public Works Department is beaten to death by rowdies for his failure to contribute a substantial sum of money to celebrate the birthday of the chief minister. A member of the legislative assembly is arrested after public uproar.
- State planning officials, suspected to be acting at the behest of a politician, take payments to approve a commercial development in a completely residential neighbourhood. The state officials reconsider after local officials deny the request; the reconsideration, presumably based on further investigation, was completed on the same day as the reconsideration directive was issued.
- A citizen pays city planning officials to get a building permit for a residence.
- A small factory owner makes monthly payments to the labour and pollution control inspectors in exchange for a compliance certification. The factory owner maintains that the regulations are so unrealistic that he could not possibly comply with them and, if he did try to comply, he would still be forced to shut down for the minutest violation unless he made the payments.
- Based on a false First Information Report filed by a well connected person to settle a personal score, police are dispatched to another state to arrest an elderly couple and bring them back in handcuffs, even though the alleged crime took place outside police jurisdiction.
- A false First Information Report is filed against the directors of a company to intimidate them into giving a share of the company to a person connected to a retired senior police official.

- A jobseeker pays 200,000 rupees to his member of the legislative assembly to obtain an appointment as a constable under the member's discretionary authority.

Although state and national institutions are in place to investigate and prosecute corruption, the Indian public has little faith in these processes. Influential people are rarely convicted, and when they are the penalties are mild. When the state *lokayukta* brought the false First Information Report against the elderly couple to the attention of the senior police officer in charge, the response received was that "the policeman responsible has been warned." In the case of the collusion between the prosecutor and the defence attorney, the high court imposed a three-month suspension on the offending lawyers. Similar conduct in developed countries would have resulted in permanent debarment from the practice of law and even criminal penalties for both lawyers. In India, even that slap on the wrist evoked the wrath of the bar association.

Thus, corruption, accepted as a way of life for citizens and businesses alike, has become a corrosive aspect of governance in India. It is also a major hurdle to economic growth and poverty alleviation. Research has established that in the long run corruption reduces productivity, lowers investment, causes fiscal drain and has a debilitating effect on efficiency. Unfortunately, these adverse effects of corruption are not generally appreciated by India's political and legal institutions or by the public.

The causes of poor governance

The fundamental cause of poor governance in India is the very low accountability of both the politicians and the bureaucrats to the people. Weak political and administrative accountability is exacerbated by many other factors:

- Overstretched central and state bureaucracies have too wide a scope of responsibility but too little ability to provide essential services, such as justice and security.

- Courts are clogged with a large backlog of pending cases, so they cannot provide recourse to aggrieved citizens.
- The police are politicized to the point that they are more a coercive than a protective force.
- Government authority remains highly centralized, despite the oft-stated intentions to decentralize.
- Transparency in government is lacking.
- Civil society—citizens and businesses alike—still has not raised its voice to demand better governance.

Weak political accountability

Like citizens in any mature democracy, Indian voters can demand accountability from elected officials by threatening to vote out the ruling party. This is the best tool, at least in theory, for holding politicians accountable, since being reelected is the prize sought by most politicians. Indian citizens over the past 20 years have routinely shown their disapproval by voting the ruling party out of office at both the national and state levels. So why has this not increased the accountability of politicians? There are several possible explanations:

- The normal five-year period between elections provides enough time for politicians to take personal advantage of their position (in economic terms, "extract rents"). The low probability of important politicians being charged, much less convicted, is hardly an effective deterrent against political corruption.
- Politicians are able to win elections through patronage and by building coalitions based on narrow interests. Patronage in India tends to be geared towards advancing the interests of individuals or narrow groups rather than towards bringing results for the broader constituency. This is a classic description of what political scientists call a "clientelistic state".
- The barriers to entry in the political process are high. Elections are becoming more and more

expensive, requiring the contestants to mobilize significant funds. Evidence also suggests that politicians use the coercive power of the state to discourage electoral competition, particularly at the state and local levels. As a result, honest and upright candidates are often discouraged from participating, and party leaders are free to handpick their nominees.

- The emergence of coalitions as a "regular" form of government over the past 20 years has shortened the life expectancy of governments, though a few manage to last their full term, as is the case with the present government. The general expectation, however, is that governments will not survive for long. If ministers expect to be in office only for a short period, the tendencies to maximize the gains of office and minimize the accountability for performance become paramount. Almost anything goes, including switching sides, in the event of loss of majority by a particular coalition of parties.

Some important measures have been undertaken in recent years to improve the electoral process. These include:

- The Central Election Commission has gained high credibility by rigorously enforcing election laws.
- The contestants are now required to declare personal assets.
- Candidates who have been charged with criminal offences are barred from office.

These are all important steps in the right direction, although it will take some time for their impact to be felt. However, significant issues remain unaddressed:

- No credible mechanisms free of political pressure yet exist for investigating charges of political corruption and holding elected officials accountable for their misdeeds. Only in rare instances are politicians ever prosecuted successfully, even in the face of well known evidence. When they are found guilty, few ever

face any sanctions. As we will discuss later, the *lokayukta*s, who were intended to pursue corruption charges against state politicians and high officials, have not been effective.

- Politicians increasingly intrude into affairs that should largely be left to the bureaucracy. The area of greatest interest to individual legislators is the placement (postings and transfers) of their favoured or disfavoured officials. Junior and senior officials alike seek support of the power-brokers for their career advancement. Just as one illustration of the problem, under the Right to Information Act the police department in Punjab disclosed that more than 1,200 recommendations for postings and transfers of police officers at various levels had been received from politicians in a four-year period, despite rules against political influence in service matters.

- At the state level, every member of the legislative assembly aspires to become a minister, but a law limits the size of a ministry to 15 percent of the number of legislators. Members of the legislative assembly who cannot be appointed ministers demand to be accommodated in another lucrative position, such as head of a public sector institution, even if they lack administrative skills and the inclination to perform effectively. The arrangement is convenient for legislators seeking to consolidate their political strength, but is often disastrous for governance.

- By and large state legislators oppose decentralization of authority to the local level, since it reduces their patronage. This is a major reason for the failure of states to empower local bodies as mandated by the 73rd and 74th Amendments to the Constitution. Similarly, the substantial discretionary funds with legislators and members of the legislative assembly for development projects militate against democratic decentralization.

> **The civil service that served India well in its initial years is now morphed into an unwieldy and unaccountable bureaucracy that is inappropriate for the much more complex and developed India of today**

- The Election Commission's efforts to bar criminals from seeking elected office have been often thwarted, and people accused of serious crimes continue to be able to compete in and win elections. In the states of Chhattisgarh, Delhi, Madhya Pradesh and Rajasthan, 20 percent of the candidates in the assembly elections of November 2008 had criminal cases pending, as do 18 percent of sitting members of parliament in the current Lok Sabha.[2]

- The election process at the state and local level is less credible than at the national level. Recent local government elections in several states were marred by improprieties.

Weak administrative accountability

In the civil service, there is virtually no accountability for performance. A public official may be transferred to a less desirable job for falling into disfavour with a politician, but is unlikely ever to be reprimanded for poor service. For the average citizen who must endure poor service, there is little recourse. Few Indians complain about petty payments or repeat visits to government offices, knowing that the complaint process is likely to be nonexistent or highly burdensome. Businesspeople dare not complain against offending officials for fear of sanctions and even bigger problems in the future. The larger businesses simply buy influence at the highest political levels or rely on intermediaries to unclog the bureaucracy.

The very nature of the Indian civil service, with its roots in British rule, makes for poor accountability to the people. The British employed an elite group of Britons and Indians in the Indian Civil Service (ICS) to administer the raj all the way down to the district level. The ICS officials at the district level maintained law and order, collected taxes and intermediated between the British rulers and the population. These district administrators exercised unfettered authority as surrogates for the British government. The British government as the "principal" picked some of the ablest Indians (alongside Britons) as "agents" to the ICS and rewarded them handsomely through power and perks. The ICS at the time was a model of good governance: the principal with clear goals and a competent agent to help the principal advance those goals.

When British rule ended, the Indian Administrative Service (IAS) became an elite all-Indian corps within the civil service modelled on the ICS. It continued to emphasize the elite nature of the service by selecting some of the best and the brightest through a highly selective nationwide competition. The IAS was maintained as a national service; to foster national unity, a deliberate attempt was made to have at least some members assigned outside their state of domicile. The individual officers were given a lot of powers and perks. The deputy commissioner, a position carried over from the ICS, was still seen as the all-powerful administrator of the district, responsible for law and order and for coordinating delivery of all state services at the district level. The system was again well suited to post-Independence India: a national government with the clear goals of providing a large number of services to the poor masses as the "principal" and an honest and competent administrative service as the "agent."

However, the civil service that served India well in its initial years is now morphed into an unwieldy and unaccountable bureaucracy that is inappropriate for the much more complex and developed India of today. The IAS officers are far removed from the average citizen, who has little influence over them. They enjoy unchecked authority and ever-growing perks—personal attendants, official cars equipped with red lights and sirens as status symbols, palatial government housing in the districts, ex-officio appointments in civic bodies and even country clubs. They are all ordained to move to the highest level of government (secretary) through a strictly seniority-based system of promotions, bypassing the "inferior" state civil service officers irrespective of performance. Appointments in the field where they are expected to serve the people most directly are simply short detours in their career path towards important positions in the

> **❝ A monolithic national service that is expected to run all levels and organs of government at the central, state, and local levels is simply not workable in a large and complex country with widely varying local needs**

state capitol or New Delhi. Performance for the public plays at best a marginal role in their careers. Indeed, it has been said that these administrators have simply replaced the British as the modern day rulers. The term "civil servant" is a complete misnomer.

As "rulers" they can be impervious to the burden of government on business or the public. This probably is the most important reason why the Indian red tape continues unchecked. The expectation is that it is the function of the "governed" to learn to cope with the rules and requirements of the government rather than the other way around. The challenge in a modern and higher-income India is to convert these public officials into genuine public servants.

Three other aspects of the IAS have made it less relevant for modern India. First, a monolithic national service that is expected to run all levels and organs of government at the central, state and local levels is simply not workable in a large and complex country with widely varying local needs. No country of any significant size has such a system.

Second, the IAS is based on the concept that everything the government does is basically a question of administration that is best handled by well trained generalists, be it education, health, infrastructure or industrial promotion. Appointments in any one field are often short—from a few months to a few years. Appointees are transferred from post to post across vastly different disciplines. Most are overloaded with mundane administrative tasks. In writing about the Indian bureaucracy *The Economist* describes the work of a collector in a district as follows:[3]

> There for the next four hours, beneath a portrait of a beaming Mohandas Gandhi, Mr. Samphel receives a stream of poor people. A turbaned flunkey regulates the flow, letting in a dozen at a time. Many are old and ragged or blind. Paraplegics slither to the collector's feet on broken limbs. Most bring a written plea, for the resumption of

a widow's pension that has mysteriously dried up; for money for an operation; for a tube-well or a blanket. Many bear complaints against corrupt officials. One supplicant wants permission to erect a statue of a dead politician: a former champion of the Hindu outcastes who comprise nearly half of Jalaun's population.

> Mr. Samphel listens, asks questions and, in red ink, scrawls on the petitions his response. For desperate cases, he orders an immediate payment of alms, typically 2,000 rupees ($50), from the district Red Cross society, of which he is president. More often, he writes a note to the official to whom the petition should have been directed in the first place—or, wretchedly often, to whom it has already been directed: "Act upon this according to the law."

The story of Mr. Samphel could just as well describe the routine of many senior bureaucrats for much of their careers. As a result, most senior civil servants develop little depth of knowledge in any field. A modern economy demands much more specialized knowledge.

Third, for many years the IAS enjoyed a high reputation for integrity and for keeping a healthy distance from politics, following the example of its ICS predecessors. This, however, has changed in the past few decades, with growing reports of IAS officers aligning themselves closely with powerful state politicians to advance their own careers.

A parliamentary form of government requires the politicians to set policy and the civil service to implement it diligently, and ultimately almost all senior civil servants serve at the pleasure of the political bosses. But in India, because of excessive political influence over transfers and postings, combined with the possibilities for corruption, the relationship between politicians and civil servants has often degenerated into an unholy alliance.

Politicized police

As enforcers of the law, the police are commonly expected to act righteously and rigorously in defence of the rule of law and adhere to its letter and spirit. Such an ideal view of the police is, sadly, not visible in India today. Instead, the police are seen as a poorly paid and inadequately trained service, whose members resort to aggressive, brutal methods in their investigative work, frequently collude with wrongdoers and sell their services. On their part, the police feel overstretched by being assigned duties that range from tracking down terrorists to guarding and escorting the growing number of local dignitaries (in Punjab, a third of the police are engaged in such security details).

In British India the police understood their role as maintaining law and order and ensuring the rule of law as defined by the imperial power. Especially during the freedom struggle, civil liberties were suppressed and any disaffection firmly quelled. Traditionally the police were allowed to wield immense power in the daily life of towns and villages and acquired a reputation as an oppressive force, even as they delivered even-handed justice in disputes between citizens. Since Independence and especially since the advent of terrorism, in many parts of India the police have acquired additional powers. While the laws for administration of criminal justice have changed little since British times, some states have enacted new local laws to deal with emergent situations.

The Indian police are organized on a federal pattern. Since constitutionally law and order is a state subject, the state government exercises organizational and operational control over the police. The states have guarded their control zealously and have furiously resisted the central government's efforts to have a federal investigation agency take responsibility for interstate crimes of an antinational or terrorist background.

The police leadership is recruited from the Indian Police Service (IPS), and all higher posts in state police organizations are filled by IPS officers. As with members of the IAS, they are appointed through a highly competitive examination. On being allocated to states, these officers come under the administrative and operational control of the respective state governments. This leads to an anomalous situation. States feel curbed in their authority over the IPS, despite the clear constitutional assignment of police supervision to the states. And IPS officers chafe at the day-to-day control over their functioning by the state governments, especially the unfettered use of the power of transfers. This conflict results in unhealthy compromises from both sides, though mainly from the side of the officers, thus undermining their integrity and independent functioning within the parameters of law. The political leadership has progressively increased its grip on the police and tends to utilize it for personal and political ends, to which purposes the organization willingly lends itself. Most of the complaints of police excesses and human rights violations flow from this configuration.

Besides the state police forces, a number of other police organizations are raised, equipped, staffed and operated exclusively by the federal government at the centre. The Intelligence Bureau is tasked with gathering intelligence on antinational activities within the country, but at times is busier collecting intelligence on the political opponents of the government in power. The Central Bureau of Investigation is more of a tool to tailor investigations to suit the government of the day. The Border Security Force is tasked with guarding the Pakistan and Bangladesh borders, while the Sashastra Seema Bal guards the Indo-Nepal and Indo-Bhutan border. The Indo-Tibetan Force and Central Industrial Security Force have self-explanatory names. The Central Reserve Police Force acts as the armed reserve of the federal government to deal with law and order problems at the request of the states. Then there are specialized organizations that do not impact the states generally, such as the elite National Security Guard for antihijacking and Special Protection Group for prime ministerial security.

When the central government gets a demand for additional force from the states, it frequently deploys whichever central force is conveniently available. These

> **The imperative of a major overhaul of police functions became apparent during the tragic events of terrorism in Mumbai in November 2008**

central police or paramilitary forces are also manned by IPS officers from the rank of deputy inspector general and above. These officers allocated to states in normal rotation thus keep shuttling between the states and the central forces. This results, as in the case of IAS, in underspecialization and poor professionalism for both the state and central organizations.

The shortcomings in police functioning have been appraised in several studies carried out at the national level, the most significant of which are the reports of the National Police Commission appointed in 1977. The main thrust of the recommendations is to professionalize the police forces and free them from unwarranted political interference. Unfortunately, the recommendations have not been implemented by successive governments over the past 30 years.

Recognizing that the executive was failing in its responsibility to provide the public the basic quality of law and order, the Supreme Court of India was compelled to question the deliberate inaction of the government in implementing the recommendations of these expert bodies. As early as September 2006 the Supreme Court issued clear directions to the central and state governments to undertake the following specific reforms in police administration:

- Constitute a State Security Commission to ensure that the state government does not exercise unwarranted influence or pressure on the police, lay down broad policy guidelines and evaluate the performance of the state police.
- Ensure that the director general of police is appointed through a merit-based, transparent process and enjoys a minimum tenure of two years.
- Ensure that other police officers on operational duties (including superintendents in charge of a police district and station house officers in charge of a police station) also have a minimum tenure of two years.
- Set up a Police Establishment Board, which will decide all transfers, postings, promotions and other service-related matters for police officers at and below the rank of deputy superintendent and make recommendations on postings and transfers for officers above that rank.
- Set up a National Security Commission at the union level to prepare a panel for selection and placement of chiefs of the Central Police Organisations, who should also be given a minimum tenure of two years.
- Set up independent Police Complaints Authorities at the state and district levels to look into public complaints against police officers in cases of serious misconduct, including custodial death, grievous hurt or rape in police custody.
- Separate the investigation and law and order functions of the police.

The various governments nevertheless have continued to drag their feet. Consequently the Supreme Court reiterates its directives and monitors compliance.[7]

The imperative of a major overhaul of police functions became apparent during the tragic events of terrorism in Mumbai in November 2008. The police response to those events revealed a lack of coordination amongst numerous intelligence and security agencies, as well as a lack of preparedness of the national and state security network to meet the looming threat. As an institutional response to the terror attack, a national intelligence agency is to be established under new central legislation enacted in December 2008. This agency should supersede the role of state agencies where national interest so demands. If the police agencies are made professional at the national level, as envisaged under the new legislation, this change should inevitably carry forward the reform process in the states, which are the main source of security and criminal justice for most Indian citizens.

Undoubtedly, Indian stakeholders at all levels of government—even up to the Supreme Court—are seriously addressing the issues of police reform. The critical question for governance: will the stakeholders in power be prepared to give up their narrow controls in the national interest? Perhaps the current national crisis arising from

IV/12

a terrorist threat will help to carry India along the reform path that has already been charted.

Centralized authority

In most advanced countries, public confidence in the quality of governance tends to be highest in the local government, where citizens directly and immediately see the results of government action (e.g. in education, roads, water, and garbage collection). Confidence decreases with successively higher levels of government. Although the national government is recognized as being important for carrying out specific major functions (such as defence and trade policy), most citizens are not directly affected by these functions in their daily lives. In India, however, the perceptions of different levels of government are exactly the opposite: local governments are seen as the weakest link in governance and the national government as the strongest. This reversal

is perhaps attributable to the fact that, despite the rhetoric for decentralization, India remains a highly centralized country.

Much of the recent debate on decentralization in India has focused on insufficient devolution of functions to the lower levels, which certainly is true. However, the more fundamental problem is the central government's dominant control over resources. In many higher income countries, the central government generates the largest share of resources (table 2). What differentiates India is the very low resource mobilization at the local government level and the relatively low percentage of resource transfers to the lower levels. State governments in India generate a significant level of resources, comparable to other countries, but they also depend on revenue passed down from the centre through revenue-sharing and various centrally sponsored schemes. State politicians expend considerable time and resources seeking

Table 2	Revenue and intergovernmental transfers, by government level, in India and comparable countries

	India (2007)	United States (2006)	Canada (2005)	Mexico (2000)	Brazil (1998)
State government revenue (% of central government revenue)	57	49	41	23	37
Local government revenue					
Share of central government revenue (%)	3	37	29	7	8
Share of state government revenue (%)	5	76	71	29	23
Transfers from central government to state government					
Share of central government revenue (%)	na	15	20	25	12
Share of state government revenue (%)	na	32	47	105	33
Transfers from central government to local government					
Share of central government revenue (%)	—	2	14	3	16
Share of local government revenue (%)	—	6	49	38	186
Transfers from state government to local government					
Share of central government revenue (%)	5	34	—	—	—
Share of local government revenue (%)	100	44	—	—	—

Notes: na is not available.

— is not applicable.

Source: Prepared by the author based on U.S. Census Bureau data; International Monetary Fund, various years, *Government Finance Statistics;* Twelfth Finance Commission data.

> **When states do provide resources to local governments to carry out specific function, they keep the local governments on a very short leash by maintaining tight control over their activities**

a greater share of central resources. It is not surprising that most Indians see the centre as the most important level of government to provide for their welfare.

The lack of resources at the local level has often led state governments to take on many of the functions that should normally be carried out by the local governments. When states do provide resources to local governments to carry out a specific function, they keep the local governments on a very short leash by maintaining tight control of their activities. Local authority was seriously eroded in the 1970s and 1980s, as the state governments routinely dissolved the local bodies and began to run local governments essentially as their departments. These arrangements persist today and contribute to the local governments' lack of standing amongst citizens.

The central government took a major step towards greater decentralization in 1992/93 with the passage of the 73rd and 74th Amendments to the Constitution. The amendments did not mandate decentralization, something that had been discussed at the time but rejected on the grounds of infringement on the powers of the states. Rather, the approach was to encourage states to delegate a suggested list of activities to Panchayati Raj institutions and urban local bodies. It also required states to set up State Finance Commissions to determine revenue-sharing mechanisms between state and local governments. For urban local bodies in 63 cities, it set up a programme to finance infrastructure development, if the concerned states agreed to reforms envisaged under the 74th Amendment.

Fifteen years after the passage of the two amendments, progress has been very slow, with half-hearted and very partial actions by most state governments. Delegation of responsibilities has often not been accompanied by the granting of any significant autonomy. Moreover, there has been little delegation of tax powers. Although most states set up State Finance Commissions to determine the resource transfers from state to local governments to accompany the transfer of responsibilities, the recommendations of these commissions have been often ignored.

The result is that in most states, Panchayati Raj institutions and urban local bodies continue to function essentially as appendages of the state governments. Karnataka is one of the few states that has made the most progress in decentralization to rural local bodies (see annex 2), but it faces continuing pressures for reversal from elected state representatives who see decentralization as a threat to their power and prestige. Although the Panchayati Raj institutions have received some additional resources, most of the resources flowing to localities continue to be provided through centre- or state-sponsored schemes. Such arrangements tax the already limited planning and administrative capacity of the Panchayati Raj institutions without granting them any more authority.

On decentralization to urban local bodies, as discussed in the chapter on urban management,[8] Gujarat provides the best example to follow in creating local governments that are close to the citizens, that derive their revenues much more directly from the citizens and that spend the resources transparently for services people can see and feel. Decentralization is the cornerstone of all efforts to improve governance in India.

Insufficient transparency

Transparency means that citizens have information at hand to monitor government actions and can use the information to hold officials and politicians accountable. Open access to information facilitates the work of the watchdogs of civil society, particularly the press. The popularization of the Internet makes that information easier for everyone to access.

Public institutions in India have been trying to become more open, although much remains to be done. The Right to Information Act (discussed later) has been a major impetus for openness in government. Most major institutions have a website, but information posted is often incomplete or outdated. Few agencies have opened their meetings to the public and, when they have, these are not publicized. The system of appointments, transfers and postings remains secretive and mysterious. There is a lot of public distrust about

> **Indian businesses need to recognize that the poor business environment cannot be divorced from the poor governance facing all citizens**

the integrity of public procurement. What is needed is proactive disclosure of all pertinent information by all public organizations.

Low public demand for better governance

Ask any Indian citizen, and you will hear a litany of problems with the government. Any Indian businessperson can relate stories of corruption, often based on personal experiences. Yet, Indians almost universally express resignation about the way things are and do not seem motivated to do anything to change the state of affairs. Why?

- *Hopelessness.* Most citizens see few avenues open to them for voicing concerns, and they have little faith that those in charge will do anything anyway. Recent initiatives like the Right to Information Act have been helpful, but overall citizens feel their complaints are futile.

- *Disconnection and self-seeking from government.* Citizens see the government as some distant body that has rewards—money, jobs—to dispense, and their ambition is to extract as much as possible for themselves. They almost never see government funds as their own money to manage prudently, perhaps because most taxation is not direct and so much government funding (*sarkari* funds) has been spent on wasteful or unproductive things.

- *Slow emergence of civil society groups.* The civil society institutions that can be useful in educating citizens about their rights and demanding change are just beginning to emerge. Some large cities now have a few activist groups rallying public opinion behind reform efforts, and some have even been successful. The effort needs to be expanded.

The business community has been equally complacent. They complain about the poor business environment but contribute to it by relying on bribery, intermediaries or connections to manoeuvre through the maze of red tape and bureaucracy. Smaller businesses do not protest for fear of retribution, and larger businesses simply find it expedient to use influence for their work. Indian businesses need to recognize that the poor business environment cannot be divorced from the poor governance facing all citizens. A government that does not serve the people well is also unlikely to serve the business interests.

Recent initiatives to improve governance

In the past few years, India has introduced some innovative mechanisms to improve the performance of its institutions. These include using computer technology to request and track service operations (e-governance), passing a modern right-to-information law, establishing ombudsmen (*lokpal* and *lokayukta*) at various levels of government and adopting citizen charters that lay out performance expectations and citizen report cards that rate actual service delivery. These are commendable initiatives, consistent with the modern thinking in developed countries.[9]

E-governance

With the easy and inexpensive availability of information technology, governments at all levels have begun to use e-governance to improve the speed, reliability and efficiency of delivering services to their citizens. Some examples include:

- *One-stop service centres.* The most common use of new technology has been to create one-stop service centres that provide a variety of public and private services to the citizens. The services include, e.g., paying utility bills, providing birth and death certificates, paying property and other local taxes, receiving land titles, purchasing train or bus tickets, filing passport applications and even purchasing and transferring shares. The centres are geographically dispersed and networked, so citizens can easily access any one of them. In many cases, the centres are funded and operated as public-private partnerships. In one state, all transactions are recorded on video camera to eliminate the possibility of under-the-table-payments. The combination of one-stop service with information technology has reduced transaction time and expense (no need for intermediaries to move paperwork along) and bureaucrat opportunities for corruption. Andhra Pradesh, Gujarat and Karnataka have the most widespread and effective service centres of this type.

- *Land records.* Computerization of land title records and maps makes them accessible to anyone. Copies of land records can be obtained from a kiosk without the need to go through the patwari, who can now concentrate on recording any changes. Gujarat and Karnataka have completely computerized their land records and made them available online.
- *Train reservations.* The most well known and highly successful case has been the computerization of train reservations, which has made travel planning easier and virtually eliminated unnecessary trips to railway reservation offices and bribery to get a seat. At the same time, it has improved revenue yield for the railways.
- *Court records.* The Supreme Court and most of the high courts are now completely computerized. As a result, courts have been able to group similar cases on the basis of points of law and thus reduce the backlog of cases.[10]

The experience of e-governance is very promising, but Indian agencies still have a long way to go to replace their manual registers with computer-based systems. The highest priority should be given to areas where the average citizen has the greatest interaction with the government or where functions have been most susceptible to corruption. Land records and transactions, property valuation and taxes, utility bill payments and arrears, land use change proceedings, school admissions and ration card use are some priority areas.

The expansion of e-governance cannot be divorced from the issue of the large number of low-level (class III)

administrative clerks. In some states (such as Punjab), although the receipt of applications for certain government services has been computerized in a one-stop window, the time for processing has not been reduced because paper copies still need to be passed through a succession of clerks. Without a retrenchment, retraining and re-orientation of the class III employees, e-governance initiatives will be thwarted.

Right to information

Accepting the premise that information freedom is a hallmark of democratic governance, as promulgated in the 1948 United Nations Universal Declaration of Human Rights, India enacted the Right to Information Act in 2005. The act empowers any Indian citizen to secure information from any public institution of the government of any state or of the central government within a timeframe of 30 days. In cases involving individual life or liberty the authority is obliged to deliver the relevant information within 48 hours.

India's legislation incorporates the best features of enactments on information freedom elsewhere in the world, and in some ways goes beyond the other models. The act enables citizens to call to account policies as well as any specific decision of public authorities at every level. It also serves as a safeguard against any possible high-handedness by the police and other powerful functionaries. Since its inception in 2005 the Right to Information Act has ensured that many important decisions of central and state governments are open to public notice.

For regulation, adjudication and enforcement of the act, autonomous Information Commissions have been established at the centre and in all the states. Committees of the prime minister or chief minister, as well as the respective leader of the opposition, select the information commissioners at the centre and in the states. This nonpartisan procedure has established the credibility of the commissions. The media, whistle-blowers from within public bodies and nongovernmental organizations are invoking the act extensively to

> **" The Right to Information Act has undoubtedly blazed a trail for empowerment of the public and for accountability and transparency in government**

demand information on sequestered official matters. Since, as a quasi-judicial authority, every commission is empowered to impose financial penalties against any defaulter, proceedings under the Right to Information Act are taken seriously by the entire government machinery. The central Information Commission has held that even notes by officials in all official files constitute "information" under the act and must be disclosed on request. This broad definition offers public access to the identity of the decisionmaker and the contents of the decisions themselves.

The Right to Information Act mandates that all government offices and public institutions must systematize their management of records and display all aspects of their working on an official website. Thus, the Right to Information Act has proved to be an impetus for scientific management of official records, which were frequently in disarray in many offices.

The Right to Information Act has undoubtedly blazed a trail for empowerment of the public and for accountability and transparency in government. As the initiative is carried forward, it must overcome three major obstacles. First, the prompt delivery of information is hampered by the inability of many government offices to systematize their records for open display. Since records are poorly kept, retrieval in response to a demand becomes difficult. Complete overhaul of the methods of working in all government offices is necessary if all the requisite information is to be properly posted on a website—a daunting task for any government. Even in the United Kingdom, the Freedom of Information Act, passed in 2000, began to operate only in 2005. A grace period of five years was allowed for records in that country to be systematized. The Right to Information Act's deadline of four months for effecting improved record management was perhaps not realistic.

Second, the seekers of information have yet to recognize the power of information freedom. Under the Act, citizens have a right to disclosure of any information that can be demanded by an elected representative in

a house of legislature (a state assembly or the national parliament). To really put the act into practice, citizens have to overcome the inertia caused by their traditional timidity in relation to powerful officials.

Third, ensuring access to information requires a change in the mindset of officials. Government functionaries have to become more responsive, better trained and prompt.

Lokpal *and* lokayuktas

As with the right to information, the institution of ombudsman, labelled as *lokpal* for the national level and *lokayukta* for every state, is expected to provide democratic support for cleansing the machinery of administration. The institution has a longer history than the Right to Information Act in India. As early as 1966, the Administrative Reforms Commission in its first report recommended that a *lokpal* be appointed under Article 323 of the Constitution as an autonomous authority to oversee and consider complaints against the highest persons in public office at the national level. Similar autonomous authorities, *lokayukta*s, were suggested for each of the states. The Commission went so far as to append a draft legislative bill incorporating the status and responsibilities of the *lokpal* and *lokayuktas*. These institutions were to keep a watchful eye on the wrongdoings of the administration, taking cognizance of complaints against corrupt elements, especially political persons holding high offices, including ministers.

The government has repeated its commitment to set up the office of the *lokpal*, but despite a lapse of more than 30 years a national ombudsman is yet to be appointed. The recommendations of the 1966 Administrative Reforms Commission have been ignored, except to the extent that many of the states have created bodies by state legislation. There is no uniformity across the states, however, in the functions and authority of the *lokayuktas*. Most appointees are distinguished jurists, being former judges or chief justices of the high courts,

> **" In the absence of a national consensus on establishing the *lokpal* and the limited role so far assigned to *lokayukta*s in the states, the potential of the ombudsmen in India is still unrealized**

but their empowerment is vague. Some states, such as Karnataka, have entrusted the *lokayukta* with wide powers for investigation, but others complain of an inadequate machinery even to look into complaints. In Karnataka, the entire Department of Vigilance has been placed under the executive control of the *lokayukta*. In most states, however, the *lokayukta* is a figurehead who sends occasional recommendations that are often ignored by the government.

The *lokayukta*s also suffer from having too wide a mandate. Although the original intent was for them to focus on allegations of corruption against politicians, in practice they have been swamped by citizens' complaints against low-level functionaries or bureaucrats' complaints against the civil service. There have been very few investigations of politicians, and even in those cases no action was taken.

In the absence of a national consensus on establishing the *lokpal* and the limited role so far assigned to *lokayukta*s in the states, the potential of the ombudsmen in India is still unrealized. The current Administrative Reforms Commission has made important recommendations regarding both the *lokpal* and the *lokayukta*s. At the time of this writing, the recommendations have not been acted upon by the government. The functions and powers of *lokpal* and *lokayukta*s need to be reconsidered. They need to focus only on political corruption, the heart of the governance issue. Their powers need to be correspondingly increased, and they should be freed from the control of the state politicians.

Citizen charters

In a citizen charter, a public service organization undertakes to provide an agreed service within certain declared norms to all citizens in the given area. The standards help set citizen expectations and remove uncertainty and unnecessary efforts in follow-up. A few years ago, almost every government department and agency launched its citizen charter. The Centre for Media Studies Survey of 2005 reported some 107 citizen charters by central government agencies or

organizations and another 629 by various state and local organizations.

Despite these good intentions, the citizen charters have in practice fallen into disuse. The principal reasons include: a lack of awareness by citizens, a lack of precision in setting service standards, a lack of commitment by employees, but most importantly, a lack of any consequences for not meeting standards. Regular monitoring of performance by the agencies and by citizens could make the charters a useful tool for improving governance.

Citizen report cards

In the context of growing urbanization and poor delivery of services, a group of citizens in Bangalore began issuing citizen report cards in 1993. The group gathered systematic feedback from citizens on the quality of services by various local government agencies and publicized the results. Some agencies took notice, possibly concerned with the adverse public reaction to their poor performance, and started to seek citizen input on improving services. The positive interest generated by the initiative led to the creation of a Public Affairs Centre, which began to replicate the process in other cities while also strengthening the Bangalore citizen report card initiative.

In 1994, 1999 and 2003, the Public Affairs Centre prepared annual citizen report cards on city services in Bangalore; they showed a significant improvement in the quality of services by most of the city agencies (figure 1). Aggregate satisfaction levels for all agencies combined rose from 9 percent in 1994 to 34 percent in 1999 to 49 percent in 2003, and perceived corruption showed a marked decline. The centre's positive assessments have been confirmed by other independent surveys.

Although still on a limited scale, India's experience with citizen report cards demonstrates the power of information, when produced without bias, in forcing change. It also shows the power of citizen involvement in improving governance, even without a formal mandate. Probably the most effective way to expand the use of citizen report cards will be to strengthen local civil society

> **All leaders at the central, state and local levels—from the president down—should sign a sworn statement every year reaffirming their commitment to govern ethically**

institutions, which are still weak or absent in most Indian cities.

Recommendations for reform

As the preceding discussion indicates, poor governance is a multifaceted problem, and solutions need to be multifaceted as well. This section recommends a variety of reforms that together are comprehensive yet manageable and, most important, achievable. The recommendations are intended to achieve six goals critical for improving India's governance:

- Raising ethical standards.
- Focusing on essential functions.
- Decentralizing authority.
- Strengthening connections between taxation and services.
- Transforming public officials to public servants.
- Mobilizing civil society.

Raising ethical standards

The political and business leaders of the country must demonstrate a commitment to ethics and integrity, both in their personal behaviour and in the processes they follow in making appointments and conducting business. Specific actions should include:

- *Personal commitments to ethical behaviour.* All leaders at the central, state and local levels— from the president down—should sign a sworn statement every year reaffirming their commitment to govern ethically. The statements should not only proscribe specific actions (such as accepting payments of any kind and accepting gifts of value), but also define clear roles and boundaries for the legislators and executives. The statements should recognize the legitimate role for legislators in setting policy and the distinct role of executives in implementation (including appointments). As has been done in Gujarat (see annex 3), legislators should be barred from serving on the boards of executive

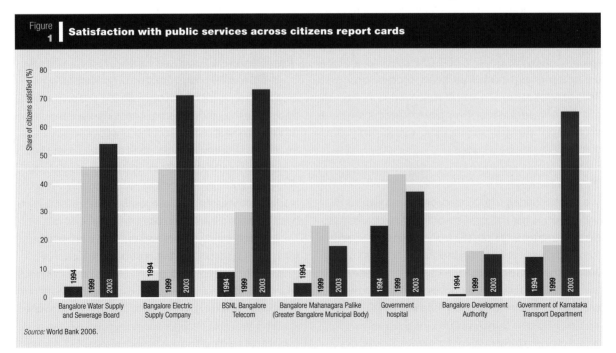

Figure 1 | **Satisfaction with public services across citizens report cards**

Share of citizens satisfied (%)

Bangalore Water Supply and Sewerage Board; Bangalore Electric Supply Company; BSNL Bangalore Telecom; Bangalore Mahanagara Palike (Greater Bangalore Municipal Body); Government hospital; Bangalore Development Authority; Government of Karnataka Transport Department

Source: World Bank 2006.

and regulatory bodies. Such statements should be publicized widely. Similar statements should be required of all heads of departments. It should be acknowledged that a violation of the ethics standards would disqualify a person from continuing to hold the office.

- *Open processes for appointments.* Appointments to the highest public offices should be made in a way that inspires people's trust. There should be full transparency in all appointments to high offices, including the Supreme Court, the high courts, information commissions, the *lokayukta*s, heads of regulatory commissions, and the like. In practice, all major appointments should be conducted through open public hearings, where citizens and other interested parties are invited to testify for or against the candidate, commenting not only on the qualifications but also on issues of ethics and integrity. An open process will also safeguard against baseless allegations and rumours that sometimes have marred the appointments of otherwise deserving individuals to such offices.

- *Business codes of ethics.* The leaders of the large business houses, perhaps starting with the companies listed on the stock exchange, should adopt ethics statements for their employees, including a no-bribery pledge.

Focusing on essential functions

An effective government is one that carries out only the essential functions. The focus on essential functions begins with a careful definition of activities deemed to be critical; the definitions should be periodically updated to eliminate functions that are no longer needed or that have proved beyond the capability of the government. Specifically, a review should be carried out of all government departments and agencies at the centre and the states to identify areas from which the government should withdraw. Such a review should result in the

elimination of some agencies, scaling down of others and strengthening of the critical ones. In addition, there is a potential for considerable downsizing of public sector employees, particularly at the lower levels where recruitments have often been made in response to pressures for patronage.

Even when the government has a clear role in a particular function, it should seek ways to get private and nonprofit sectors involved in delivery, with government providing financing. This approach is particularly relevant for basic public services, such as education, health, garbage collection, road maintenance, public transport, and the like. The central government can reinforce the recent movement towards such public-private partnerships by providing guidelines, models, expertise and financing.

At the same time, there are three basic functions that any government must perform effectively: protecting citizens against crime, violence and, increasingly, acts of terrorism; ensuring fair and speedy justice; and maintaining public trust in the functioning of the state. Unfortunately, India falls short in each of these three functions: the first because of the poor quality and politicization of the police; the second because of the enormous backlog of cases in the judiciary and growing perception of corruption; and the third because of weak institutions for holding elected officials accountable for misdeeds. The critical actions needed in each area include:

- *Police reform.* The actions recommended in the orders of the Supreme Court (discussed earlier) would go a long way towards professionalizing the police and protecting its leaders from political influence. In addition, the central government needs to strengthen its capability to respond to acts of terrorism by expanding the National Security Guard, with stronger capability in intelligence and rapid deployment, a glaring deficiency revealed by the events in Mumbai in November 2008.

> **Bringing government closer to the people will require much more determined decentralization than has been done in the 15 years since the passage of the 73rd and 74th Amendments**

- *Judicial reforms.* To clear the backlog of cases and make sure that capacity keeps up with caseloads, more judges should be appointed, the working hours of judicial officials and staff should be increased, and evening courts should be set up (as has been done in Gujarat). India can also emulate the practice of other countries to reduce caseload by encouraging out-of-court settlements, plea bargain agreements[11] and a more restrictive practice of accepting appeals. At the High Court and Supreme Court levels, the best of the recent law school graduates could serve as clerks to the justices, as is the practice in the United States. The government, in cooperation with the judiciary, can take a lead in this effort by setting the target of eliminating the backlog in five years, rooting out judicial corruption and bringing the guilty to justice and establishing open processes of appointment of all judges.

- *Ethical reform.* Aggressively pursuing corruption and ethical violations is critical to restoring citizens' trust in the integrity of the government. The *lokayukta*s have not proved effective in this regard. Specific steps needed are making political corruption a federal crime; establishing the office of the *lokpal* at the center to specifically be responsible (only) for investigating and prosecuting charges of corruption against elected officials; making *lokayukta*s at the state subservient to the *lokpal*, with the responsibility of pursuing political corruption investigations at the state and local levels under the supervision of, and in collaboration with, the *lokpal*; and providing sufficient investigative resources to the *lokpal* and *lokayukta*s. The additional resources could come from savings from having *lokpal* and *lokayukta*s focus exclusively on political corruption and having *lokayukta*s cover multiple states and share resources across states when needed. The functions of

addressing citizen grievance should be left to the ombudsmen or citizen advocates within the bureaucracy. Corruption charges against public servants should be the responsibility of vigilance bureaus.

Decentralizing authority

Bringing government closer to the people will require much more determined decentralization than has been done in the 15 years since the passage of the 73rd and 74th Amendments. The United States, as the country most like India in geography, diversity, structure of government and legal origins in British institutions, provides the most appropriate model for India. The U.S. Constitution, like the Indian Constitution, prescribes distinct roles and responsibilities only to federal and state levels of government and is silent about local governments. The local governments in the United States also emerged through local demands for self-governance. In addition, the current system of county, village, township and city governments maps almost fully to the Indian districts, villages, towns and municipal corporations.

Specific recommendations to achieve a much more decentralized government are as follows:

- Central, state and local governments should be viewed as three spheres of government, each with distinct and complementary roles and responsibilities, rather than the current view of these being three hierarchical tiers of government.

- Cities above a certain population (say, 100,000), should enjoy full autonomy in planning, expenditures, resource mobilization and personnel within certain parameters prescribed under law. The role of the state governments should be circumscribed in the law. As recommended elsewhere in this chapter, a start should be made by granting such autonomy immediately to the 100 largest cities.

- Zila Parishads, Panchayats and town councils should similarly assume responsibility

> **Public demand for good governance is strongest when citizens see a link between the taxes they pay and the services they receive**

for all functions designated under the 73rd Amendment, with their relative authority determined by negotiation and agreement amongst them, taking into account the unique characteristics of each district. However, in view of their much weaker capacity and fewer resources than urban areas, full autonomy should be phased in over time. In the short term, they should be assigned unequivocal responsibility for local health services, basic education, social welfare, water and sanitation, solid waste management and roads, at a minimum. Funding should be in the form of revenue-sharing, instead of coming through various vertical programmes of the state and central government. Staff (including teachers and health workers) should be recruited specifically by districts or towns and should report to them, not to the state government. State governments should provide technical support and oversight until the local districts can assume full autonomy. Blocks, administrative units created by the state governments to manage the districts, would have no role under the decentralized structure and should be abolished.

- States should undertake a massive programme of staff training for all local bodies.

Decentralization should also ensure accountability to the people by:

- Requiring full transparency in all matters related to planning, expenditures and personnel. Proactive disclosure should be the norm in all such matters. Public comment and hearings should be required for all planning, budget and taxation matters. The Janaagraha, a nongovernmental organization working in Bangalore, has drafted useful model codes of information-sharing for urban areas that can be adapted by localities.
- Establishing ombudsmen at the municipal and district levels to investigate citizen complaints about malfeasance or lack of performance. The findings should be made public.
- Encouraging civil society groups to monitor performance and publish periodic report cards of results. The Indian business community and philanthropic organizations should provide financial support to selected nongovernmental organizations to perform these functions.

Indeed, decentralizing authority along the lines suggested here would greatly diminish the role of the state governments in local affairs, something the states may resist. Only strong and selfless leaders at the state level can make the necessary changes. However, the central government can play a catalytic role by providing additional funding to local bodies in cases where a state takes significant steps towards decentralization. Such funding should be in the form of reliable budget support over a number of years (not as a centrally funded special project) and should be linked to increased resource mobilization efforts and tangible actions, rather than promises of action.

Strengthening connections between taxation and services

Public demand for good governance is strongest when citizens see a link between the taxes they pay and the services they receive. Strengthening that link in India will require building a much stronger tax base at the local and state levels, with a correspondingly smaller base at the central level. Specific actions that should be taken include:

- The centre should limit its taxation to amounts that meet its Constitutionally prescribed functions and support a small number of centrally sponsored programmes that can help promote social inclusion or advance other specific national goals. The centre should not mobilize resources simply to pass them on through general revenue-sharing to lower levels. Nor has the centre achieved much progress in "lagging states" through higher levels of budget-sharing.

> **The IAS as a national civil service should be abolished and replaced by civil service recruitment unique to the central and the state levels**

The centre can better assist lagging states by tilting certain central schemes towards them.

- The states should individually determine their own taxation sources and levels. They may piggyback a surcharge on certain central taxes (such as the income tax, value added tax, gasoline tax and so on). But each state must determine the level with due deliberation and make sure that the population understands the decisions taken and thus holds state officials accountable.

- The biggest effort needed is in taxation at the local level, particularly in the cities. Each local government, with due deliberation in their elected bodies and with public consultation, should determine the types and levels of taxes and be held accountable for results.

Transforming public officials to public servants

Establishing accountability to the people as the guiding principle at all levels of government will require significant changes in the attitudes of civil servants and the structure of the civil service. These recommendations would make the civil service in India at par with the practice of most developed countries:

- The IAS as a national civil service should be abolished and replaced by civil service recruitment unique to the central and the state levels of government. However, the selection for civil service should continue to be done by the centre and the states in a competitive and transparent manner, as is currently done for the IAS. Each local government should similarly have its own staffing and recruitment.

- All professional employees should be recruited through the civil service at the relevant level of government, with progression from one level to the next done competitively based on merit. There should not be a separate elite programme for the "officers". The focus instead should be on recruiting professionals with the requisite expertise and experience.

- The only rationale for continuing a national recruitment programme like the IAS for the state governments is to ensure constant infusion of young and bright Indians to the civil service and to encourage cross-state fertilization. If the IAS does continue, three conditions are essential: the numbers should be kept very small; the centrally selected civil servants should be assigned exclusively to states other than their domicile state; and once selected and trained, the young recruits should start their careers at the lowest professional level and work their way up in competition with all other civil servants, rather than being immediately anointed as managers, as in the current IAS.

- With each government level having its own civil service, the present system of transfers and postings between them should be abolished. Each level should have a competitive application and selection process to attract staff from other levels.

- The professional civil service should become more specialized, with people assigned to specific functions after their selection in the civil service. Movement across functions should be encouraged over time through a competitive application and appointment process, instead of the current system of transfers and postings.

- All mid- and senior-level appointments at the centre and state levels should be open to applicants from outside the government.

- Heads of departments and agencies should serve fixed terms and not be subject to removal by incoming politicians, except for cause.

- The current system of perks should be abolished and its value monetized in salaries. Only those at the highest levels should be provided housing and official cars, and none should be entitled to servants and orderlies for their houses. This change will not only reduce government expenditures, since most perks are expensive and tend to come at an inordinate hidden cost, but also improve the public image of a civil servant. The change should be made first at the local level to reverse the worrisome trends already being observed, but should then be extended to all levels of government.

- Class III employment should be reduced to a fraction of professional staff and limited to only a few support positions, such as messengers, secretaries and personal assistants. A drastic reduction of current Class III will be required over time, with a small portion replaced by recruitment at the professional levels.

Mobilizing civil society

All Indians need to take a much more active role in demanding good governance. The changes recommended above should help citizens feel that their government is becoming more responsive, but should also make them feel more empowered and obliged to let their voices be heard on the major issues. Civil society organizations can play a much more prominent role in this process. Already civil society organizations in some states have taken advantage of available instruments, such as right to information and public interest litigation, to raise awareness and demand change. However, such cases are still limited in numbers.

India should embark on a proactive programme to develop civil society groups that can act as watchdogs on government performance. A start can be made in the 100 largest cities, which are recommended here to recieve a grant of full autonomy. It is likely to be easier to find and nurture such organizations in the larger cities. The organizations will need autonomous and stable sources of funding for several years. The Indian private sector should be prepared to provide some funds. In addition, the central government can approve selected

bilateral and multilateral sources of grant funds to provide direct support.

Good governance for a modern society

As India leapfrogs into the ranks of affluent countries, no challenge is greater or more important than improving governance. Businesses and investors will increasingly expect good governance as a precondition of high economic growth, and citizens will expect it commensurate with their improved economic status. Most of the first-generation reforms that opened up the economy could be accomplished without major changes in India's outmoded institutions, but basic institutional reforms that improve the quality of governance are now critical. The recommendations in this chapter provide the essential elements of a package that the country's leaders need to consider.

Unquestionably, implementation will not be easy. While there is widely shared dissatisfaction about the current state of affairs, there is far less consensus on whether governance is an issue that should or can be tackled.

There are two prevalent views—pessimistic and gradualist. The most common is the highly pessimistic view that change is impossible, given the entrenched interests and deep scepticism about the political system. The pessimists cite as evidence inaction or half-hearted action on the recommendations of numerous commissions going as far back as the 1960s, and they are equally negative about the current Administrative Reform Commission.

The gradualists argue instead that governance improves in a slow endogenous process as incomes rise and not much needs to be done to accelerate the process. They cite the United States as an example, which also had serious problems of political corruption and collusion between politicians and business in the early part of the 20th century (and some would argue that it does even now in some places).

This chapter disagrees with both views. While there is justification for pessimism based on the past record

IV/12

of government action (or more appropriately, inaction), some progressive state leaders have begun to show a commitment to improving governance, with Gujarat generally recognized as having taken the most steps (see annex 3). Enlightened leadership, particularly at the state level, can have a tremendous beneficial effect.

Improvement in governance is not some automatic process of historical development—it requires enlightened leadership. Certainly, in advanced countries such as the United States governance changed as incomes rose. In fact, there was considerable citizen activism and local control, as well as a significant effort to fight corruption, in part by breaking up the monopoly power of business. The changes in the United States also took place in the context of opening up new frontiers that provided economic opportunities. India today has to grow in a highly competitive environment in a globalized world. It cannot afford to follow the precedents of a century ago and must be more proactive in creating the right conditions for greater prosperity.

Even amongst those who agree with the need for the reforms recommended here, there will be resistance to change. Vested interests will argue against specific proposals. Some will assert that decentralization will increase corruption, as has been observed in other countries. But these arguments ignore this chapter's main contention: it is inconceivable that a country as large and diverse as India can continue to be governed as it is now. Centralized power has simply not delivered and cannot be expected to do better in the future.

Some will find the dramatic shift in the focus of the civil service too extreme. The strong and elite IAS lobby will argue against state-level recruitment as "diluting national unity" and removing barriers to political corruption, despite their own assessment that over the past two decades they have become enmeshed in corruption along with the politicians. These arguments need to be considered against the basic premises here that the civil service should function as public servants and not as rulers and should be close to the people and not imposed from far away.

Finally, the political class that has devised ways to benefit from the current misgovernance is likely to resist more accountability. But a visible improvement in public integrity is essential to restore much-needed public confidence in the government. This must start at the top of both the central and the state governments.

Whatever problems decentralization may pose—and it will surely pose many—the solution is not to centralize but to strengthen local institutions. As Mahatma Gandhi replied to Lord Mountbatten's concern about the possible chaos India would face if the British withdrew suddenly: "But it will be our chaos." The words hold just as true for decentralization. There will no doubt be chaos, but the people must own the problems and find their own solutions. Strong and committed political leadership will also be critical, because proposed reforms will have to be implemented as a complete package and not piecemeal. Guiding such significant changes will require political courage to overcome all the objections of the many entrenched groups. Yet this cannot be a time for marginal tinkering and partisan bickering. The reforms to transform India's governance will never be implemented unless leaders put their personal and party interests behind the interests of the public.

Annex 1

Doing business in India: A saga of visa extension, as narrated by a nonresident Indian

We landed at Delhi only to find that while we had our U.S. passports, our Persons of Indian Origin (PIO) cards were missing. Somehow, we had lost them between the time we boarded the plane at Washington Dulles and our arrival in Delhi. We were panicked since we knew that India does not grant visas on arrival.

Much to our relief, the immigration officer was very helpful. He told us that while under normal circumstances he would have sent us back to Paris where we had taken our connecting flight, given our circumstances he would use his authority to grant us a visa but only for two weeks. He told us that we would have to apply to the Ministry of Home Affairs (MOHA) for an extension beyond two weeks. We were relieved and thanked him profusely. At least we were in the country and surely we would find some way to get the Ministry of Home Affairs to give us an extension. I was impressed to see one of the much-maligned Indian bureaucrats making a decision on the spot. Maybe Indian bureaucracy had changed after all.

On arriving in my hometown in Punjab, my family immediately found a friend of friend who occupied a senior position in the MOHA. I called and got through to his personal assistant, who had already been told about me. The personal assistant directed me to the MOHA website to find the two-page form for visa extensions that I was to fill out and courier to him. The form was relatively straightforward, not too different from what I would have expected to see in the United States for similar matters. I attached a cover letter explaining my situation. I was slightly embarrassed to think why I did not do all this myself given the simplicity of the process, without having to call on an influential contact. Maybe I too had been a creature of habit and unable to fathom that the Indian bureaucracy had changed.

My positive view was short-lived. The personal assistant called back the next day, after he had received the forms, to tell me that the matter was not so simple after all. I had to file a police report for my lost PIO cards and take the police report to the foreigners' cell at the district police headquarters, who would process my application and send it on to MOHA. But he also assured me to not worry. "Everything will be taken care of. This is just the process you have to follow." Thus began my saga with the real Indian bureaucracy.

Filing a police report was not so simple. After two hours at the police station being given the run-around from one desk to another, with some desks unattended for "tea break", I returned home frustrated. But an employee of the family business came to my rescue. "Never mind, uncle. I deal with these people every day and know what to do. Just give me the stuff and I will take care of it." He disappeared with our passports and my letter to the police explaining our lost PIOs. Raj returned after four hours, all sweaty and hassled, with a sheath of papers in his hands. These were stamp papers on which an affidavit had been typed saying that we had accidentally dropped the PIO cards while walking down the street in the city. It turned out that the police could only take a police report if the PIO cards had been lost in their jurisdiction. If they were lost in the air between Washington and Delhi, we should have filed the report with the Delhi airport police, which of course was before we cleared immigration! Moreover, you cannot file a report by simply telling the police or sending them something in writing. It has to be an "affidavit" on a "stamp paper" that costs a few rupees. Raj assured me that it does not matter at all that my affidavit will be false. "No one will read it. All they need is a piece of paper." Besides, what other choice did I have?

The affidavits returned later in the evening with an unintelligible scribble in Punjabi by the police department on the top margin. It apparently indicated that the report had been filed with the police.

The next step was to take it to the "foreigners' cell" at the district police headquarters to file my application. I was in no mood to go again from desk to desk in futility. So I fell back on the common Indian trait of finding a friend, who knew some high-ranking police official, who arranged for me to be received at the foreigners' cell. Inspector Singh was most cordial, offering me a warm cup of tea on arrival. He patiently explained to me the procedure: I was to go out to one of the "*Munshi*" sheds in the parking lot, pay him a fee and have him prepare the paperwork, which consisted of yet another affidavit on a stamp paper, this time saying that I will not become a public ward. Then I was to have someone known to me in the town certify that he will be responsible financially if I became indigent, and after this is done, I should go to the local branch of State Bank of India and deposit a processing fee and come back with the receipt from the bank and the completed affidavits along with three photographs. It took me a whole day to complete the process. Mr. Singh welcomed me back at the end of the day. He registered each of the three applications in longhand in duplicate in his "foreigners' register" and fixed one picture in the register. (I thumbed through the pages and found not a single foreign name. There were pictures of men, women, and children of all ages, most adorned in nice Punjabi garb!) But then he apologized and said that my daughters had to be with me in person, since we now have to appear before his senior officer. I returned home and collected them and brought them back to Mr. Singh's office.

We waited patiently for "*sahib*" to appear in his office. After an hour, Mr. Singh's phone rang. We all followed him hurriedly to the office of the assistant superintendent of police. A smartly dressed, somber-looking man sat behind a large desk. He never lifted his head. He did not offer us the chairs in front of him. We all stood there while he shuffled his papers. After a couple of minutes, he looked up with a little disdain to ask: "How long have you been in the United States?" and began signing the forms barely paying attention to my answer "40 years." My daughters were amused by his officiousness, but fortunately only joked about it outside his presence.

We returned with Mr. Singh to his office. He penned in some more entries in his register next to our names. I couriered the entire paperwork to the personal assistant in Delhi.

We received a call three days later from Mr. Singh saying that our visa renewal had been approved by Delhi and we could pick them up at his office. Again, another two hours sitting in his office while he filled in some forms, placed several different stamps on them, each time making a loud thump, and insisted that we have tea. When I thanked him at the end, he smiled and said: "You must be an important man with such a high approach. Normally, Delhi never approves and if they do approve, it is never for more than a few days. You asked for two weeks and they gave you four weeks." I muttered something polite to appear humble. My work had been done, and I was grateful.

I left the office thinking that if this is what it took someone who knew someone high up to get this simple matter dealt with, what is the chance of someone simply walking into these offices and getting attention? What took me numerous forms, visits to several different offices, at least two full days of chasing personally, the cost of various steps and not to mention the payments that I did not see would in developed countries have been a simple application with a one- or two-step process.

Annex 2
Karnataka's decentralization to Panchayati Raj institutions

Karnataka has had a long history of Panchayati Raj institutions. The Karnataka Zila Parishad, Taluk Panchayat Samithis, Mandal Panchayats and Nyaya Panchayat Act of 1983 were brought into operation in 1983 when some 2,469 Mandal Panchayats and 19 Zila Parishads came into existence. Some 257 plan schemes were transferred from the state government to Zila Parishads, and 89 plan schemes to Mandal Panchayats.

Following the 73rd Constitutional Amendment in 1993, Karnataka enacted a revised Karnataka Panchayat Raj Act with these provisions:

- Three Panchayta Raj institutions (PRIs) were recognized: Zila Parishads (ZP) at the district level, Taluka Panchayat (TP) at the taluka level and a Gram Panchayat (GP) at the village level. Subsequently (in 2003), a detailed activity mapping assigned distinct functions and responsibilities for each of the three PRIs, following the principle of subsidiarity.
- Some 29 subjects previously handled by the state were transferred to the PRIs in accordance with the 73rd Amendment.
- More than 100,000 government servants were transferred to the PRIs on deputation. A senior IAS officer was assigned as the executive head of the district reporting to the Zila Parishad. All employees in the district reported to him.
- Fiscal authority along with expenditure control authority was decentralized to PRIs, with a significant growth in allocated resources (from nearly 16 billion rupees in 2004/05 to 51.6 billion rupees in 2007/08 in plan and nonplan allocations).
- Certain tax powers were assigned to the PRIs that, along with reforms in property taxation, resulted in significantly higher collection.
- Elections were held in 2005 for all three PRIs: 5,628 Gram Panchayats, 176 Taluka Panchayats and 27 Zila Parishads for total elected representatives of 91,402 for GPs, 3,683 TPs and 1,005 ZPs. About 40 percent of the elected members are women, and 28 percent are from scheduled castes and scheduled tribes.
- Full transparency was instituted in PRIs by requiring:
  o Monthly meetings at the GP level.
  o Disclosure of pecuniary interest by PRI members in any matters coming before them.
  o Declaration of assets and liabilities annually by TP and ZP members.
  o Declaration of election expenses by TP and ZP members.
  o All proceedings to be made public within 72 hours.
  o Conduct minimum of two Ward Sabhas and Gram Sabhas each year.
  o Annual audits by comptroller and auditor general for ZPs and TPs and by the Local Audit Circle for GPs. Internal audits done by chief administrative officer of the ZP.
  o Jamabandhi (social audit) conducted each year of all GPs between August 16 and September 15, with all records made available to the public.
  o An extensive programme for training elected representatives and staff of PRIs by the Administrative Training Institute in Mysore.

Some issues arising from the implementation need to be addressed:

- PRIs are often seen as rivals for influence by state legislators with periodic attempts to weaken their role.
- The state bureaucracy has resisted working under PRIs, resulting in attempts to thwart some aspects of decentralization.
- There is no separate cadre and recruitment policy in place for PRI employees.
- Large numbers of specialized centre- and state-sponsored schemes drain limited planning and implementation capacity.

- GPs and TPs lack administrative support.
- Elected representatives of PRIs also lack of capacity and skills.
- TP does not have a clear role at the intermediate level.

- Unscientific rotation of the heads (*adhyaksha*) and deputy head (*upadhyaksha*) of the districts results in a lack of continuity and weak accountability.

Annex 3
Gujarat's approach: "Minimum government and maximum governance"

Gujarat is widely recognized throughout India as one state that has made a concerted effort to improve governance in the last five years. Today, the state ranks high amongst the Indian states in the quality of its investment climate and its control of corruption. As a result, it has become the state most favoured by investors, accounting for the lion's share (25.8 percent) of all investments in India in 2006/07, well ahead of all other states in India.

The state government has taken a number of initiatives to improve governance in the delivery of services to citizens and to create an enabling environment for investors. These initiatives can be categorized under the following key principles:

Empowered civil servants

- Instilling in all civil servants the notion of not government employees (*karam chari*) but public servants (*karam yogi*).
- Training of all government employees (350,000 out of 500,000 total completed to date) in carrying out their functions more effectively. Every employee is expected to undergo at least three days of continuing training each year.
- Convening of Chintan Shibir, an annual three-day conclave of the chief minister, all ministers, secretaries to the government, department heads, and all district collectors and district development officers (some 250 in total) to review progress in the state, to discuss challenges, to share best practices and management approaches, and to generate new ideas to improve governance. Ideas are generated freely without consideration of rank or hierarchy.
- A clear separation between the elected officials and the civil servants, with the former framing policies and programmes and the latter responsible for implementation. No minister or member of the legislature is allowed to serve in an executive capacity or on the board of a public corporation.
- Improved job satisfaction of civil servants through initiatives such as Swant Sukhai, which allows district collectors and district development officers

to implement any project during the year that they consider to be a personal priority, free from implementation rules and regulations.

Decentralization

- Implementation of the 73rd and 74th Constitutional Amendments on decentralization. The municipal corporations are particularly empowered to assume all responsibilities and enjoy considerable autonomy not only in functions but also in personnel and finances.

Open government

- A state-of-the-art information centre (BISAG) makes available all data and other information on the state for shared use by all departments, breaking down the traditional bureaucratic barriers to information sharing. BISAG makes extensive use of satellite imagery to generate information on land, water and other resources in the state.
- An open presentation by all department heads of their priorities and vision to a meeting chaired by the chief minister, with comments and suggestions sought from other departments.
- A determined effort to make available on the Internet as much information as possible on the functions, procedures and priorities of the government.

Citizen-centered government services

- An extensive network of Jan Sewa Centres in all 25 districts and 225 talukas, with single-window service for the public services (about 40 in total) most commonly accessed by citizens. The centres are networked through the Gujarat State-Wide Network to allow the citizens to access the services in any of the centres. Service standards are set, with rigorous daily monitoring to ensure compliance and to identify weak links in the system. Many services are provided the same day. Similar centres have been introduced in all 141 municipalities.

- Computerization of all 14,000 Gram Panchayats under the e-Gram programme that allows instant processing of birth and death registration and issuance of certificates for certain services administered by the Panchayats.
- All land records in the state have been computerized and made accessible instantaneously to the citizens through the e-Dhara project.
- State-Wide Attention on Grievances by Application of Technology (SWAGAT), a mechanism set up in the Office of the Chief Minister to deal with citizen grievances. Complaints can be sent over the Internet. The SWAGAT secretariat, led by a senior officer, channels each complaint to the relevant office and ensures prompt response. Citizens also have an opportunity to meet personally with the chief minister one fixed day of the month.
- SWAGAT programmes have also been instituted at the district and taluka level, where public complaints can be addressed to the collector or the district development officer.
- All ministers and officials are required to be present in their offices on two fixed days during the week, when any citizen can meet them on a walk-in basis.
- A video conference network covering the entire state down to the village level maintained by BISAG is used regularly for public consultation and information-sharing.
- In cooperation with the state high court, evening courts have been introduced and working days extended (by half an hour a day and seven days a year) to make the court more accessible to citizens and to reduce the backlog of cases. The chief minister plans to reduce the backlog completely by the end of 2010.

Focus on results

- The state leadership emphasizes timely completion of development schemes rather than merely publicizing the launch of initiatives. Some examples include: construction of some numerous small check dams throughout the state that have helped reverse the serious problem of groundwater depletion, 24/7 power supply to all villages as demanded by the citizens, complete unbundling of the power sector with promising outcomes, construction of world-class rapid transit corridors for buses, riverfront development of the famed Sabarmati River in Ahmadabad, door-to-door garbage collection throughout the state and improvements in the nutritional status of children.
- A statewide initiative is launched each year to focus on a specific problem and mobilize the citizens and the state machinery to tackle the problem. Recent initiatives have included controlling pollution, increasing literacy, helping the environment and improving nutrition.

Public-private partnerships

- The state seeks private partnerships wherever possible in all its major initiatives.

INDIA
2039

Part IV

Chapter

13

Governance
and
administrative
reforms

Governance and administrative reforms: Reforming the public administration and civil service

C. M. Vasudev, Hariharan Ramachandran, and Vivek K. Agnihotri

Importance of governance and administrative reforms

In the past two decades, the world has witnessed tumultuous changes in the economic arena and in global expectations. Many countries have learned that unregulated markets can play havoc with the domestic and global economy and more importantly, that the state also matters and that it cannot abdicate critical responsibilities to the market. Each country must choose not only its role in this new world economic order but also its goals, developing a blueprint of where it wants to be some decades into the future. While the blueprint must be developed by the political leadership, the civil service and bureaucracy must be prepared to implement it. Alongside the political leadership and the bureaucracy, the judiciary, the media and civil society also have important roles in shaping governance.

Policy reforms in India have focussed on liberalizing the economy and reducing the role of an overextended government in order to move the economy to a higher growth trajectory. While these efforts must continue, the next generation of reforms will also need to address governance improvement and the government's ability to provide security to its citizens, to frame clear laws and to enforce them effectively.[1] A World Bank study of 150 countries finds positive causal relationships between measures of perceived quality of governance and development outcomes.[2] Public administration and civil service reforms and reform of the judicial infrastructure will be critical for improving the governance framework.

It is now conventional wisdom amongst development practitioners that governance is a critical variable in development. This chapter focuses on administrative reforms at several levels—governance issues relating to the civil service, public order, internal security, and judicial reforms; the changing role of the state in economic administration; institution building, including strengthening regulatory systems and competition; and delivery of social services such as education, health and social security to safeguard the interests of vulnerable groups.

To meet the needs of the growing and modernizing Indian economy, fundamental administrative reforms are needed in a system that has experienced numerous incremental changes to the original colonial system developed by the British. Past attempts at administrative reforms have had little success. As the recent report of the Second Administrative Reform Commission (2007) observes:

> It is ironical that there has been no sincere attempt to restructure the civil service although more than six hundred committees and commissions[3] have looked into different aspects of public administration in the country. Rather, the Indian reform effort has been unfailingly conservative, with limited impact. Rapid and fundamental changes are taking place in the political, economic and technological fields. These call for major reform in the civil service.[4]

Current state of affairs

The public administration system is plagued by inefficiency, incompetence and corruption. This results in reduced development impact of economic growth and efficacy of public expenditure and poor delivery of public services to the citizens.

The seriousness of the situation can be gauged by the fact that the President of India in her speech on the eve of the 63rd Independence Day Speech (August 14, 2009) felt compelled to highlight the ill effects of these governance deficiencies. In her Address, the President said:

> **"** There is outrage when money meant
> for welfare schemes is pilfered out by
> corrupt practices.... Hence, the emphasis
> on reform of governance for effective
> delivery of public services is critical
> to change the lives of the people

Facilities, amenities and services meant for them [the people] whether they are living in rural or urban areas can be delivered smoothly only if there is an effective governance system that is less cumbersome but more transparent and accountable. There is outrage when money meant for welfare schemes is pilfered out by corrupt practices.... Hence, the emphasis on reform of governance for effective delivery of public services is critical to change the lives of the people.[5]

Shourie,[6] in a review of procedural delays in decision making in government, gives a detailed account of the persistent delays in decision making, with attendant high transaction costs, because of time spent by senior civil servants on trivial matters. The report led to wide ranging discussion of a host of ideas for improving governance, such as greater transparency, accountability, best practices and citizen's charters.

Blurring of boundaries

An increased blurring of the boundaries between the three pillars of democracy—Legislature, Executive and Judiciary—is a matter of concern. Members of Parliament and of State Legislatures have increasingly wanted to have a greater role in the executive functions, thereby further eroding the checks and balances in the system and leading to further politicization of the civil services. This trend is also indicative of the growing impatience with the inability of the civil services to deliver on the mandates given during elections by the political executive. The judiciary's growing pronouncements on issues in the domain of the Executive is generally attributed to the failure of the bureaucracy and the executive to perform the tasks entrusted to them.

Civil Service: Federal or State?

The role of the All India Services and their continued relevance is a contentious issue which attracts extreme views. Of the All India Services, the Indian Administration Service (IAS) is seen as the symbol of civil service and often all the ills that plague the system are laid at its door. Also under attack is Article 312 of the Constitution of India which provides for creation of the All India Services, including the IAS. The current structure of the All India Services is one where the central government recruits officers on behalf of the state governments and officers are allocated to cadres of different states. Under All India Services rules, the appointing authority is the President of India and the central government of India has the final say in all service related matters including disciplinary action. Accordingly, there is dual control over the service conditions of civil servants. The state governments do not find this arrangement to be very satisfactory, and feel that it leads to increased influence of the central government over the states and dilution of their control over the All India Services officers. It also erodes continuity in administration and has the effect of poaching of talented officers of the State Cadre by the central government.[7]

Supporters of the All India Services system argue that, in view of their national vision and perspective, these services have been instrumental in promoting national integration. By virtue of serving in the state as well as the central governments, AIS officers are able to build bridges between the two levels of the Indian federal system. They are able to balance the state level perspectives with national perspectives. When sent on deputation from the states to the centre they are seen to be contributing to participation by the states in management of the central government. On account of their selection through an All India competitive examination, the caliber of the officers selected is significantly higher than that of officers recruited at the state level. Moreover, on account of the constitutional safeguards provided to them, the officers of All India Services can afford to give independent advice to the political executives.[8]

Be that as it may, the officers of All India Services have not always covered themselves with glory. Being at the pinnacle of the civil services pyramid, they cannot escape the responsibility for the many ills that plague the

" **A major area of concern in Indian administration is the civil servant–politician relationship**

system. Several of them have been found wanting in professional competence, integrity and intellectual honesty and have been alleged to have aligned themselves with the politicians in power, not always in the best interests of the society at large. They have not shown the leadership needed to improve the civil service apparatus and are often perceived to be self serving. Frequent transfers across sectors and between states and centre contribute to weakening their commitment to the jobs they are assigned to. They are also often seen as representing a vested interest that obstructs reforms aimed at reducing the role and the scope of government activities and also do not encourage lateral entry of specialists into higher echelons of civil service or autonomous regulatory bodies. Any agenda for civil service reforms should address theses deficiencies.

Politicization

A major area of concern in Indian administration is the civil servant–politician relationship. The need to motivate All India Services to discharge their duties and responsibilities without fear and favour has been enshrined in law. In practice, however, because of the weaknesses of the officers themselves or excessive political pressures, the civil servants are increasingly becoming subservient to the political executive of the day. Over the years, a healthy respect for each other's role has come to be replaced by sycophancy and mutual aggrandizement. This has altered the basic structure which had envisaged an anonymous civil service with some degree of responsibility to the society at large instead of accountability only to the political executive of the day. Politicians tend to have a short time horizon, constrained by electoral considerations, and this myopia is transmitted to the patronage-seeking bureaucracy, thus weakening institutions and seriously damaging effective governance. Increasing political interference in the administrative domain is also a result of political patronage in the transfer and posting of civil servants.

The political executive has used the tools of frequent transfers, arbitrary promotions, and appointments to make the civil servants subservient and in many cases their partners for furthering their objectives. In one state, orders for the transfer of 1000 officials were effected in a short period of two years and in one instance transfers ran at an average of seven per day! Such widespread politicization has led to collusion between legislature and executive with widespread adverse consequences for internal accountability. Managerial functions which should be in the professional domain of civil servants are being encroached upon by the political executives or legislators. There is a need to have an unbiased look at the system so that the roles of professional civil servants and political executives and legislators are clearly defined and understood and respected.

Cost reduction and rightsizing

One strand of administrative reforms in India concerns the need to drastically reduce non-development expenditures and transaction costs. In early efforts, this led to solutions for downsizing the government by freezing recruitment across the board. Later, rightsizing became the guiding principle for dealing with the need to expand the government's role in internal security, regulation and law enforcement and in some sectors, such as elementary education and primary health care, while contracting it out in others, especially in general administration, and at the lower rungs across the board. Increasing use of e-governance will also create demands for rightsizing and for the right skill mix of staff. Many government offices are increasingly resorting to outsourcing services such as sanitation and housekeeping to move out of areas that are better handled by the private sector and reduce the wage burden.

Implementation of government programs and projects also suffers from a number of deficiencies and needs specific remedial actions, including a focus on objectives, monitoring, and evaluation (see box 1).

The challenge for the government is to be able to redeploy its work force and have the right skill mix of employees to meet the needs of the changing role of government. Attempts to create an inventory of surplus

> **While systemic changes may have improved some aspects of the business climate, many governance-related shortcomings still present obstacles to growth, especially for small businesses**

Box 1 | Performance of programs and projects

For improving performance and monitoring of programs and projects, problems at two levels need to be tackled. First, there is the need to address the high cost of implementation and multiple layers of administration and supervision with limited skills and capacities. When a former Prime Minister had said that only 14 paise out of a rupee allocated for a particular project reaches the intended beneficiary, it was not so much a reflection of leakage of funds (which is also not insignificant) as the layers of administration through which funds flow and supervision of implementation is done. Apart from the number of layers, the skills available with the implementing staff are often highly inadequate. Capacity building is rarely given the attention it deserves.

Second, since programs are driven by procedures and rules, the system tends to lose sight of the objectives and often misses the forest for the trees. Concepts like performance budgeting or zero-based budgeting remain a paper exercise devoid of any practical utility. Measures that can be taken to remedy the situation include framing of programs and schemes with a clear description of objectives and physical targets, and linking allocation of funds and disbursements to realization of the stated objectives. There should also be effective monitoring and evaluation and periodic impact assessment of every program by agencies outside the government, and the results used for improved implementation and for designing future programs.

personnel, so that workers in contracting sectors could be redeployed to expanding sectors, have had only limited success. The success of all these civil service reform measures would need to be measured in terms of results and national as well as international perceptions about the efficiency, effectiveness, transparency, quality of service, citizen centricity, and, above all, ethics, fairness and equity in the delivery of public goods and services by the civil servants. Achieving success will require a significant, sustained effort over a long period to make fundamental changes in the way in which public administration systems are structured and implemented. As in all other areas of reforms success will, above all, require visionary political leadership and a bipartisan understanding across the political spectrum.

Business climate and subsidies

The business environment for new enterprises has been vastly improved in India over the last two decades, through the dismantling of "the license and inspector Raj" and the successful courting of members of the Indian diasporas by the government, particularly

state governments. While systemic changes may have improved some aspects of the business climate, many governance-related shortcomings still present obstacles to growth, especially for small businesses.

The Doing Business Surveys conducted by the World Bank have highlighted deficiencies in regulations for starting new businesses, hiring and firing workers, transferring property, protecting legal rights, establishing adequate credit information systems and bankruptcy laws, and enforcing contracts and corporate governance. There is evidence that subsidies such as low interest credit, and the Public Distribution System meant for the poorer segments of business and society fail to reach them, while large investors reap huge direct benefits through tax holidays and land allotment at prices below market values.

Subsidies—their size, transparency, and target population—underlie many of the issues affecting the efficiency of social service delivery. Non-transparent subsidies hide inefficiencies, and their benefits do not always reach the intended beneficiaries. For example, a cost-plus pricing regime in the fertilizer industry means

> **The need for comprehensive reforms in the Criminal Justice System and Police has been highlighted by many commissions, committees and judicial pronouncements**

that subsidies may be going to inefficient producers in the name of subsidizing farmers. Similarly, food subsidies may be rewarding the inefficient practices of the Food Corporation of India rather than benefiting poor consumers.

The business climate at the state level is driven primarily by subsidies and incentives. States compete to provide the most generous incentives, even though the costs and benefits of such incentives remain unclear.

Consider the contrasting experience in the states of Gujarat and West Bengal. While the former records one of the highest committed investments among all the states, the latter experienced investment being pulled out.[9] Gujarat's economic successes, and its perceived positive investment climate appears to be more personality driven than systems driven.

Judicial and police reforms

Maintenance of public order and internal security is a basic function of the state and is critical for fostering development. Considerable empirical evidence links performance of the legal system and a country's economic development. Clear and swift enforcement of contractual and property rights is crucial for the functioning of an efficient market economy. India faces many challenges and grave problems in this sphere. These problems relate to a diverse set of issues comprising communal strife, terrorism, militancy in certain parts, and left wing extremism in the form of naxalism. A mixture of social, economic, political, and administrative factors contribute to these problems, and solutions will need to address these causative factors. Experience over the years has underscored major weaknesses in the institutions responsible for maintaining internal security and public order. The need for comprehensive reforms in the Criminal Justice System and Police has been highlighted by many commissions, committees, and judicial pronouncements.

The Committee on Reforms of Criminal Justice System set up by the government in 2003 has observed:

A former Chief Justice of India warned about a decade ago that the Criminal Justice System in India was about to collapse. It is common knowledge that the two major problems confronting the Criminal Justice System are huge pendency of criminal cases and the inordinate delay in disposal of criminal cases on the one hand and the very low rate of conviction in cases involving serious crimes on the other. This has encouraged crime. Violent organized crimes have become the order of the day. As chances of conviction are remote, crime has become a profitable business. Life has become unsafe and people live in constant fear. Law and order situation has deteriorated and the citizens have lost confidence in the criminal justice system.

India can ill afford any delay in reforming and improving the Police and Criminal Justice System. The government is fully cognizant of the problems but solutions do not seem to be emerging. The Second Administrative Reforms Commission has addressed these issues in its report of June, 2007. The Law Commission has given several reports on reforming the criminal justice system as have the National Police Commission, State Administrative Reform Commissions, and several State Police Commissions.

As of the end of 2005, there were 2.9 million pending civil cases in the high courts of various states and 650,000 criminal cases. In subordinate courts there were 7.2 million pending civil cases and 18.4 million criminal cases. Just to clear this backlog within a year would take an estimated 1,434 high court judges and 18,376 subordinate court judges.[10] As many as 2,860 judicial officer positions were vacant in subordinate courts as of 30 April 2006. The number of courts in India is woefully inadequate. The judge to population ratio is 11 to 1 million whereas in many developed countries it is 100 to 1 million. This along with outdated and complex procedures makes the system slow, inaccessible, and unaffordable. The problem is further compounded by

> **The police has become a major instrument in the hands of the political executive in the states leading to criminalisation of politics and other related ills**

the plethora of laws, regulations, and administrative directions at both the central and state levels, with their multiple layers and lack of clarity. Even as simple a task as hiring employees is burdened by layers of legal requirements, and employers often do not even know whether they are in compliance with all of them, putting them at the mercy of local government functionaries.

At a structural level, there is also a need to examine the judicial framework itself and to consider alternative frameworks for dispensing justice. At the operational level, several changes are needed: shifting from resolving conflicts to dispensing justice, strengthening judicial enforcement of socioeconomic rights to improving outcomes for the poor, introducing management and information technology practices that reduce the time spent on process issues,[11] and broadening use of alternative dispute resolution processes.

The police system in India and its functioning is still based on the Police Act framed in 1861 to serve the interests of a colonial rule. Barring incremental changes in the Act, its basic foundations have remained unchanged. The Police Act Drafting Committee, 2006, has recommended a Model Police Act for adoption by the states. The Supreme Court of India has also issued directions covering several aspects of police reforms. There are also a number of other reports and recommendations of expert bodies. Lack of political will at the state level coupled with certain entrenched vested interests come in the way of introducing the much needed reforms.

Under the Constitution, "Public Order" and "Police" are part of the State List implying that the responsibility for maintaining public order and administration of police functions rests with the state. Reform of the Police system to enable it to fulfil the needs of a modern fast developing democratic country is a major challenge for the policy makers. The police has become a major instrument in the hands of the political executive in the states leading to criminalization of politics and other related ills. A key common theme of recommendations in the reports of numerous commissions is the need to depoliticize the

functioning of the police.[12] Other basic reforms needed in police functioning relate to separation of crime prevention, crime investigation, and maintenance of law and order functions. The current system is unable to professionalize and insulate crime investigation and prosecution from the vagaries of partisan politics The Administrative Reform Commission, in its 2007 Report, has endorsed these suggestions and has also observed that a "holistic examination of the police and criminal justice system is needed for comprehensive reforms."

Given the political interests of the political executive in the states, a fundamental reform of the police system requires a more proactive stance by the Central Government and the national Parliament. This will need to be combined with a massive programme of modernization and professionalization of the police force. Police reforms will need to be complemented by improvements in other parts of the criminal justice system as discussed earlier.

Accountability, transparency, and performance

Accountability

Accountability, or the lack of it, in governance generally, and civil services, in particular, is a major factor underlying the deficiencies in governance and public administration. Designing an effective framework for improving accountability has been a key element of the reform agenda. A fundamental issue is whether civil services should be accountable to the political executive of the day or to society at large. In other words, how should internal and external accountability be reconciled? Internal accountability is sought to be achieved by internal performance monitoring, official oversight by bodies like the Central Vigilance Commission and Comptroller and Auditor General, and judicial review of executive decisions. Articles 311 and 312 of the Indian Constitution provide job security and safeguards to the civil services, especially the All India Services. The framers of the Constitution had envisaged that provision of these safeguards would result in a civil service that is

" **The Hong Kong-based Political & Economic Risk Consultancy, which conducted a survey of 12 Asian economies recently, has ranked India's "suffocating bureaucracy" as the least efficient**

not totally subservient to the political executive but will have the strength to function in larger public interest. The need to balance internal and external accountability is thus built into the Constitution. The issue is where to draw the line. Over the years, the emphasis seems to have tilted in favour of greater internal accountability of the civil services to the political leaders of the day who in turn are expected to be externally accountable to the society at large through the election process. This system for seeking accountability to society has not worked out, and has lead to several adverse consequences for governance. A paper brought out by the Department of Administrative Reforms for a conference on the occasion of Civil Services Day 2009 observes:

> For a variety of reasons, elections as an instrument for external accountability have some well known weaknesses. In India, these weaknesses are exacerbated by the particular nature of the evolution of Indian democracy. Politics in India is marked by a conception of competition where to hold the state accountable is to gain access to its power and the goods it provides. Clientelism and patronage are rife and voters are mobilized more on the politics of caste, regional or religious identity than on the politics of accountability and initiatives that bring long term benefits to the public as a whole. Consequently, the state and its apparatus, including the bureaucracy are treated not so much as a means of generating public goods but as a means of generating benefits for the particular group that controls the state.[13]

This problem is further compounded by what the Second Administrative Reforms Commission[14] has described as the Hegelian dictum ingrained in the conduct of Indian bureaucracy, which believes that its authority and legitimacy is derived not from the mandate of the people but from an immutable corpus of rules and regulations. This has resulted in Indian civil servants being perceived as "slow and painful" and resistant

to change. Little wonder that the Hong Kong-based Political & Economic Risk Consultancy, which conducted a survey of 12 Asian economies recently, has ranked India's "suffocating bureaucracy" as the least efficient.

Some specific measures can be considered for improving accountability in civil services. Provisions of Articles 311 and 312 should be reviewed and laws and regulations framed to improve external accountability of civil services. The proposed Civil Services Bill seeks to address some of these requirements. The respective roles of professional civil services and the political executive should be defined so that professional managerial functions and management of civil services are depoliticized. For this purpose, effective statutory civil service boards should be created at the centre and in the states.

A number of measures are being considered to bring civil service reforms to strengthen accountability and to improve public service delivery (see box 2).

Transparency

Greater transparency should be introduced in decisions taken by governments. The government seeks to achieve transparency and accountability through increased use of information technology (see box 3) and e-governance and through citizen empowerment based on citizen charters and the Right to Information Act. Several initiatives at the central and state levels using information and communication technology are intended to improve service delivery, reduce costs, and refine administrative processes; computerize records and automate office operations, such as the recording of decisions and the maintenance and archiving of files; and help to redress and monitor the resolution of public grievances. Though implementation has been sporadic and piecemeal, consumer response has been positive and expansion to other areas of governance is recommended.

> **Specific measures should be implemented to make the use of the Right to Information Act more citizen-friendly and to remove certain impediments in its use**

Box 2 | **Delivery of public services**

A Framework for Assessment (*sevottam*) has been developed to bring about excellence in public service delivery. Simultaneously, piloting of quality management systems at districts and sub-districts levels has been taken up.[15]

A Public Services Bill on the anvil aims to provide a statutory basis for the regulation of public services in India, to regulate the appointment and conditions of the public servant, to lay down and review the fundamental values of public services, the Public Service Code of Ethics, and the Public Service Management Code. It also seeks to establish a Public Service Authority for facilitating review and development of public services as a professional, neutral, merit based, and accountable instrument for promoting good governance and better delivery of services to the citizens. Further, All India Services (Performance Appraisal) Rules, 2007, have been prescribed with a view to improving the performance

evaluation and appraisal of all senior civil servants for better human resource management.[16]

Several arrangements have been put in place in order to benefit from international experience in improving public service delivery through civil service reforms. Thus a UK Department of International Development (DFID) assisted project on Capacity Building for Poverty Reduction, is under implementation since 2005-06. A Memorandum of Understanding has been signed with the Government of Malaysia to work jointly on areas of mutual interest, including Human Resource Management and Governance, Civil Service Matters and Service Delivery and Productivity Enhancement. Co-operation with Brazil, China, South Africa, and several other countries has been structured to focus, inter alia, on civil service reforms, capacity building, and citizen empowerment.[17]

Right to Information Act of 2005

The Right to Information Act of 2005 empowers citizens to enquire into the decisionmaking processes of government, long obscured by a tangled web of complex rules, regulations, and opinions. Those seeking information are not required to explain why they are doing so, whereas information providers must cite reasons for not providing the information.

About 70 countries have information access legislation. India's is considered to be among the most progressive, since it includes every level of government from the president and prime minister to the chief ministers and almost everyone else and because penalties are imposed for failing to provide requested information. Decisions of the Information Commission are binding. The sweeping coverage may have been overambitious; Japan and the United States, among others, exclude the legislature and the judiciary in their information access legislation. The Indian government has recently taken

the position that the Act does not cover the legislature, and the judiciary is taking a similar stance on the law's jurisdiction over the judicial system. Other amendments to the Act are likely to emerge, in part to ensure that its ambitious measures do not clog the system and add to the red tape. The Act's impact over the last four years has been uneven, demonstrating successes as well as misuse and obstruction.[18] An amendment to the Act now excludes some information contained in "file-notings", which reveal the rationale behind government decisions.

Specific measures should be implemented to make the use of the Right to Information Act more citizen-friendly and to remove certain impediments in its use.

Citizen's Charters

One manifestation of improved governance is the issuance of citizen charters. The main objective of issuing the Citizen's Charter of an organization is to improve

❝ **To improve citizen–government exchanges, personal interactions need to be minimized and electronic interactions promoted**

To improve citizen–government exchanges, personal interactions need to be minimized and electronic interactions promoted. This would improve efficiency and help to reduce corruption. A National e-governance Plan (NeGP) has been proposed to be implemented.[19] Technology based solutions could serve the increasing demands of citizens more effectively in terms of improving the quality, cost, and delivery of services, simultaneously reducing day-to-day corruption.

It is ironical that Indian IT professionals have contributed to improving efficiency and productivity in many developed countries but India has not been able

to provide benefits from IT for its own society. The initiatives in the sphere of e-governance have provided limited gains.

The enormous knowledge and skills available in the country in the field of IT should be harnessed to provide societal benefits by wider adoption of e-governance in all activities involving citizen state interface as well as vigorous institutionalization of Information Technology enabled Services (ITeS). A major nationwide initiative needs to be launched to spread the use of e-governance in all areas of government functioning both in the centre and the states.

---

the quality of public services. This is done by letting people know the mandate of the concerned Ministry/ Department/ Organization, how one can get in touch with its officials, what to expect by way of services and how to seek a remedy if something goes wrong. The Citizen's Charter does not by itself create new legal rights, but surely helps in enforcing existing rights. As of February 2008, 115 union ministries, departments, and other government agencies finalized citizen charters, and 650 departments and organizations of the state governments prepared charters. However, some large ministries, such as Human Resources Development (which includes education and health), Rural Development, Panchayati Raj and Women and Child Development have not prepared citizen charters. Critics consider the charters to be mainly ceremonial documents[20] because implementation of the charters is non-justiciable.

Decentralization

Decentralization and devolution of authority to bring government and decision-making closer to the people also helps to enhance accountability. In India, government decentralization and greater citizen empowerment were initiated from the top down rather than emerging from

the ground up. Over time, however, grass roots demand has started to build.

Decentralizing administration, and governance responsibilities to local government bodies is envisaged in the 73rd and 74th Amendments of the Constitution in spirit. In practice, in many states there is reluctance to transfer functions and functionaries to local bodies. For decentralization to be really meaningful it should involve devolution of both expenditure and revenue-raising functions. So far, the thrust has been limited to decentralizing expenditure functions. Unfortunately, this approach has the unhealthy consequence of bidding for more funds by local bodies without commensurate responsibility for expenditure effectiveness.

At the same time, the changes brought about by decentralization have generated social and political tensions that need to be addressed collectively at all levels of government by politicians, bureaucrats, non-governmental organizations, and the media. While many in the bureaucracy and the established political powers are resisting the ongoing changes, others see decentralization as a positive step. Achieving effective decentralization across all states will require much more active involvement by non-governmental organizations and favorably disposed elements in the bureaucracy.[21]

> **"** The Government of India has, in the past, taken several initiatives to improve the level of motivation, competence, performance, and the image of Indian bureaucracy

---

Box 4 | Career path of a typical IAS officer

The career path of a typical IAS officer starts with working on field assignments at the district or sub-district level in the states where he/she deals with cutting edge administrative issues, internal security, and implementation of development schemes. This is a good grounding and gives him/her a grass root level understanding of public administration issues. The officer then works in the Secretariat of the state government and deals with policy level issues and formulation of development schemes at the state level. He/she can also be assigned to state Public Sector Undertakings or specialised departments dealing with state taxes, industrial development, and rural development, etc. Typically, after 15 years or so the officer is ready to move to the federal government where he/she works for 5 years in a ministry and then returns to the state.

Performance, evaluation, and management

Putting in place robust and effective performance management systems is another key element for improving accountability. The Second Administrative Reforms Commission has this to say about plan implementation and performance management systems in government:

> Traditionally governance structures in India are characterized by rule-based approaches…. The main performance measure thus is the amount of money spent; and the success of schemes, programs and projects is therefore eventually evaluated in terms of the inputs consumed.

The task of designing a performance evaluation system for civil servants poses a challenge. The objective of any evaluation system should be to drive superior performance and judge the suitability and merit for placements and promotions so that the system can match the person with the job requirements. Many reports within and outside government have struggled with this issue but the design of a suitable evaluation framework has eluded policy makers. Knowledge deficit in the civil service is a major shortcoming as is the tendency of the system to be somewhat inward looking. The system works on the basis of near automatic promotions after completion of prescribed years of service and highly subjective systems for merit evaluation (see box 4 for the typical career path of an IAS officer). Systems like 360 degree evaluation are non existent. The immediate superior is the sole determinant of merit. Much needed skills and behaviors such as relationships of the officer with officers in other ministries, coordination skills, teamwork or leadership skills, and relationships with subordinates are rarely captured in the evaluations. The system encourages sycophancy at the expense of professional growth. The evaluating officer is expected to grade the officer in categories of outstanding, very good, good, or poor. Superior officers rarely grade their subordinates below outstanding or very good and are reluctant to highlight any shortcomings for fear having to deal with representations which often cast aspersions and impute ulterior motives. The result is that the evaluation is rarely seen as a good determinant of merit or suitability for promotions. There is a strong case for introducing a system of mid career tests and interview for evaluating the suitability of officers for promotions and even continued retention in the service.

The Government of India has, in the recent past, taken several initiatives to improve the level of motivation, competence, performance, and the image of Indian bureaucracy. A welcome step in this direction is the institution of the Prime Minister's Award for Excellence in Public Administration to acknowledge the outstanding and exemplary performance of Indian civil servants.[22] These steps are, however, sporadic and are merely indicative of the government's desire to affect improvements in the functioning of the civil services. The malaise

❝ Decisionmaking in an integrated global economy has become extremely complex, requiring a broad base of knowledge among civil services employees. The current system suffers from a knowledge deficit in critical areas

is much deeper and requires more fundamental changes and overhaul of the system. Another significant set of initiatives pertains to improvement in the delivery of public services (box 2).

The Second Administrative Reforms Commission in its Tenth Report has made a number of suggestions which are worth looking at. It advocates inter alia, a comprehensive and continuous Performance Management System, coupled with a Code of Ethics and a more stringent disciplinary action framework and procedures to be managed through a comprehensive Civil Services Law and a Central Civil Services Authority.[23]

Social auditing should be widely used and systems introduced for sharing of social audit findings with government together with measures for ensuring timely follow-up action. Performance benchmarks in different spheres of administration for evaluating performance and outcomes should be clearly defined.

Needed skills and qualifications

A major determinant of performance in the civil service, as elsewhere, is their skills, qualifications, and training for their responsibilities. In this context, one of the structural issues relates to the generalists vs. specialists dichotomy. The particular context has to do with the positioning of the IAS officers (generalists) to head various departments, including those staffed predominantly by specialists. Over the years, this controversy has gained momentum to an extent where it is felt that, on the one hand, the technical departments should be headed only by specialists and, on the other hand, even the generalist services should be made to specialise in different sectors of public administration.

Most secretaries of departments are drawn from the IAS. There is a limited but increasing trend of officers of other specialised services like Audit and Accounts, Railways, Revenue, etc. being appointed as Secretaries, which needs to be further encouraged. There are hardly any instances of appointment of persons from outside the government as Secretaries, with the exception of

a few reputed economists. At mid career level or even senior levels, some proportion for lateral entry should be considered for some proportion of the positions. At the same time, efforts should also be made to encourage greater specialization at mid career level and officers encouraged to develop specialised knowledge and skills for sectors to which they are assigned.

An important area that merits consideration for reform is entry-level skills for civil servants. The present practice is of a minimum qualification of a graduate degree in any discipline for All India Services such as IFS, IAS, Income Tax, Customs, Audit, Accounts, and Railways, etc. In recent times, there has been a large inflow of specialists, such as engineers, doctors, MBAs, agriculture scientists, and PhDs in the so-called generalist civil services. This trend is more a reflection of personal preferences rather than related to job requirement. The time has come to revisit the entry-level qualifications so that new entrants have some degree of specialised job-related knowledge.

Some further suggestions made by the Second Administrative Reforms Commission in its Tenth Report for improved performance of Civil Services[24] pertain to: the stage of entry into the Civil Services; the structure of the Civil Services Examination; other modes of induction into the civil service;[25] and placements at middle and top management levels.[26] The report also includes a section on lessons from multi-country experience in civil service reform. These include training civil servants in domain knowledge, lowering the entry age, fostering competition for appointments to senior executive positions, and creating a central civil service authority with responsibility for preparing recommendations on appointments to senior positions and for overseeing lateral entry at higher levels.

Decision making in an integrated global economy has become extremely complex, requiring a broad base of knowledge among civil services employees. The current system suffers from a knowledge deficit in critical areas. The civil service is unable to attract professional talent at key policy making levels. There is a need to

257

> **Action must start immediately because the impact will be fully realized over a long period**

and mismanagement. Care is also poor in higher-level facilities because of overcrowding.

Improving these facilities through better management could substantially reduce out of pocket expenditures, particularly among the poor, and increase returns on investments in public health infrastructure.[35] The government could adopt a more strategic approach, leaving the day to day management of public facilities to the private sector and focussing instead on the drivers of long-term value, setting targets, and encouraging alliances and partnerships with the private sector. A major focus under the Eleventh Five Year Plan should be on strengthening the public health sector.[36]

Social security. Market-driven economic policies are widely believed to have marginalized large segments of the population, especially the socially deprived (Scheduled Caste and Scheduled Tribes): "As a result of receding social security and [the public distribution system], displacement of traditional labour in the agrarian economy and privatization of jobs, the Dalits will encounter a major threat to their survival."[37] Plans are under consideration for an equal-opportunity commission. However, almost 94 percent of employment is in the informal sector, out of the reach of labour laws.

India still lacks a comprehensive national social security policy that would cover the entire population. The National Commission for Enterprises in the Unorganized Sector, established in September 2004, presented its report on Social Security for Unorganized Workers to the Prime Minister in May 2006. The report calls for bringing agricultural workers into an overarching social security scheme for unorganized workers that is based on defined contributions. The three-part scheme would include social assistance (financed by the state budget or by community funds) for citizens who lack the financial means to meet their basic needs, a compulsory social insurance scheme financed by employers and employees, and voluntary private insurance for people who wish to take out additional insurance. Some states are seeking their own solutions to meeting the social

security needs of the informal sector. Clearly, the issue of providing decent social security for a major segment of the population that is outside the ambit of the formal sector is a challenging agenda. In this context, the Parliament has since enacted the Unorganised Sector Workers' Social Security Act, 2008.[38]

Priority agenda

Countless commissions and other reports have pointed out many of the existing inefficiencies in India's public administration. As in other areas, the issue is not policy formulation but implementation. What is most desperately needed now is not further analysis or discussion, but concrete action.

Also, action must start immediately because the impact will be fully realized over a long period. In this context, the following key recommendations merit immediate attention.

1. Civil Service reforms are needed in order to inculcate professionalism amongst public servants and make them increasingly responsiveness to societal needs. This will require basic changes, including: changes in recruitment practices, fostering more specialisation, introducing a robust and transparent performance evaluation mechanism including mid career evaluation through tests and interviews, increasing external accountability (see point 3) of civil servants, increasing lateral recruitment at higher levels, and introducing higher ethical standards. Specific measure are also needed to curtail pervasive day-to-day corruption, break down the unhealthy civil servant politician nexus, and minimize role transgression of various arms of the state—Legislature, Judiciary, and Bureaucracy.

2. Comprehensive reforms in the police and criminal justice system are required to fulfill the needs of a modern fast developing democratic country. Maintenance of public order and internal security is critical. Depoliticization of

❝❝ Implementation of this agenda for change depends critically on political vision and bipartisan support across the political spectrum

the police force, making it professional and equipping it with modern tools and skills cannot be delayed any further. Areas of reform should also include separation of crime prevention, crime investigation, and maintenance of law and order functions and insulation of crime investigation and prosecution from the vagaries of partisan politics. Suggestions contained in the Police Act Drafting Committee 2006 should be implemented. Judicial reform should encompass reduction of large pendency of cases at different layers of the judiciary and making dispensation of justice affordable and speedy. Reports of many commissions like the Law Commission, Second Administrative Reforms Commission, and Committee on Reform of the Criminal Justice System contain many useful suggestions. Immediate steps should be taken for early implementation of these recommendations.

3. Accountability of the civil services must be improved. Measures for doing so include: (a) depoliticizing the professional managerial functions and management of civil services by creating effective civil service boards at the centre and in the states; (b) imparting greater transparency in public administration, including by making the Right to Information Act more citizen-friendly and removing certain impediments in its use; (c) greater use of IT for providing societal benefits and wider adoption of e-governance and IT-enabled services in all activities involving citizen state interface; (d) wider acceptance of social auditing, and sharing of social audit findings with government; (e) creating performance benchmarks for provision of services in different spheres of administration and linking performance with outcomes; (f) greater decentralization of administration and governance responsibilities to local government bodies as envisaged in the

73rd and 74th Amendments of the Constitution, combined with the removal of the hurdles placed in many states for transfer of functions and functionaries to local bodies—both expenditure and revenue-raising.

4. A robust and effective system for monitoring, evaluating, and managing performance under public programs and projects is also essential for improving accountability. Some measures that can be taken in this regard are: (a) framing of any program or scheme should be preceded by a clear description of objectives and physical targets; (b) allocation of funds and disbursements should be linked to realization of these objectives; (c) for every program there should be a sunset clause after which its impact should be assessed; (d) evaluation and impact assessments should be done by agencies outside the government and their results used for improved implementation and for designing future programs; and (e) capacity building should form an integral part of all programs and schemes.

5. Regulatory bodies have been set up in many sectors. The key governance challenge in this area is to select competent regulators, ensure their autonomy across all critical sectors, and frame clear, transparent, and predictable regulations.

6. More efficient delivery of social services, particularly education, health and social security, is vital for both, moving India to an affluent society and reducing inequities to build a cohesive society. The challenge of sustaining and improving selected ongoing programs and implementing others (e.g., for social security) merits immediate attention.

Implementation of this agenda for change depends critically on political vision and bipartisan support across the political spectrum.

Notes

Part I

Chapter 1

1. The main criteria used by the IMF's *World Economic Outlook* are income, diversification of exports, and integration into the global financial system. But there is no fixed formula.

2. The founding members were France, Italy, Japan, the United Kingdom, the United States, and West Germany.

3. Of course, a cross-country comparable system of national income accounts was not introduced until 1953, so the early years are very rough estimates.

4. Mearsheimer (2001, p. 2) argues that "the overriding goal of each state is to maximize its share of world power, which means gaining power at the expense of other states."

5. The White House 2009.

6. Elwell 2006.

7. For example, Dani Rodrik.

8. For example, Arvind Virmani.

9. Virmani 2008.

10. McKinsey Global Institute 2001.

11. Oura 2007.

12. Gupta 2008.

13. Bhalla 2008.

14. Farrell 2007. McKinsey's definition of the middle class is between $23,000 and $118,000, a somewhat narrower band than proposed here.

15. The previous discussion has emphasized increasing returns to scale. This is perhaps best thought of in the model as the presence of Arrow "learning-by-doing" externalities, where catch-up total factor productivity growth depends on the level of output.

16. Hawksworth and Cookson 2008; Wilson and Purushothaman 2003.

17. See Aghion and Hewitt (1997) on why Europe converged with the United States after World War II, but more recently has faced slower total factor productivity growth.

18. For transition economies, the criterion is 3.5 percent per capita growth or more between 1995 and 2005.

19. This total factor productivity rate is consistent with the U.S. long-term labor productivity growth of 1.8 percent.

20. Goldman Sachs first looked only at six developed countries and four BRIC countries, and then extended their analysis to a further 11 emerging economies. PricewaterhouseCoopers looked at 30 emerging economies.

21. Indeed, in their 2007 update, Goldman Sachs analysts Poddar and Yi raised their sustainable growth forecast for India to 8 percent through 2020.

22. Bhalla 2008

Chapter 2

1. The Commission on Growth and Development (2008), chaired by A. Michael Spence, identified 13 success stories including Botswana, Brazil, China, Hong Kong, Indonesia, Japan, Malaysia, Malta, Oman, Singapore, South Korea, Taiwan, and Thailand.

2. Together, these factors are sometimes called "innovation capacity". The ability for innovation to drive economic growth depends on factors that evolve over time. Complex university-business linkages, state support, flexible factor markets, connectivity, and other forces are thought to be important, but even EU countries have faced difficulties in understanding how to advance this agenda. The Lisbon process has yet to deliver significant results.

3. Gill and Kharas 2007.

4. Imbs and Wacziarg 2003.

5. Kharas et al. 2008.

6. Voynets n.d.

Chapter 3

1. World Bank 2008.

Chapter 4

1. Government of India, Ministry of Personnel, Public Grievances and Pensions, Department of Administrative

the conclusions appear to be quite tentative, given that the program was still at an early stage.

16. Second Administrative Reform Commission 2007.

Part III

Chapter 8

1. Haldea 2008.

2. Araujo et al. 2007.

3. Araujo and Kohli 2008.

Chapter 9

The authors are grateful to all the experts and officials in the Indian academic and R&D community, government, private sector, and independent leaders and thinkers who provided great insights, candid advice, and useful information. The work has also benefited immensely from the valuable guidance and support of Harinder S. Kohli, Anil Sood, and the India 2039 Study Team. The authors are grateful to Varun Shiva Goel for assisting in research and preparation of the report. They also acknowledge assistance from K. Radahkrishnan and Yanbei Yao in data collection.

1. Studies tracing the relationship between the stock of education and GDP find that a one-year increase in average education attainment raises output per capita 3–6 percentage points and the GDP growth rate about 1 percentage point (Dahlman 2008). The cumulative impact of a 1 percentage point increase in the rate of growth soon exceeds the one-time increase in output.

2. This number masks many disparities—in 2004/05 the gross enrolment ratio in higher education was 19.0 percent for the urban population but 6.7 percent for the rural population, and 12.4 percent for men and 9.1 percent for women, contributing to the lower productivity levels in the informal sector and thus to large productivity dispersion.

3. The number of children aged between 14–18 is estimated at 120 million in 2006. In 2005/06, enrolment was 132.1 million in primary education, 52.2 million in middle/upper primary, and 38.4 million in secondary and upper secondary education. The combined gross primary and secondary enrolment ratio was 39.9 percent. The dropout rate was 25.7 percent in primary school, 48.8 percent in middle/upper primary school, and 61.6 percent in secondary school.

4. NASSCOM and McKinsey & Company 2005.

5. Central universities are established by the central government; deemed universities are institutions that are awarded university status by the University Grants Commission; and institutes of national importance include Indian Institutes of Technology, Indian Institutes of Management, Indian Institute of Science, and the like.

6. China's rapid expansion of higher education may eventually give it supremacy over India even in services, particularly in knowledge and knowledge-based industries. China's 1998 Higher Education Law facilitated large-scale expansion, consolidation, and quality improvement in higher education. The gross enrolment ratio in tertiary education rose from 2.9 percent in 1985 to 21.6 percent in 2006 and is expected to rise to 40 percent by 2020 and 55 percent by 2050. Enrolment in regular institutions of higher education rose from 3.2 million in 1997 to more than 9 million in 2002. China is also working to raise the level of some 100 of its universities to become world-class institutions and has already established 53 high-technology development zones to synergize the efforts of universities and business houses. There has also been an exceptional increase in governmental allocation for R&D, which rose more than 22-fold, from $660 million in 1978 to $14.6 billion in 2004, and more thereafter (Jha 2006).

7. Shanghai Jiao Tong University, Graduate School of Education 2005.

8. Most public universities in Europe and the United States are large, with 10,000–75,000 students. In contrast, the University of Pune has only 7,500 students, and the Indian Institutes of Technology have 3,000–4,000 students. Universities in Australia, China, Singapore, and the United States have budgets of $1 billion and more compared with about $50 million for the Indian Institutes of Technology.

9. Each Indian Institute of Science Education and Research has been allocated 5 billion rupees ($120 million). Each will have 200 faculty and 2,000 students (500 PhDs), with an annual intake of 200 undergraduate and 200 graduate students, offering BS degrees and integrated five-year MS/PhD programs. The Indian Institute of Science

Education and Research at Pune has so far attracted 80 percent of its faculty from nonresident Indians returning to India. A new campus is under construction inside the campus of the National Chemical Laboratory. Within five years, the two institutions will be producing some 1,000 science and engineering PhDs.

10. The Eleventh Plan envisages an outlay of 2.74 trillion rupees ($60 billion) for education—an increase from 7.7 percent to 19.3 percent of the total. Around 50 percent of the education outlay is for elementary education and literacy, 20 percent for secondary education, and 30 percent for higher education, including technical education (Indian Planning Commission 2008). During the Tenth Plan the share of private unaided higher education institutions increased from 42.6 percent in 2001 to 63.2 percent in 2006 (Indian Planning Commission 2002). Their share of enrolments also increased, from 32.9 percent to 51.5 percent. This trend is likely to continue in the Eleventh Plan and therefore, about half of incremental enrolment targeted for higher education is likely to come from private providers.

11. Dutz 2007.

12. Murthy 2008.

13. Murthy 2008.

14. In pre-liberalized (pre-1991) India, the private sector was protected through high tariff barriers. Indian industry responded with import substitution applying reverse engineering. Industry developed several products that were "first to India" in pesticides, drugs, and pharmaceuticals, auto industry, and other sectors. Taking advantage of the fact that before January 1, 2005, when the Indian patent laws came into compliance with the Trade-Related Aspects of International Property Rights agreement, the Indian drug industry used its skills in process chemistry and engineering to create a strong base producing generic drugs, which were among the cheapest in the world.

15. *Management Today* 2007.

16. Indian Planning Commission 2002, 2008.

17. Dutz 2007.

18. For example, the idea of increasing R&D expenses to 2 percent was first presented by Prime Minister Rajiv Gandhi (in 1989), formally announced by Prime Minister Atal Bihari Vajpayee in the Indian Science Congress (in 2000), and by Prime Minister Manmohan Singh (in 2007) (Ramachandran 2007). Yet during the period 1989–2008 (20 years), India's R&D expenditures never exceeded 1 percent.

19. On December 13, 2008, Prime Minister Manmohan Singh announced plans to launch an integrated knowledge network that would have nodes at all major institutions of higher education and learning for carrying out inter-disciplinary dialogue. While a step in right direction, India needs more, including a national research and education network. As the Prime Minister said, India needs to leverage its technology strengths.

20. For example, the University of Pune system has some 423 affiliated colleges, more than 200 institutions with more than 400,000 students, but only 7,500 on campus, one-third of them foreign students.

21. The latest effort was made by the Indian Institute of Management Ahmadabad Review Committee (September 2008), but in December 2008, the institution's board, in an unprecedented move, rejected the review committee's report.

22. Dar et al. 2006.

23. Wessner 2006

24. Lakshman 2006.

25. UNESCO 2008.

26. Böhm et al. 2004, p. 4.

27. In the United States, a significant percentage of all PhD recipients are reported to be non-U.S. citizens: 41 percent of graduate students in sciences and 51 percent in engineering are from other countries, and half of all international students studying in United States are at the graduate level (Jha 2006). Students come from many countries, the major ones being China, India, Japan, and South Korea.

28. Dutz 2007.

29. Dutz 2007.

Chapter 10

1. IEA 2008.

2. EIA 2008.

3. Lorenz et al. 2008.

4. ERI 2006.

5. Indian Planning Commission 2006.

6. IEA 2008.

7. India deliberated the topic of energy security while preparing its energy policy. It defined energy security as the ability "to supply lifeline energy to all citizens as well as meeting their effective demand for safe and convenient energy to satisfy various needs at affordable costs at all times with a prescribed confidence level considering shocks and disruptions that can be reasonably expected" (see Indian Planning Commission 2006).

8. The Iran–Pakistan–India project was conceptualized in 1989 and has gone through many negotiation cycles. The pipeline would be 2,775 kilometers long and would be supplied from the South Pars field in the Persian Gulf. The initial annual capacity of the pipeline would be 22 bcm of natural gas, with capacity eventually reaching 55 bcm. It would cost $7.5 billion. The latest negotiations indicate a construction start date in 2009 and a completion date of September 2012. The deal encountered a setback in July 2006 when Iran demanded a price of $7.20 per million Btu against India's offer of $4.20. The long-stalled talks were revived in April 2008 when the Iranian president visited India and Pakistan.

9. There are no accurate estimates of India's technical and nontechnical losses. The gains from loss reduction pertain to technical losses. Half of transmission and distribution losses are assumed to be technical.

10. The typical nuclear fuel cycle starts with refined uranium ore, composed mainly of uranium 238 (U-238). U-238 is not fissile—the process by which the nucleus of the atom splits, releasing tremendous quantities of energy. Uranium ore normally contains very small percentages of U-235, which is fissile. When a U-235 atom splits, it releases a spread of high-energy neutrons. If one of these neutrons collides with another U-235 atom, it can cause the atom to split, releasing more neutrons. This chain reaction could create an explosive power for a nuclear bomb or the meltdown of a nuclear reactor. Since there is too little U-235 in mined uranium ore, the ore needs to be "enriched" to around 3–5 percent U-235 for nuclear fuel (and 85 percent for a nuclear weapon). Once a sufficient proportion of U-235 is achieved, the ore is made into fuel suitable for a reactor. While U-235 is necessary for fission, U-238 is "fertile," which means that it can transmute into other fissile elements in a process called "breeding." In this process, when an atom of U-238 absorbs a neutron, such as one thrown out by a nearby splitting U-235 atom, it can transmute into U-239, then quickly into neptunium-239 and then to plutonium-239 (PU-239). PU-239, like U-235, is fissile and can maintain a chain reaction. The spent fuel can be reprocessed. The problem is that many reactors are not optimized for burning plutonium, and as a consequence, large quantities of PU-239 remain as a waste by-product in spent fuel rods. This means that much of the spent fuel—highly radioactive—becomes waste that needs to be stored for a very long time. This waste PU-239 also represents the greatest weapons proliferation threat because of the possibility that some of the waste could fall into the wrong hands.

11. IEA 2008.

12. The Solar American Initiative, a program of the U.S. Department of Energy, has a goal of bringing solar to grid parity by 2015. Photovoltaic electricity cost is expected to drop from 35 cents a kilowatt hour to 10 cents a kilowatt hour within this timeframe. The IEA also projects that the cost of solar photovoltaic and concentrated solar power will decline substantially and become economically viable before 2020. Furthermore, IEA's assessment indicates that while most solar capacity is being installed in industrial countries, future solar capacity will be concentrated in countries like those in the Middle East and North Africa, where there is abundance of strong solar resources.

13. IEA 2008.

14. Indian Planning Commission 2006.

15. IEA 2008.

16. The United Nations Framework Convention on Climate Change is an international environment treaty declared at the UN Conference on Environment and Development, known as the Earth Summit, held in Rio de Janeiro in 1992. The parties agreed to recognize "common but differentiated responsibilities", with greater responsibility of industrial countries (called Annex 1 countries) for reducing greenhouse gas emissions in the near term. The treaty includes provisions for updates, called "protocols". The principal update is the Kyoto Protocol, adopted in 1997. Most industrial countries and some Central European

economies in transition (called Annex B countries) agreed to legally binding reductions of 6–8 percent below 1990 levels in greenhouse gas emissions over 2008–12, defined as the first emissions budget period. The United States would be required to reduce its emissions by an average of 7 percent below 1990 levels. The administration of President George W. Bush explicitly rejected the protocol in 2001. Since then, a series of meetings have helped resolve many practical issues, such as agreement on a flexible mechanism, which provides for emissions trading instruments such as the Joint Implementation and the Clean Development Mechanism, which allow industrial countries to fund emission reduction activities in developing countries as an alternative to domestic emission reduction. At the latest meeting, held in Bali, Indonesia, in December 2007, agreement was reached on a timetable for negotiating the post-2012 framework or successor to the Kyoto Protocol. At the upcoming meeting in Copenhagen, in December 2009, negotiations are expected to lead to an ambitious global climate agreement for the period after the commitment under the Kyoto Protocol expires, in 2012. At a meeting in July 2008 in Japan, the G-8 leaders agreed on a 50 percent emission reduction target by 2050 but asked that other major economies, such as India and China, also limit emissions. It is therefore expected that the Kyoto Protocol's reliance on industrial countries for the major reductions in greenhouse gas emissions might not hold in the next round of negotiations.

17. India has not signed the Nuclear Non-Proliferation Treaty (NPT). It carried out its first nuclear test in May 1974 and subsequently became subject to a nuclear trade embargo, which the Nuclear Suppliers Group (NSG) imposes on countries that are not signatories of the NPT and conduct nuclear activity. After more than 30 years of embargo, a U.S.–India agreement was signed in March 2006 that would allow India to buy nuclear technology and nuclear fuel from the United States as long as India separates its military and civilian nuclear facilities and agrees to supervision by International Atomic Energy Agency (IAEA). The agreement has cleared the Indian parliament. IAEA also approved the deal by signing a nuclear safeguards agreement with India in August 2008. The agreement to allow nuclear fuel and technology exports to India for its civilian use was also cleared by the 45-member NSG and would need to go to the U.S. Congress for approval. However, critics say that implementation of the U.S.–India nuclear cooperation agreement will be a breach of the NPT, thus undermining international nonproliferation efforts. The international community hopes that India will eventually sign the NPT.

18. See, for example, Dean (2006).

19. See, for example, IEA (2008); Madan (2006); Taylor et al. (2008); Indian Planning Commission (2006).

20. In June 2008 the Prime Minister announced a climate change plan with a vision of making India's economic development energy efficient, placing solar power at center stage and pooling India's scientific, technical and managerial talents, and financial resources to develop solar energy. However, the plan makes no commitment to reducing carbon emissions.

Part IV

Chapter 12

1. Transparency International India 2005, 2008.

2. Chhokar 2008.

3. *The Economist* 2008.

4. *The Economist* 2008.

5. Such litigation by bureaucrats also contributes to the judicial backlog.

6. The high court judges blamed poor governance by unaccountable civil servants as a leading cause of litigation. They estimated that as much as 50 percent of their caseload would disappear if civil servants performed the job that they are supposed to perform and took citizen grievances seriously.

7. While such direction by the Supreme Court is often applauded by the public, it raises the disturbing possibility of judicial overreach into matters that should essentially lie under the purview of the executive. It is hoped that better governance would reduce, if not eliminate, the need for excessive judicial intervention in public policy, freeing up judicial resources for adjudicating the laws.

8. Sud 2009.

9. A more extensive description of these initiatives can be found in Government of India, Department of

Administrative Reforms and Public Grievances, Ministry of Personnel, Public Grievances and Pensions (2008), and World Bank (2006).

10. Transparency International India 2005.

11. A recent amendment to the Criminal Court Procedure allows plea bargaining in cases in which punishment is up to seven years of imprisonment. Plea bargaining has not been used much because prosecutors, lawyers and judges are still unsure about how to apply the concept and defence lawyers often advise the accused to go forward with the trial knowing that the process is likely to take years and conviction is never a certainty.

Chapter 13

1. For a detailed exposition of the concerns relating to internal security and possible state interventions see Government of India (2008a). The government has announced an ambitious unique identification project that would assign a unique identification number to each resident of the country. The Unique Identification Authority of India has been constituted as an attached office of the Indian Planning Commission to eliminate the multiple identification mechanisms prevalent across various government departments.

2. Kaufmann et al. 1999.

3. Government of India 2008b, p. iv.

4. Government of India, Ministry of Personnel, Public Grievances and Pensions, Department of Administrative Reforms and Public Grievances, in collaboration with Indian Institute of Public Administration, New Delhi, has brought out a Digital Repository of 73 Reports of Commissions/Committees on Administration, covering a period from 1812 to 2004, on a CD.

5. See http://presidentofindia.nic.in/speeches/html

6. Shourie 2004.

7. Arora and Goyal 1995, p. 320.

8. Arora and Goyal 1995, p. 319.

9. The small car project of an Indian MNC withdrew its production facility from West Bengal and relocated in Gujarat.

10. Sabharwal 2006.

11. The world over, court management and case-flow management are recognized as specialized skills that need to be adopted by the judiciary.

12. A Police Act Drafting Committee was set up by the Government of India in 2005. This Committee has made many recommendations for granting functional autonomy to the police while vesting the authority to lay down policies and guidelines to the state governments.

13. Government of India, Department of Administrative Reforms, Civil Service Day 2009, Panel Discussion, Theme Papers.

14. Government of India 2008b, p. v.

15. Government of India 2008c, pp. 154–55, 162.

16. Government of India 2008c, pp. VIII–IX.

17. Government of India 2008c:160–62, 166–68.

18. Centre for Public Policy 2008.

19. Government of India, Department of Information Technology n.d.

20. Arora 2008.

21. Agnihotri 2003; see also Tandon, Agnihotri et al. 2001.

22. These awards are conferred on the selected individuals on 21 April every year, which is designated as the Civil Services Day. A complementary initiative taken by the Department of Administrative Reforms and Public grievances is documentation and dissemination of good governance practices, including a World Bank Project on 'Capacity Building for Good Governance' (Government of India 2008c, 149–52, 162, 168–70).

23. Government of India 2008b, p. 326–35.

24. Government of India, Second Administrative Reforms Commission 2008b.

25. Government of India 2007, p. 315–19.

26. Government of India 2007, p. 324–26.

27. They have also contributed to a rising trend of blatant corruption. India was ranked 74th most corrupt country among 180 countries surveyed for Corruption Perception Index, 2008 by Transparency International.

28. See Panagariya (2008) for a review of issues relating to privatization and regulation of these sectors.

29. Section 60.

30. High Level Committee on Competition Policy and Law. 2000.

31. Competition Commission of India 2004.

32. There as some exceptions. For instance, Peru's competition law does not prohibit anticompetitive mergers, and Mexico's competition law has no provisions on abuse of dominance (Chakravarthi 2001).

33. Bhattacharjea 2008, p. 609.

34. Chaudhury et al. 2006.

35. Government of India, Ministry of Health and Family Welfare 2006.

36. Government of India, Task Force on Public-Private Partnership constituted by the Planning Commission on 25 May 2006.

37. Jogdand 2000, p. 11.

38. Act 33 of 2008.

References

Part I

Chapter 1

Aghion, Philippe and Peter Howitt. 1997. *Endogenous Growth Theory.* Cambridge, MA: MIT Press.

———. 2008. "Indian Economic Growth 1950–2008: Facts & Beliefs, Puzzles & Policies." New Delhi: Oxus Research & Investments.

Bosworth, Barry P. and Susan M. Collins. 2006. "Accounting for Growth: Comparing China and India," NBER Working Paper No. 12943. Cambridge, Massachusetts: National Bureau of Economic Research.

Centennial Group. 2009. Centennial Group in-house database, June 2009. Washington, D.C.

Elwell, Craig. 2006. "Long-Term Growth of the US Economy: Significance, Congressional Research Service, Washington, D.C.

Farrell, Diana. 2007. "Next Big Spenders: India's Middle Class." *Business Week*, May 19.

Gupta, Anil. 2008. "The Future of India-China Trade." *The Economic Times*, January 14.

Hawksworth, John, and Gordon Cookson. 2008. "The World in 2050: Beyond the BRICs: A Broader Look at Emerging Market Growth Prospects." PriceWaterhouseCoopers, New York.

International Monetary Fund. 2006. *World Economic Outlook, September 2006: Asia Rising: Patterns of Economic Development and Growth.* Washington, D.C.: World Economic and Financial Surveys.

Maddison, Angus. 2009. "Statistics on World Population, GDP and Per Capita GDP, 1-2006 AD" (Last update March 2009, *horizontal file*, copyright Angus Maddison).

McKinsey Global Institute. 2001. "India: The Growth Imperative." New York: McKinsey Global Institute.

Mearsheimer, John. 2001. *The Tragedy of Great Power Politics.* New York: W. W. Norton & Company.

Oura, Hiroko. 2007. "Wild or Tamed: India's Potential Growth." IMF Working Paper WP/07/224. Washington, D.C.: International Monetary Fund.

Poddar, Tushar and Eva Yi. 2007. "India's Rising Growth Potential," Global Economics Paper No. 152. New York: Goldman Sachs Global Research Centres.

Rodrik, Dani and Arvind Subramanian. 2004. "Why India Can Grow at 7 Percent a Year or More: Projections and Reflections," IMF Working Paper WP/04/118. Washington: International Monetary Fund.

PovCal database [http://go.worldbank.org/NTZAIXUWPO, accessed December 2008].

The Brookings Institution. Forthcoming. The Four Speed World. Wolfersohn Center for Deveopment, The Brookings Institution.

The White House. 2009. *Economic Report of the President.* Washington, D.C.: United States Government Printing Office.

Virmani, Arvind. 2008. "India Has 9 per cent Medium-Term Growth Potential: Chief Economic Adviser." October 1.

Wilson, Dominic, and Roopa Purushothaman. 2003. "Dreaming with BRICs: The Path to 2050." Global Economics Paper 99. Goldman Sachs, New York.

World Bank. 2009. World Development Indicators database [http://go.worldbank.org/UOFSM7AQ40, accessed January 2009].

World Values Survey. Various years. Available online at http://www.worldvaluessurvey.org/

Chapter 2

Commission on Growth and Development. 2008. *The Growth Report: Strategies for Sustained Growth and Inclusive Development.* Washington, D.C.: Commission on Growth and Development.

Centennial Group. 2009. Centennial Group in-house database, June 2009, Washington, D.C.

Gill, Indermit, and Homi Kharas. 2007. *An East Asian Renaissance: Ideas for Economic Growth.* Washington, D.C.: World Bank.

Imbs, Jean and Romain Wacziarg. 2003. "Stages of Diversification." *American Economic Review* 93 (1): 63–86.

Kharas, Homi, Danny Leipziger, William Maloney, R. Thillaintathan, and Heiko Hesse. 2008. *Chilean Growth through East Asian Eyes.* Working Paper 31. Washington, D.C.: Commission Growth and Development.

Maddison, Angus. 2006. "Statistics on World Population, GDP and Per Capita GDP, 1-2006 AD (copyright Angus Maddison, accessed January 2006).

World Bank. 2009. World Development Indicators database [http://go.worldbank.org/UOFSM7AQ40, accessed January 2009].

Volynets, Alexey. n.d. "The Story of One 'Vision.'" [http://web. worldbank.org/WBSITE/EXTERNAL/WBI/WBIPROGRAMS/ KFDLP/0,,contentMDK:21014147~menuPK:2500572 ~pagePK:64156158~piPK:64152884~theSitePK:461198,00. html].

Chapter 3

IMF (International Monetary Fund). 2009. IMF World Economic Outlook, April 2009, Washington, D.C.

World Bank. 2008. *World Development Report 2009: Reshaping Economic Geography.* Washington, D.C.: World Bank.

Part II

Chapter 5

Ahmed, Sadiq and Ashutosh Varshney. 2007. *Battles Half Won: Political Economy of India's Growth and Economic Policy since Independence.* Working Paper 15. Washington, D.C.: Commission on Growth and Development.

ASER Institute. 2008. *The Annual Status of Education Report.* New Delhi: The ASER Institute.

Banerjee, Abhijit and Thomas Piketty. 2005. "Are the Rich Growing Richer? Evidence from Indian Tax Data." In Deaton and Kozel, eds, *The Great Indian Poverty Debate.* New Delhi: Macmillan India Ltd.

Banerjee, Abhijit and Rohini Somanathan. 2007. "The Political Economy of Public Goods: Some Evidence from India." *Journal of Development Economics* 82(2): 287–314.

Bertrand, Marianne, Rema Hanna, and Sendhil Mullainathan. 2008. "Affirmative Action: Evidence from College Admissions in India." NBER Working Paper 13926. Cambridge, MA: National Bureau of Economic Research.

Bertrand, Marianne, Paras Mehta, and Sendhil Mullainathan. 2002. "Ferreting Out Tunnelling: An Application to Indian Business Groups." *Quarterly Journal of Economics* 117 (1): 121–48.

Besley, Timothy and Robin Burgess. 2004. "Can Labour Regulation Hinder Economic Performance? Evidence from India." *Quarterly Journal of Economics* 119 (1): 91–134.

Besley, Timothy, Rohini Pande, and Vijayendra Rao. 2004. "The Politics of Public Good Provision: Evidence From Indian Local Governments." *Journal of the European Economic Association* 2 (2–3): 416–26.

Bhattacharjea, Aditya. 2008. "India's New Competition Law: A Comparative Assessment." *Journal of Competition Law and Economics* 4 (3): 609–38.

Center for International Comparisons of Production, Income and Prices. 2008. Penn World Tables, version 6. 2. [http://pwt.econ.upenn.edu/, accessed March 2008].

Central Statistical Organisation. Available online at http:// mospi.gov.in/mospi_cso_rept-pubn.htm, accessed August 2008.

Chakravorty, Sanjoy, and Somik Lall. 2007. *Made in India— The Economic Geography and Political Economy of Industrialization.* New Delhi: Oxford University Press.

Chandra, Kanchan. 2004. *Why Ethnic Parties Succeed: Patronage and Ethnic Headcounts in India.* Cambridge and New York: Cambridge University Press.

Damodaran, Harish. 2008. *India's New Capitalists—Caste, Business and Industry in a Modern Nation.* New Delhi: Permanent Black.

Das, Veena. 2004. "The Signature of the State: The Paradox of Illegibility." In Veena Das and Deborah Poole, eds, *Anthropology in the Margins of the State.* Santa Fe, N.M.: School of American Research Advanced Seminar Series.

Deaton, Angus and Valerie Kozel. 2005. *The Great Indian Poverty Debate.* New Delhi: Macmillan India Ltd.

De Ferranti, David, Guillermo Perry, Francisco Ferreira and Michael Walton. 2004. *Inequality in Latin America: Breaking with History?* Washington, D.C.: World Bank.

Del Villar, Rafael. 2009. "Competition and Equity in Telecommunications." In Santiago Levy and Michael Walton, eds, *No Growth without Equity? Inequality, Interests and Competition in Mexico.* New York: Palgrave-MacMillan.

Evans, Peter 1995. *Embedded Autonomy: States and Industrial Transformation.* Princeton, NJ: Princeton University Press.

FOCUS Survey. 2006. *Focus on Children under Six.* New Delhi: Citizen's Initiative for the Rights of Children under Six.

Forbes.com. 2008. Available online at http://www.forbes.com/2008/worlds-richest-people-billionaires-2008-billionaires_land.html, accessed December 15, 2008.

Gill, Indermit and Homi Kharas. 2007. *An East Asian Renaissance: Ideas for Economic Growth.* Washington DC: The World Bank.

Guha, Ramachandra. 2007. "Adivasis, Naxalites and Indian Democracy." *Economic and Political Weekly* August 11–18, 42(32): 3305–12.

Himanshu. 2007. "Recent Trends in Poverty and Inequality: Some Preliminary Results." *Economic and Political Weekly,* February 10–16, 42(6): 497–508.

International Country Risk Services. 2008. *Political Risk Services.* [http://www.prsgroup.com/ICRS.aspx, accessed March 2008.

Kaufmann, Daniel, Aart Kray, and Massimo Mastruzzi. 2008. "Governance Matters VII: Aggregate and Individual Governance Indicators, 1996–2007." Policy Research Working Paper 4654. Washington, D.C.: World Bank.

Kharas, Homi. 2009. The Promise: Makings of a Determined Marathoner. India 2039 Policy Paper 1. Washington, D.C.: Centennial Group.

Kochhar, Kalpana, Utsav Kumar, Raghuram Rajan, Arvind Subramanian, and Ioannis Tokatlidis. 2006. "India's Pattern of Development: What Happened, What Follows." Working Paper WP/06/22. Washington, D.C.: International Monetary Fund.

Kohli, Atul. 2006a. "Politics of Economic Growth in India, 1980–2005." *Economic and Political Weekly* 41 (13): 1251–59.

——. 2006b. "Politics of Economic Growth in India, 1980–2005." *Economic and Political Weekly* 41 (14): 1361–70.

López, Calva, Luis Felipe, Isabel Guerrero, and Michael Walton. 2009. "The Inequality Trap and its Links to Low Growth." In Santiago Levy and Michael Walton, eds., *No Growth without Equity? Inequality, Interests and Competition in Mexico.* New York: Palgrave-MacMillan.

Loury, Glenn. 2002. *The Anatomy of Racial Inequality.* Cambridge, Mass.: Harvard University Press.

Morck, Randall and Masao Nakamura. 2007. "Business Groups and the Big Push: Meiji Japan's Mass Privatization and Subsequent Growth." NBER Working Paper 13171. Cambridge, MA: National Bureau of Economic Research.

——. Forthcoming. "Citizenship and Accountability: The Case of India." In Anis Dani and Ashutosh Varshney, eds, *Citizenship, Governance, and Social Policy in the Developing World.* Washington, D.C.: World Bank.

Noll, Roger. 2009. "Priorities for Telecommunications Reform in Mexico." In Santiago Levy and Michael Walton, eds, *No Growth without Equity? Inequality, Interests and Competition in Mexico.* New York: Palgrave-MacMillan.

Panagariya, Arvind. 2008. *India: The Emerging Giant.* New York and New Delhi: Oxford University Press.

Pande, Rohini. 2003. "Can Mandated Political Representation Increase Policy Influence for Disadvantaged Minorities? Theory and Evidence from India." *The American Economic Review,* 93 (4): 1132–51.

Pritchett, Lant. 2008. "Is India a Flailing State? Detours on the Four Lane Highway to Modernization." Cambridge, MA: Harvard Kennedy School.

Pritchett, Lant and Rinku Murgai. 2007. "Teacher Compensation: Can Decentralization to Local Bodies Take India from Perfect Storm Through Troubled Waters to Clear Sailing?" In Suman Bery, Barry P. Bosworth, and Arvind Panagariya, eds, *India Policy Forum 2006–07, Vol. 3,* pp. 123–68. Washington, D.C.: Brookings Institution.

PROBE Team. 1999. *The Public Report on Basic Education.* New Delhi: Oxford University Press.

Rajan, Raghuram. 2008. "Is There a Threat of Oligarchy in India?" Speech to the Bombay Chamber of Commerce on its Founders Day celebration, September 10, Bombay, India.

Rajan Committee. 2008. *A Hundred Small Steps: Report of the Committee on Financial Sector Reforms.* New Delhi: Planning Commission, Government of India.

Rajan, Raghuram and Luigi Zingales. 2003. *Saving Capitalism from the Capitalists: Unleashing the Power of Financial Markets to create Wealth and Spread Opportunity.* New York: Crown Business.

Ramaswamy, K. V. 2006. "State of Competition in the Indian Manufacturing Sector." In Pradeep S. Mehta, ed., *Towards a Functional Competition Policy for India.* New Delhi: Academic Foundation.

Rao, Vijayendra and Paromita Sanyal. 2008. "Dignity through Discourse: Poverty and the Culture of Deliberation in Indian Village Democracies." Washington, D.C., and Wesleyan University, Middletown, Conn: World Bank.

Robinson, James. 2009. "The Political Economy of Equality and Growth in Mexico: Lessons from the History of the United States." In Santiago Levy and Michael Walton, eds, *No Growth without Equity? Inequality, Interests and Competition in Mexico.* New York: Palgrave-MacMillan.

Rudolph, Lloyd and Susanne Hoeber Rudolph. 2008 (1987). "State Formation in India: Building and Wasting Assets." In *Explaining Indian Democracy: A Fifty-Year Perspective, 1956–2006. Volume II.* New Delhi: Oxford University Press.

Sachar Committee. 2006. *Social, Economic and Educational Status of the Muslim Community of India: A Report.* Prime Minister's High Level Committee, Cabinet Secretariat. New Delhi: Government of India.

Sinha, Aseem. 2005. *The Regional Roots of Development Politics in India: A Divided Leviathan.* New Delhi: Oxford University Press.

Somanathan, Rohini. 2007. "The Demand for Disadvantage." Paper presented at the Fifth Annual Agence Française de Développement/European Development Research Network conference, October, Paris.

Sud, Inder. 2009a. *Governance for a Modern Society: Combining Smarter Government Decentralization and Accountability to People.* India 2039 Policy Paper 6. Washington, D.C.: Centennial Group.

——. 2009b. *Urbanization and Public Services: Creating Functioning Cities for Sustaining Growth.* India 2039 Policy Paper 3. Washington, D.C.: Centennial Group.

Thorat, Sukhadeo. 2007. *Human Poverty and Socially Disadvantaged Groups in India.* New Delhi: United Nations Development Programme.

Varshney, Ashutosh. 2002. *Ethnic Conflict and Civic Life: Hindus and Muslims in India.* New Haven: Yale University Press; and Delhi: Oxford University Press.

Walton, Michael. Forthcoming. "The Political Economy of India's Malnutrition Puzzle." Institute of Development Studies Bulletin.

World Bank. 1998. *World Development Indicators.* Washington, D.C.: World Bank.

——. 2005. *India: Re-energizing the Agricultural Sector to Sustain Growth and Reduce Poverty.* New Delhi: Oxford University Press.

——. 2008. *World Development Indicators 2008.* Washington D.C.: World Bank.

World Bank Institute. *Governance Indicators.* Available online at www.worldbank.org/wbi/governance/data, accessed March 2008.

Chapter 6

3iNetwork. 2006. *India Infrastructure Report 2006—Urban Infrastructure.* New Delhi: Oxford University Press.

Bagchi, Amresh. 1998. "Reforming the Property Tax: Need for a New Direction." Working Paper 98/1. New Delhi: National Institute for Public Finance and Policy.

Bahl, Roy. 2003. *The Property Tax in Developing Countries: Where Are We in 2002.* Atlanta, GA: Georgia State University, Andrew Young School of Policy Studies.

Bahl, Roy and Johannes Linn. 1992. *Urban Finance in Developing Countries.* Washington, D.C.: World Bank.

Mathur, Om Prakash. 2001. *Approach to State-Municipal Fiscal Relations: Options and Perspectives.* New Delhi: National Institute for Public Finance and Policy.

Mehta, Arun C. 2005. *Elementary Education in India: Progress Towards UEE: Analytical Report 2005–06.* New Delhi: National Institute for Education Policy and Administration and Department of Elementary Education and Literacy.

International Monetary Fund. Various years. *Government Finance Statistics.*

National Institute for Public Finance and Policy. 2005. *Redefining State-Municipal Fiscal Relations: Options and Perspectives for the State Finance Commission.* New Delhi: National Institute for Public Finance and Policy.

———. 2007. *India Urban Report.* New Delhi: National Institute for Public Finance and Policy.

National Sample Survey Organization. 1990. "National Sample Surveys (NSS)." New Delhi: National Sample Survey Organization, Ministry of Statistics and Programme.

Ravindra, D. A. and Vasanth Rao. 2002. *Property Reform in India.* New York: United Nations Development Programme.

Second Administrative Reform Commission. 2007. *Local Governance, Sixth Report.* New Delhi: Government of India.

United Nations. 2008. *World Urbanization Prospects: The 2007 Revision.* New York: United Nations. [http://esa.un.org/unup, accessed October 29, 2008].

United Nations Population Division. 2009. "World Population Estimates and Prospects Report," New York, January 2009.

World Bank. 2004. *India Urban Finance and Governance Review.* Washington, D.C.: World Bank.

———. 2005. *Brazil: Inputs for a Strategy for Cities.* Washington, D.C.: World Bank.

———. 2006. *India Water Supply and Sanitation: Bridging the Gap between Infrastructure and Services.* Urban Water Supply and Sanitation Background Paper. Washington, D.C.: World Bank.

Chapter 7

Amarasinghe, U.A., T. Shah, H. Turral, and B.K. Anand. 2007. "India's Water Future to 2025–2050: Business-as-usual Scenario and Deviations," IWMI Research Report 123, p. 47. Colombo, Sri Lanka: International Water Management Institute.

IWMI (International Water Management Institute). 2006. *India's Water Futures to 2025/2050—Issues and Scenarios.* Sri Lanka: IWMI.

Planning Commission. 2007. "Ground Water Management and Ownership—Report of the Expert Group," September 2007. New Delhi, India: Government of India, Planning Commission.

Shah, Tushaar. 2007. "Co-management of Electricity and Groundwater: Gujarat's Jyotigram Yojana," Regional Workshop, Hyderabad, August 29.

Shah, Tushaar and Shilp Verma. 2008. "Co-management of Electricity and Groundwater: An Assessment of Gujarat's Jyotigram Scheme." *Economic & Political Weekly.* February 16, pp. 59–66.

Part III

Chapter 8

Araujo, Armando, Luis Avella, Harinder Kohli, and Richard Scurfeld. 2007. "Political Economy of Infrastructure Reforms in India for Japan Bank for International Cooperation." Centennial Group Study, Washington D.C.

Centennial Group. 2007. "Challenges in Introducing Public Private Partnerships in India." Unpublished report, October. Washington D.C.: Japan Bank for International Cooperation.

———. 2009. "India's Infrastructure Investment Requirements during 2009–2039," Background study by Armando Araujo and Harinder Kohli, unpublished, Washington D.C., January.

Haldea, Gajendra. 2008. "Infrastructure at Crossroads," Unpublished manuscript. New Delhi.

Chapter 9

Böhm, Anthony, Marcelo Follari, Andrew Hewett, Sarah Jones, Neil Kemp, Denis Meares, David Pearce, and Kevin Van Cauter. 2004. *Vision 2020: Forecasting International Student Mobility.* London: British Council.

China National Bureau of Statistics. 2007. *China Statistical Yearbook 2007.* Beijing: China National Bureau of Statistics.

Dahlman, Carl. 2008. "Innovation Strategies of the BRICKS: Brazil, Russia, India, China, and Korea—Different Strategies, Different Results." OECD–World Bank Conference on Innovation and Sustainable Growth in a Globalized, Paris, November 18.

Dar, Amit, Kin Bing Wu, Alan Abrahart, S.A.A. Alvi, Prema Clarke, Sangeeta Goyal, Venita Kaul, Ashish Narain, Deepa Sankar, Yevgeniya Savchenko, Hong Tan, and Anuja Utz. 2006. "Skill Development in India: The Vocational Education and Training System." Washington, D.C.: World Bank, Human Development Unit.

Dutz, Mark. 2007. *Unleashing India's Innovation: Toward Sustainable and Inclusive Growth.* Washington, D.C.: World Bank.

IANS (Indo-Asian News Service). 2008. "Nandan Nilekani Confident of Changing India with Ideas." November 25.

India Department of Heavy Industries. 2006. *Automotive Mission Plan 2006–2016.* New Delhi: Government of India, Department of Heavy Industries.

Indian National Assessment and Accreditation Council. Available online at http://naacindia.org/

——. 2008. "Recommendations, Engineering Education." Report of a Working Group on Engineering Education, Sam Pitroda, Chairman. New Delhi. www.knowledgecommission.gov.in/recommendations/engineer.asp.

Indian Planning Commission. 2002. *Tenth Five-Year Plan: 2002–07.* Delhi: Controller of Publication, Department of Publication, Civil Lines. [http://planningcommission.nic.in/plans/planrel/fiveyr/welcome.html].

——. 2008. *Eleventh Five-Year Plan: 2007–12.* New Delhi: Oxford University Press. [http://planningcommission.nic.in/plans/planrel/fiveyr/welcome.html].

India, Prime Minister's Council on Climate Change. 2008. *National Action Plan on Climate Change.* New Delhi: Office of the Prime Minister. [http://pmindia.nic.in/Pg01-52.pdf].

Jha, C. S. 2006. "Higher Education in India: Restructuring for Increased Innovation." World Bank, South Asia Region, Finance and Private Sector Development, Washington, DC.

Lakshman, Nandini. 2006. "Will Foreign Universities Come to India?" *Business Week,* October 9.

Management Today. 2007. "Global Innovation Index". London: *Management Today.* [www.managementtoday.co.uk/news/610009/].

MHRD (Ministry of Human Resource Development). 2007. *Annual Report.* New Delhi: Government of India, Ministry of Human Resource Development.

Murthy, N. R. Narayana. 2008. "Why Do We Need World-class Educational Institutions and How Do We Create Them?" Lecture at the Platinum Jubilee Celebrations of the University Institute of Chemical Technology, Mumbai, October 1.

NASSCOM and McKinsey & Company. 2005. Extending India's Leadership in the Global IT and BPO Industries. New Delhi: NASSCOM.

Ramachandran, R. 2007. "Obstacle Race." *Frontline* 24 (1): 126–30.

Shanghai Jiao Tong University, Graduate School of Education. 2005. *Academic Ranking of World Universities.* Shanghai, China: Shanghai Jiao Tong University, Graduate School of Education. [www.arwu.org].

Summers, Lawrence. 2006. Speech at the Federation of Indian Chambers of Commerce and Industry Education Summit, New Delhi, March 23.

UNESCO (United Nations Educational, Scientific, and Cultural Organization). 2008. World Education Indicators database. Paris: United Nations Economic, Scientific and Cultural Organization. [www.unesco.org/education/information/wer/htmlENG/tablesmenu.htm].

University Grants Commission. Available online at http://www.ugc.ac.in

WEF (World Economic Forum). 2008. *Global Competitiveness Report 2008–09.* Geneva: World Economic Forum.

Wessner, Charles W., ed. 2006. *Assessment of the Small Business Innovation Research Program.* Washington, D.C.: National Academies.

World Bank. 2008a. Key Knowledge Economy Resources. World Bank, Washington, D.C. [http://go.worldbank.org/2LC65DBYS0].

World Bank. 2008b. Public Expenditure Database, Education Statistics. Summary Education Profile. World Bank, Washington, D.C. [http://go.worldbank.org/ITABCOGIV1].

Zakaria, Fareed. 2008. *The Post-American World*. New York: W.W. Norton & Company.

Chapter 10

Adelman, A. and G. Watkins. 2008. "Reserve Prices and Mineral Resource Theory." *Energy Journal* 29 (Special Issue to Acknowledge the Contribution of Campbell Watkins to Energy Economics): 1–16.

BP (British Petroleum). 2008. "BP Statistical Review of World Energy." London: British Petroleum.

Dean, Tim. 2006. "New Age Nuclear." *Cosmos Magazine* Issue no. 8, April.

EIA (Energy Information Administration). 2008. *Annual Energy Outlook*. Washington, D.C.: U.S. Department of Energy.

ERI (Energy Resources Institute of India). 2006. "India's Energy Growth." Presentation to the Executive Management Training, Indian School of Business, Hyderabad, June 16, 2006.

ESMAP (Energy Sector Management Assistance Program). 2008. "Study of Equipment Prices in the Power Sector." Washington, D.C.: World Bank.

IEA (International Energy Agency). 2008. *Energy Technology Perspectives: Scenarios and Strategies to 2050*. Paris: Organisation for Economic Co-operation and Development, International Energy Agency.

Indian Planning Commission. 2006. *Report of the Expert Committee on Integrated Energy Policy*. New Delhi: Government of India.

Kemp, A. G. and A. S. Kasim. 2008. "A Least-Cost Optimization Model of CO_2 Capture Applied to Major Power Plants within the EU-ETS Framework." *Energy Journal* 29 (Special Issue to Acknowledge the Contribution of Campbell Watkins to Energy Economics): 99–134.

Lorenz, Peter, Dickon Pinner, and Thomas Seitz. 2008. "The Economics of Solar Power." *McKinsey Quarterly*, June, pp. 1–38.

Madan, Tanvi. 2006. "Energy Security Series: India." Washington, D.C.: Brookings Foreign Policy Studies, Brookings Institution.

Mao, Jiaxiong. 2008. "Status and Development of China's Electric Power." Paper presented at the Asia Clean Energy Forum, Manila, June 2–6.

McKinsey and Co. 2008. *The Carbon Productivity Challenge: Curbing Climate Change and Sustaining Economic Growth*. New York: McKinsey Global Institute.

NETL (National Energy Technology Laboratory) 2007. "Cost and Performance Baseline for Fossil Energy Plants." Washington, D.C.: U.S. Department of Energy.

OPEC (Organization of the Petroleum Exporting Countries). 2008. *World Oil Outlook*. Vienna: Organization of the Petroleum Exporting Countries.

Taylor, Robert P., Chandrasekar Govindarajalu, Jeremy Levin, Anke S. Meyer, and William A. Ward. 2008. *Financing Energy Efficiency: Lessons from Brazil, China, India, and Beyond*. Washington, D.C.: World Bank.

Part IV

Chapter 12

Chhokar, Jagdeep S. 2008. "Criminals in Elections." *The Tribune*, New Delhi, India, November 23.

The Economist. 2008. "Battling the Babu Raj." London, U.K., March 6.

Sud, Inder. 2009. *Urbanization and Public Services: Creating Functioning Cities for Sustaining Growth*. India 2039 Policy Paper 3. Washington, D.C.: Centennial Group.

Supreme Court of India. 2008. *Court News*. July–September. [http://www.supremecourtofindia.nic.in/court%20news%20July_Sept2008.pdf, accessed February–May 2008].

Transparency International India. 2005. *India Corruption Study 2005*. New Delhi: Transparency International India.

———. 2008. *India Corruption Study 2007*. New Delhi: Transparency International India.

World Bank. 2006. *Reforming Public Service in India—Drawing Lessons from Successes*. Report 35041-IN. Washington, D.C.: World Bank.

Chapter 13

Agnihotri, V. K. 2003. *Effective and Responsive Administration.* New Delhi: Macmillan India Ltd.

Arora, D. 2008. *Citizen's Charters in India: Formulation, Implementation and Evaluation.* New Delhi: Indian Institute of Public Administration.

Arora, R. K. 2008. *Ethics in Governance: Innovations, Issues and Instrumentalities.* Jaipur: Aalekh Publishers.

Arora, Ramesh K. and Rajni Goyal. 1995. *Indian Public Administration—Institutions and Issues.* Wishwa Prakashan.

Bhattacharjea, Aditya. 2008. "India's New Competition Law: A Comparative Assessment." *Journal of Competition Law & Economics* 4 (3): 609.

Centre for Public Policy. 2008. *Right to Information Act—Revisiting the Act.* New Delhi: Centre for Public Policy.

Chakravarthi, S. 2001. "New Indian Competition Law on the Anvil." *Corporate Law Adviser* 42 (1): 8–23.

Chaudhury, N, J. Hammer, M. Kremer, K. Muralidharan, and H. Rogers. 2006. "Missing in Action: Teacher and Health Care Worker Absence in Developing Countries." *Journal of Economic Perspectives* 20 (1): 91–116.

Competition Commission of India. 2004. *Activities and Progress.* New Delhi: Competition Commission of India.

Government of India, Department of Information Technology. u.d. Status Note on NeGP.

Government of India, High Level Committee on Competition Policy and Law. 2000. "Executive Summary." "Report of the High Level Committee on Competition Policy and Law." New Delhi: High Level Committee on Competition Policy and Law [www.edepositoryindia.com/index6d.html, accessed May 2000].

Government of India, Ministry of Health and Family Welfare. 2006. "Report of the Working Group on Health Care Financing Including Health Insurance for the 11th Five Year Plan." New Delhi: Government of India.

Government of India, Ministry of Personnel, Public Grievances and Pensions. 2008. *Annual Report 2008–09.* New Delhi: Government of India.

Government of India, Second Administrative Reforms Commission. 2007. "Public Order." Fifth Report of the Second Administrative Reforms Commission. New Delhi: Government of India.

——. 2008a. "Combating Terrorism: Protecting by Righteousness." Tenth Report of the Second Administrative Reforms Commission. New Delhi: Government of India.

——. 2008b. "Refurbishing of Personnel Administration." Tenth Report of the Second Administrative Reforms Commission. New Delhi: Government of India.

Government of India, Task Force on Public-Private Partnership. u.d. "Draft Report on Recommendations of the Task Force on Public-Private Partnership for the 11th Plan." New Delhi: Government of India.

Jogdand, P. G., ed. 2000. *New Economic Policy and Dalits.* New Delhi: Rawat Publications.

Kaufmann D, A. Kraay, and P. Zoido-Lobatón. 1999. "Governance Matters." Policy Research Working Paper 2196. Washington, D.C.: World Bank.

Panagariya, A. 2008. *India: The Emerging Giant.* New York: Oxford University Press.

Sabharwal, Shri Y. K. 2006. "Justice Sobhag Mal Jain Memorial Lecture on Delayed Justice." July 25, New Delhi.

Shourie, A. 2004. *Governance and the Sclerosis That Set In.* New Delhi: Rupa.

Tandon, B. B., V. K. Agnihotri, and H. Ramachandran. 2001. "Globalization and Decentralization—Emerging Issues from the Indian Experience." *International Review of Administrative Sciences* 67 (3): 505–23.

About the Editors and Contributors

Editors

Harinder S. Kohli is the Founding Director and Chief Executive of the Emerging Markets Forum as well as President and CEO of Centennial Group, both based in Washington, D.C. He is also the Editor of *Global Journal of Emerging Markets Economies* and serves as Vice Chairman of the institution-wide Advisory Group of Asian Institute of Technology (Thailand). Prior to starting his current ventures, he served for some 25 years in various senior managerial positions at the World Bank. He has published two other books, and written extensively on emergence of Asia and other emerging market economies, financial development, and private capital flows, and on infrastructure. He is working on the long-term economic prospects of Latin America.

Anil Sood, in his 30-year career at the World Bank, occupied many senior positions including Vice President, Strategy and Resource Management, and Special Advisor to the Managing Directors. He has since advised chief executives and senior management of a number of development organizations including the African Development Bank, the Islamic Development Bank, the United Nations Development Programme, and the United Nations Economic Commission of Africa, on matters of strategy and development effectiveness.

Contributors

Richard Ackermann served for seven years as the World Bank's South Asia Director for Social Development and Environment. He holds degrees from the California Institute of Technology and the London School of Economics.

Vivek K. Agnihotri is currently Secretary General Rajya Sabha (upper house of Indian Parliament), retired as Secretary to Government of India in the Ministry of Parliamentary Affairs. During his career of over 37 years as a civil servant, he spent more than a decade dealing with personnel matters as a trainer and as head of the Department of Administrative Reforms. He holds a PhD degree in public policy from the Indian Institute of Technology, Delhi.

Vinod K. Goel, a former World Bank official, is Head of Global Knowledge and Innovation Practice at the Centennial Group, and consultant for the World Bank and other international organizations. He is a leading expert on private and financial sectors issues and is well-known in the international community for his pioneering work on higher education, technology, and innovation, including publishing books on the subject. He has a PhD and MBA from Cornell University, USA and Masters of Technology from the National Dairy Research Institute, India.

Bimal Jalan is an Honorary Fellow of National Council of Applied Economic Research (NCAER) and Chairman of Public Interest Foundation, Delhi. Formerly, he was Governor of Reserve Bank of India, Member of Parliament, Chairman of NCAER, Executive Director of the World Bank, and Chairman of Economic Advisory Council to the Prime Minister.

Homi Kharas is a Senior Fellow at the Wolfensohn Center for Development at the Brookings Institution in Washington, D.C. Kharas is also a member of the Working Group for the Commission on Growth and Development, chaired by Michael Spence, a nonresident Fellow of the Organisation for Economic Co-operation and Development's (OECD) Development Centre, and a member of the National Economic Advisory Council to the Prime Minister of Malaysia. His research interests are now focused on global trends, Asian growth and development, and international aid for the poorest countries.

R. A. Mashelkar is President of the Global Research Alliance, a network of public research institutions globally. He is Chairman of the National Innovation Foundation and the Reliance Innovation Council.

He serves on the boards of several companies and educational and research organizations. He served for 11 years as the Director General of the Council of Scientific and Industrial Research. He is a Fellow of the Royal Society (U.K.), Foreign Associate of the National Academy of Science (U.S.), and Foreign Fellow of the National Academy of Engineering (U.S.). He has played a key role in shaping India's science and technology (S&T) policies. He lectures widely and consults for national and international organizations on innovation and restructuring public research and development (R&D) institutions worldwide. He has more than 50 awards and medals including the Padma Shri and Padma Bhushan, two of India's highest civilian honors.

Hariharan Ramachandran is currently Professor at University of Delhi. He has earlier been Director, Institute of Applied Manpower Research, New Delhi and Executive Director, National Research and Resource Centre, LBS National Academy of Administration, Mussoorie. He has authored/edited eight books and published over 50 articles in national and international journals.

Hossein Razavi is the former Director of the Energy and Infrastructure Department of the World Bank. During his 25-year tenure at the World Bank he served a number of managerial and professional positions including the Chief of Oil and Gas Division, and the Director of The Private Sector Development Department. Dr Razavi is well-known in the international financial community for his pioneering work on structuring financial vehicles suitable to the energy sector. His book on Energy Finance was published by Pennwell Books, first in 1996, and a new edition in 2007. He holds an MS in engineering and a PhD in economics, and serves on the editorial boards of the *Energy Journal* and *Energy Economics*.

Inder Sud has over 35 years of experience in international development. He has held several senior positions at the World Bank, in country economic and sector operations, policy, and finance. He currently consults for a number of multilateral and bilateral organizations, developing country governments and private foundations, and teaches at The George Washington University and Duke University.

C. M. Vasudev has worked as a civil servant in the Indian Administrative Service for nearly 40 years. During his career he held several key positions in the state government of Uttar Pradesh and the Government of India. In the Ministry of Finance he worked as Secretary in the Departments of Economic Affairs, Public Expenditure, and Banking and spearheaded economic reforms in different sectors, specially, in fiscal and financial sectors. He has also worked as Executive Director at the World Bank where he chaired the Bank's Committee on Development Effectiveness.

Michael Walton is Senior Visiting Fellow at the Centre for Policy Research, Delhi, and Adjunct Lecturer in International Development at the Harvard Kennedy School. He is also the VKRV Rao Chair Professor for 2008 and 2009 in the Institute for Social and Economic Change, Bangalore. From 1980–2004, Michael Walton worked at the World Bank, where his positions included Chief Economist for East Asia and the Pacific (1995–97) and Director for Poverty Reduction (1997–2000). He is co-editor of *Culture and Public Action* (Stanford University Press, 2004), co-director of the World Bank's *World Development Report 2005/06 on Equity and Development*, and has a co-edited a volume on equity and growth in Mexico. Michael Walton studied at Oxford University.